Modern Political
Geography

Modern Political Geography

Richard Muir
Cambridgeshire College of Arts and Technology

M

First published 1975 by
THE MACMILLAN PRESS LTD
London and Basingstoke
Associated companies in New York Dublin
Melbourne Johannesburg and Madras

SBN 333 17692 8   (hard cover)
333 17693 6 (paper cover)

Photoset, printed and bound
in Great Britain by
REDWOOD BURN LIMITED
Trowbridge and Esher

Distributed in the United States
by Halsted Press, a Division of
John Wiley & Sons, Inc., New York

Library of Congress Catalog Card No. 75–2233

To my parents
and
J., C., D., M. and T.

Contents

Preface

Through lecturing in political geography I have become aware of the need for a textbook that will provide the student with a concise introduction to recent developments in the field and in related fields of study. This is what I have attempted to write. Having so attempted, I anticipate criticism both from those who feel that there is little or no place in political geography for quantitative techniques, models and the like, and from those who consider that I have not progressed far enough in the direction of quantification and abstract theory. I have tried, not consciously to steer a middle course, but to introduce to the reader what are considered to be some valuable innovations which are otherwise accessible only in article form, while at the same time including sufficient descriptive and empirical material to link the more abstract concepts and methodologies firmly to the real world and to allow the work to stand as a textbook in its own right.

Probably the most difficult problem has been that of dividing and subdividing the material, and rather than include numerous short chapters I have used a subdivision based on parts and sections. It appears to me that a useful subdivision of material relating to political regions may be based on a consideration of morphological structure, political process and stage of evolution, provided that the analogies with geomorphology are not stretched too far. Another division can be made on the bases of scale and statehood, separating that material which is internal to the state and that which relates to its external relationships. When these divisions are introduced, it becomes apparent that a great deal of overlap remains, for example in relation to state boundaries, perception and decision-making.

Political geographers are particularly exposed to allegations of subjectivity and political bias; it is inevitable that any piece of writing will be coloured to a greater or lesser extent by the author's opinions and prejudices, and among the more insidious writings are those for which claims of objectivity are advanced. I belong to no organised political group or party, and evidence may be found here firstly of my belief in the fundamental equality of men and women of all races and classes, and secondly of my doubts that the sovereign state provides the most suitable framework for satisfying the individual and aggregate needs of men. It may prove difficult to uncover here evidence of partisanship which cannot be reconciled with one or other of these stated biases.

My interest in the interactions between politics and geography developed during my first year at Aberdeen University, when I attended a course of lectures on international relations given by Dr Joseph Frankel, now Professor of Politics at Southampton University. I subsequently joined a special option course in political geography presented by Professor Roy E. H. Mellor, who later supervised my postgraduate research. I was fascinated by his expert descriptions of political-geographical phenomena in Central Europe, and have been grateful for his advice on several occasions since, though I doubt that he would wish to be associated with all the ideas and points of view included here. To Professor Frankel and Professor Mellor, my thanks.

I would also like to thank my geography teacher, Miss L. Davison; that I ever passed my 'A' level is a tribute as much to her patience as to her teaching ability. In the preparation of this book I have been indebted to a number of overworked colleagues: Bronwen Morgan, who drew some of the maps; Russell Gent and Bernard Fingleton, who gave advice on quantitative methods; and Patrick Armstrong, for help in deciphering some systems. Thanks too to June, with whom I do not share the art of spelling.

R. M.

Acknowledgements

The author and publisher express thanks for permission granted to reproduce the following diagrams.

Figure 4.3 (a): originally published as Figure 3.9 (b) in Brian P. FitzGerald, *Developments in Geographical Method*, Oxford University Press (1974); reproduced by permission of The Delegates of the Oxford University Press.

Figure 5.2 (c): originally published in an article by Stanko Zuljic in *Geografiski Glasnik*, no. 32, Zagreb (1971), subsequently adapted by Jean Hannford of the Department of Geography, University of Texas at Austin and published in Gary M. Bertsch, The revival of nationalism *Problems of Communism*, issue 22, no. 6, (1973), 22; reproduced by permission of the University of Texas.

Figure 6.3: originally published as Figure 60 in August Lösch, *The Economics of Location*, Yale University Press (1954); reproduced by permission of Gustav Fischer Verlag, publishers of the original German edition.

Figure 7.1: originally published in Richard L. Merritt, Systems and the disintegration of empires, *General Systems*, VIII (1963), subsequently republished as Figures 20.1, 20.2, 20.3 in R. K. Kasperson and J. V. Minghi (eds), *The Structure of Political Geography*, Aldine (1969), University of London Press (1973); reproduced by permission of the Aldine Publishing Company.

Figure 7.6: reproduced by permission of the Embassy of the Republic of Iceland, London.

Figure 8.10: prepared for a seminar held in July 1964 and published in Derek Senior (ed.), *The Regional City*, Longman (1966), p. 19; reproduced by permission of Mr. Senior and Messrs. Longman.

PART 1

Introductory

Political geography is simultaneously one of the most retarded and most undervalued branches of geography, and one that offers the greatest potential for both theoretical and practical advance. Many fundamental questions remain to be decided, and unanimity is lacking concerning definitions of the subject, the relative importance that should be attached to its political and geographical aspects and the value of quantitative approaches. There is even disagreement as to the causes of political geography's backwardness, though only a minority of students would deny that the subject is in such a condition when compared to other branches of geography, many of which are of much more recent origin as coherent fields of study. The political-geographical malaise has led to a disregard for, or an awkwardness in the handling of political factors encountered in research by numerous regional and economic geographers, while the geographical preoccupation with (unattainable) objectivity and sometimes embarrassment when confronted with political realities has frequently led to subjectivity in the omission of relevant information of a political nature. Since of all geographers the student of the political branch will be the most exposed to accusations of partisanship, it is of particular importance that his explanations and findings should rest on a sound theoretical base and be supported by a well-stocked arsenal of relevant techniques and methodologies.

1.1 Definitions and approaches

The most frequently quoted definition of political geography was provided in 1954 by Hartshorne, who described the subject as 'the study of the areal differences and similarities in political character as an interrelated part of the total complex of areal differences and similarities'.[1] It would be possible here to provide the reader with a long list of alternative definitions presented by different writers at different times, though a principal outcome would be his or her needless confusion. Naturally one is anxious to justify political geography as a coherent field of study with its own subject matter, approaches and methodologies, but it is doubtful whether such extensive topics can effectively be encapsulated within a sentence or a paragraph. The urge to define in geography dates from an earlier period, and may reflect territoriality on the part of geographers anxious to protect, legitimise and defend a discipline new to university syllabuses (this urge has been reinforced by undergraduates eager for glib and easily remembered definitions suitable for repetition in the examination hall). It is hoped that this work as a whole, like others of its type, will demonstrate and justify the existence of political geography as a valuable field of social science, linking geography and political science, and in the meantime Hartshorne's definition may be sufficient even though there is little in political geography that remains settled and uncontroversial.

Political geography is concerned with the spatial interaction between political and geographical phenomena, and one of the most fundamental issues concerns the location of the subject on the spectrum between geography and political science. An extreme viewpoint was taken by Alexander, who wrote that political geographers 'are not concerned with the form or structure of the government by itself, that is, the division of functions among the executive, legislative and judicial branches or whether it is democratic or totalitarian'.[2] Jackson, however, in 1958, was concerned that students were overemphasising geographical factors and neglecting the human element, dynamic processes and the basic relevant theories formulated by political scientists.[3] This argument was restated by Cohen and Rosenthal in 1971, the writers feeling that '. . . without more attention to the political, our geographical insights are likely to be limited and sterile'.[4] In fact, since geography and politics have reciprocal relations, 'Political geography may be defined from the disciplinary perspective of either geography or political science'.[5] For a geographer to attempt to investigate political-geographical phenomena with a smug disregard for their political *milieu* would be analogous to a geomorphologist studying landforms in terms of their structure and in ignorance of process, or like studying the spatial consequences of the Molotov–Ribbentrop agreement without reference to the totalitarian characteristics of the Nazi and Soviet governments, their political perspectives, or indeed the agreement itself.

On the other hand, studies in political geography should clearly demonstrate the spatial causes and effects of political processes; if neither of these are apparent, the subject is not a political-geographical one. Geographers who become severed from their geographical roots are both denying themselves the advantages of their specialist training and, in the case of political geography, neglecting a branch of the discipline which is in great need of development. Just as the geographer has much to learn from the political scientist, so also he has much to offer, but his words will only carry a ring of authority if they relate to the spatial perspective, the hallmark of his discipline. This having been said, the overriding concern of all scientists is with problems of both a practical and a theoretical nature, and since the problems themselves seldom respect the man-made boundaries between disciplines, their solution is of greater significance than the academic pedigree of the sleuth.

The future development of political geography will be partly based on interdisciplinary research and borrowing, of which more rather than less is desirable. It may appear strange that so many of the 'great names' in political geography have a joint or ancillary training in history rather than in political science; this probably relates to the period when geography and history were favoured combinations in degrees in the humanities, while today geography is more usually (and perhaps more appropriately) grouped with the social sciences. The modern political geographer is confronted by a daunting list of subjects which bear upon his chosen field of study. In a very rough order of importance these include political science and international relations, statistics, sociology, international law, economics, psychology and ethology, with history perhaps intervening somewhere in the middle of this list. No single brain can encompass the totality of these disciplines, and sheer practicality encourages the trained geographer to refine his spatial perspectives.

There are a number of established approaches to political geography, though few can be justified as holistic approaches. Cole and King list seven conceptual and four applied approaches to political geography,[6] though most of these are of localised relevance and are flattered by their inclusion. It is currently conventional to recognise historical, morphological, functional and power analysis approaches, though the latter, concerned with the assessment and comparison of the power of states, is a branch of rather than an approach to political geography. The historical approach is generally adopted in studies which describe the evolution of a political or social unit through time. The morphological approach 'calls for a descriptive and interpretative analysis of the external and internal structure of the state area as a geographic object'.[7] The external morphological attributes include size, shape, location and boundaries, and internal morphological subdivisions include core areas, the capital, cultural regions and so on. This approach was pioneered by Hartshorne in 1935,[8] and later rejected by him as being static and dull; he replaced it in 1950 with his functional approach,[9] which emphasised the dynamic relationship of the human and morphological contents of the state to each other and to the whole. Though this approach comes the closest, none of those so far mentioned can be regarded as appropriate to the entire subject matter of political geography; rather, they emphasise different aspects of the subject.

Thus, in a study of the evolution of the state of France, a historical approach would be favoured; in a study of the core area of Poland, the morphological; while a study of Bangladesh separatism might be more amenable to the functional approach. To pursue further loose (very loose) analogies with geomorphology, just as a landform can be studied in respect of structure, process and time, and a full understanding will require reference to each of these phenomena, so a political-geographical phenomenon is to be understood in terms of its morphological, functional and historical characteristics, and no single approach is adequate to its interpretation in full.

There are several other candidates for the holistic mantle, though none has as yet gained great support. The longest established and best known of these is Jones's unified field theory (see section 2.4); this has a better potential for universality, though it does tend to be historically orientated and to impose a rather restrictive analytical sequence upon the researcher.[10] McColl's political-ecological approach was briefly stated, and does not appear to offer much more than an exhortation to political geographers to do what by the time of its publication most of them already were doing, namely to emphasise the description, analysis and evaluation of the interrelation between geography and politics while keeping a proper perspective upon each and noting their basic unity.[11] Most promising is the geographical model for political systems analysis proposed by Cohen and Rosenthal, who began with the premise that 'Political geography is concerned with the spatial attributes of political process',[12] and continued to dissect political process and its spatial attributes within the framework of a systems approach sufficiently broad to encompass the overall political man–environment interrelationship and to embrace existing political-geographical concepts such as Whittlesey's law–landscapes thread, territoriality, political place perception and decision making among others (see section 4.1). The general acceptance of this systems approach will await further testing by empirical studies—as yet it is only three years old—though it is at present being applied on the urban scale and to the question of agricultural policy in Australia.[13]

1.2 Past development

The emergence of political geography as a coherent branch of geography is essentially a phenomenon of this century, though interactions between political man and his environment are so pervasive and profound that political-geographical allusions are to be found in the works of many great writers of the past. Herodotus, Plato, Aristotle, Rousseau, Montesquieu, Herder and Hegel have variously been mentioned as describers of political-geographical observations, though none was conscious of the subject as a distinct discipline.

The real founder of political geography was the German geographer Friedrich Ratzel (1844–1904), whose writings closely reflect the location of their author in time and space, being coloured by Darwinistic notions about the survival of the fittest and by the environmental determinism of the late nineteenth-century German school of geography. The state was regarded as an organic entity, its success depending largely upon its ability to obtain space, and itself an expression of the imperishable ties between men and the land. Ratzel formulated a potentially dangerous view of the world in which the competitive aspects of state behaviour were flattered with the dignity of natural laws. Elsewhere his ideas were less controversial and more realistically based, and his attempt to systematise contemporary political-geographical knowledge appeared in 1897.[14] Ratzel's ideas provided a link and a starting point for both political geography and geopolitics, though the two subjects have not managed to coexist with much harmony since his passing.

The subsequent development of political geography might best be described as patchy, and though political-geographical works of considerable quality were produced at various intervals during this century, in general students of the subject were slow to consolidate and build upon foundations already laid down. Two texts in particular merit special mention, Isaiah Bowman's *The New World* and Derwent Whittlesey's *Earth and the State*.[15] Bowman, as chief American territorial specialist at the Versailles peace negotiations, was intimately connected with the politics and geography of the post-1918 settlement and produced an optimistic, objective and authoritative survey of the new world which was emerging from the wreckage of war, while Whittlesey's book, though methodologically dated, retains a remarkable freshness and succeeds in emphasising wider interrelationships when focusing on the local level.

During the first third of this century, a number of essentially political-geographical books and articles were produced, while the application of the principle of self-determination in Europe demonstrated to all the importance of the subject in practical terms and provided material for innumerable discourses. Yet the subject as a whole remained disorganised and frequently misunderstood; as in other branches of geography at this time, theories and concepts were presented in a loose verbal form and lacked scientific authentication (attempts at which would have led to the timely interment of many of them). Further, several texts which purported to be political-geographical consisted of regional description with historical annotations, or were tedious compendia of statistics that were dull and largely worthless without further quantitative processing.

While political geography in the West was pursuing its rather aimless course, in Germany the development of geopolitics proceeded with a more definite if sinister sense of direction. This study was given its name by a Swede, Kjellen, in 1899; he had shown an early interest in the role of state power, and went on to explore and develop Ratzel's organic view of the state.[16] His opinions, which gave a pseudo-scientific justification to the rights of strong states to expand by any means possible, found an avid readership among extreme nationalists in Germany. The foreword to Kjellen's book of 1921 was written by Haushofer, a German soldier, traveller and geographer who, having spent some years in Japan before the 1914-18 war, had been much impressed by the autocratic nature of the Japanese state and the discipline of its society. Around Haushofer there coalesced a group of German geographers, some much more extreme than himself (he was a disciple of Hess rather than of Hitler), and their speculations produced an amalgamation of the organic state notions of Ratzel, Mackinder's global system and heartland thesis, macro-regionalism, postwar paranoia and the supposed German right to *Lebensraum*.[17] These ideas were mainly articulated in the pages of the periodical *Zeitschrift für Geopolitik* which first appeared in 1924 and continued for twenty years. Within the *Zeitschrift, Geopolitik* was developed as the 'geographical conscience of the state', though certainly moral and scientific consciences must have been abandoned, for data were either presented in subjective and misleading forms or, more simply, falsified, in order to suggest directions or to enlist support for Nazi war aims.

The launching of *Geopolitiik* in Germany rightly inspired profound reactions of disgust in the geographical world outside. Though several German geographers, to their credit, had the courage and integrity to stand apart from *Geopolitik*, in Germany the subject had in fact harboured nationalistic and deterministic undertones, identified by Roncagli as early as 1919—'German geographers have long ago tried to make physical geography one of the moral weapons with which Germany prepared to carry out her plans of dominating the world'[18]—and *Geopolitik* represented the grotesque eruption of a long-seated blemish, a rationalisation of the basest policies. In 1932 the French geographer Demangeon wrote (in translation), 'We are able to establish that German geopolitics deliberately renounces all scientific spirit. Since Ratzel it has not progressed, it is diverted to the arena of controversies and national hatreds.'[19] To Bowman, 'There is no sure "science" to bring us out of these new depths of international difficulty. Geopolitics is simple and sure, but, as demonstrated in German writings and policy, it is also illusion, mummery, an apology for theft.'[20]

It is widely suggested that political geography suffered as a result of the general outcry against *Geopolitik*. Certainly most Western geographers were extremely wary of accusations of subjectivity, and at the end of the last century Mackinder apparently faced a certain hostility in the establishment of a School of Geography at Oxford, partly on the grounds that it might 'subvert' geographical techniques to the study of international politics.[21] Yet all political geographers had been aware of the distinctions between political geography and *Geopolitik*, as was explained, for example, by the geopolitician Maull: 'Geopolitik is concerned with the spatial *requirements* of a state while political geography examines only its spatial conditions'.[22] But

Because the Nazis agitated for *Lebensraum* and exploited other geographic concepts for aggressive political purposes, it was illogically assumed that any mixing of geography and politics must be orientated towards war and conquest. Geographers insisted that geopolitics was a branch of political science. Political scientists tossed the pariah subject right back to geographers. In the American political climate of the 1930s, anything that could be branded geopolitics became much 'too hot to handle'.[23]

After the 1939–45 war, geopolitics of the Haushofer variety was extinguished while a rather dishevelled political geography staggered on to be overtaken by accelerating development in other branches of geography. Its post-war development was much as before. In the 1950s, a number of important theoretical innovations appeared (notably Hartshorne's functional approach and Jones's unified field theory) which seemed to promise further conceptual advances, but, as previously, the discipline as a whole was slow to consolidate and slower to initiate. The relative importance of political geography in university geography syllabuses and establishments had declined, and in consequence fewer specialist political geographers were being trained. Political-geographical topics continued to find a reasonable representation in the academic press, partly, however, because the subject was so impoverished in its theories and techniques that almost any geographer, historian or traveller, on coming across an appropriate topic, could easily turn his or her hand to political-geographical writing (so that the impoverishment was not entirely a bad thing).

Since at least 1967, I have heard numerous predictions that a large-scale political-geographical revival is imminent; so far it has not arrived. A number of very promising publications have appeared in the course of the last decade, many by non-political geographers, but they have not yet been fully absorbed into the theoretical basis of the subject. Political geography is quite rich in regional descriptions, particularly those concerning boundary studies, but the resumption of its rightful status as a branch of geography, the equal and essential companion of the economic, historical and social branches, will depend upon the development and refinement of theoretical and analytical techniques appropriate to the subject matter. It is to some extent encouraging that, while in the post-war period the political-geographical content of many university geography degree courses shrivelled, to amount to perhaps a couple of lectures within human or social geography courses, the subject stands in its own right in at least three of the new CNAA degree courses in geography which have recently been adopted in England.

1.3 Prospects

To support my contention that political geography is a retarded branch of geography, and has been for some time, I can invoke the opinions of some of the subject's leading practitioners.

[Hartshorne]: In perhaps no other branch of geography has the attempt to teach others gone so far ahead of the pursuit of learning by the teachers.[24]

[Jackson]: There is a real need for the development of systematic thinking in political geography. The elements and principles which have been described and
analysed in recent systematic texts are sometimes trivial, disconnected and undyna-
mic. The so-called human element receives but superficial treatment and attitudes
and motivations with respect to politics are virtually ignored. Lip service is paid to
the close relationship between political geography and political science, but fresh
insights into political reality might be gained if geographers would sincerely study
political science—and perhaps social psychology.[25]

[McColl]: In the modern trend toward increasing 'scientism', political geography,
as other social sciences, has suffered from a lack of formalization and thus clarity as
to its techniques and objectives.[26]

A leading American quantitative geographer, Berry, is even more direct:
'. . . political geography, that moribund backwater. . . . Certainly any
change would be a step in the right direction.'[27]

Among those who accept that the condition of contemporary political
geography leaves much to be desired, a variety of diagnoses and remedies
are offered. It is most widely suggested that the political-geographical
dilemma is the result of an adverse reaction to geopolitics. Certainly political geography suffered as a result, but Schat probably comes closest to the
truth in stating

It cannot be denied, of course, that German geopolitics did have a detrimental effect on interest in political geography. Nevertheless it is more probable that the
reason for the apathetic attitude shown by many geographers with regard to political geography, has to be found in the lack of consensus of opinion concerning the
object of political geography; this is one of the reasons why the theoretical foundation of this branch of geography has remained rudimentary.[28]

As the years go by, the geopolitical explanation appears more as an
excuse than a cause, and other fields of study have survived misap-
plications of their knowledge. 'Very few university administrations would
withhold funds from scientific research because the product of that research might be utilised to make H-bombs, bacteriological weapons, bal-
listic missiles, or other apparatus of statecraft.'[29] Since it now appears that
the influence of *Geopolitik*, at least upon Nazi policy-making, was small,
does not the lack of united and vociferous academic reaction against the
inestimably more serious application of knowledge gained in physics,
chemistry, biochemistry, biology and psychology to militaristic uses indicate a certain duality of standards? The reaction against *Geopolitik* was
justified at the time, but the distinction between it and political geography
was always clear.

It may be suggested that political geography has not benefited from
cross-fertilisation in the way that economic geography benefited from the
geographical contributions of great analysts such as Weber and Lösch.

Prescott points out that 'political scientists have made much less contribution to the field than geographers'.[30] So perhaps Muhammad should go to the mountain, since 'The experience of other parts of geography is that a little opportunistic borrowing never hurts. In political geography a lot might help; for the need is great.'[31]

Jackson, with the periodic support of other distinguished political geographers, has consistently argued that political geographers must familiarise themselves with the approaches, concepts and techniques of political scientists; though this need would appear to be self-evident, it has been widely disregarded. He is joined by Cohen and Rosenthal, who claim that '. . . without more attention to the political, our geographical insights are likely to be limited and sterile'; they offer the promising definition that 'Political geography is concerned with the spatial attributes of political process'.[32]

In former years as much emphasis was given to the effects of geography on politics as to the effects of politics on geography. More recently, however, it has become clear that the first relationship involves causes that are difficult to isolate and evaluate while the climate of opinion in the social sciences is opposed to reductionist approaches, and studies of the effects of geography on politics would, if indiscriminately carried out, lead in the direction of environmental determinism. Consequently modern political geography has drifted in the direction of studying politics as an agent involved in landscape change, though good studies of the reverse relationship will always be welcomed.

While most leading political geographers would probably agree that the regional approaches to their subject have frequently been undertaken by writers unaware of the (rather meagre) conceptual bases of political geography, Prescott (who has consistently encouraged students to gain familiarity with political science methodologies) fears that the younger generation of political geographers are neglecting the finer points of regional description.[33] This cannot be taken as a cause of the political-geographical malaise; its literature is fairly rich in regional description but impoverished in its concepts and methodologies. Consequently the future of regional description would seem to be dependent upon the prior development of the necessary theories and techniques appropriate to regional survey. This is not to belittle the importance of regional studies, and work of the quality of Burghardt's *Borderland* is most valuable.[34]

The rejuvenation of other branches of geography, both human and physical, has largely been achieved by the assimilation of what may loosely be bracketed together as quantitative techniques. One of the minor tragedies of modern geography has been the reluctance of many, quantifiers and traditionalists alike, to temper their criticisms of opposed viewpoints with moderation and understanding. Prescott, not a partisan traditionalist, reacted strongly to Berry's description of political geography as a moribund backwater with the suggestion that the effect of a further infusion of techniques of the sort recommended 'must be that the moribund backwater would become a dangerous swamp. Political geographers trapped there would be uncertain of their footing and orientation and would soon exhaust their energy.'[35] The attitudes of the more partisan are best imagined.

Statistical techniques are a good servant but a dangerous master; to be of value in political geography they should be applied with discretion and with attention to their nature and limitations. Their presentation is also a matter of importance; some articles have been produced which are incomprehensible to the majority of potentially interested students, and approaches which seem designed to create mystique for both their authors and for quantification in general are to be deplored. It is notable that the best writings in modern political geography, such as those by Soja, Witthuhn and Merritt, have included a succinct and unpretentious description of the techniques employed.[36] Examples will be found of the use of formulae, graphs and so on to dignify conclusions which can be stated more simply in verbal form, to disguise ill-considered reasoning or to grace the irrelevant.

The case for quantification is best presented in terms of the needs of political geography. Prescott has attempted to tabulate political-geographical topics amenable and inappropriate to quantitative analysis, but this constitutes the weakest and least complete section in a generally authoritative and closely researched survey.[37] The advantages of quantification are, firstly, that it can frequently be applied to support or refute the unvalidated conceptual elements in the basis of the subject. As an example, East's asumption[38] that landlocked states tend to be weak can be validated by comparing landlocked states as a group with coastal states as a group in terms of a parameter which relates to relative strength; GNP is perhaps convenient. Or the relationship between economic strength, the area of states and their populations can be more effectively described and more precisely demonstrated using Spearman correlation coefficients than is possible using literary forms or subjective assessment. Secondly, many political-geographical phenomena can be summarised in terms of an index, such as indices of shape or of ethnic segregation, which not only provide a more accurate description of the phenomenon concerned but can also be used as a basis for comparison. Thirdly, quantification can be used to reveal underlying relationships which would otherwise remain undetected; examples here would include the use of factor analysis to detect hidden patterns of conflict and grouping at international conferences or of association and homogeneity among groups of states.

The wealth of empirical studies in political geography is not counterbalanced by an equally impressive array of generic studies or viable generalisations. With particular regard to the teaching of the subject, there is a need for the construction of more models, for which the empirical basis must largely exist. The systems approach may be regarded by some to be

limited in its powers of explanation, but it can most usefully be applied in
the organisation of disjointed elements and formulation of hypotheses,
and is particularly effective when applied in relating international behaviour to the global context.[39]

If the backward nature of political geography derives (as several, myself
included, would suggest) from the weakness of its political insights, the
shortage of sound theoretical bases, the absence of proof for many of the
notions which are currently taught and the dearth of precise measurements
and comparative studies, then the remedy must clearly lie in the assimilation of proven techniques and approaches from political science and international relations, the development and adoption of appropriate
quantitative techniques and a greater emphasis on generic studies.

Present indications are that the rehabilitation and revitalisation of political geography will take place during the next ten years or so, mainly
through the judicious adoption and creation of more accurate techniques
of measurement and analysis. Not all of the leading contributions will be
of a quantitative nature; for example, three of the foremost contributions
to political geography since the war (Hartshorne's functional approach,
Jones's unified field theory, and Cohen and Rosenthal's systems approach) were non-quantitative in essence, though each could be enhanced
by the addition of quantitative refinements.

Case study

The stunting of political geography may lead to the devaluation of political
factors as agents in landscape development and change. Few patterns of
human activity can be adequately described without reference to the effects, direct and indirect, of politics, and a lack of appreciation for political
factors will result in an improper emphasis being placed on environmental
and simplified economic forces. In order to demonstrate the importance of
politics in human and regional geographical explanation, a brief case study
of post-revolutionary Soviet development follows. Critics may argue that
in selecting an ideologically defined state with a command economy I have
chosen an extreme case to support my contentions. The choice is justified
on the grounds that, although Western democracies, for example, practis-
ing free-enterprise or mixed economies constitute equally individualistic
political entities, politics exerts its effects in more subtle ways in a state
such as the United Kingdom. In the space available it would not be possible to document the implications of the various systems of quotas and
tariffs, which create a special environment for domestic producers, legislation concerning development areas, the role of nationalised industries,
taxation and numerous other forms of government intervention. In the
Soviet Union, however, the political factor stands out in much starker reality.

Two developments in particular characterised the changing geography of post-revolutionary Russia: the collectivisation of agriculture, and the drive for industrialisation with the emphasis upon producer rather than consumer goods with urbanisation developing rapidly from the indus-trialisation. The explanation of these developments is not to be found by reference to the Russian physical environment or to simple economic re-lationships.

The Bolshevik party which gained control of Russia as an outcome of the revolutions of 1917 was essentially the party of the minority Russian industrial proletariat, the class to which Marxism accorded the social revolutionary mantle and at which it directed its appeal; at the time of the revolutions almost 10 per cent of industrial workers were actually mem-bers of the party, though other classes in Russia looked to other parties. Had Lenin not succeeded in convincing his Bolsheviks that the Russian circumstance need not be covered by the Marxist statement that socialist revolution is only possible when the industrial proletariat constitutes an increasing majority in society, then there would have been no Bolshevik revolution, and for many years to come Russia would have remained a quasi-colony of the industrial powers of Europe, a supplier of primary pro-ducts, an importer of manufactured goods, and dependent upon foreign investment to subsidise its development along directions chosen by the investors.

Post-revolutionary Russia was weak and unstable, and in the chaos of the civil war and foreign intervention, industry collapsed, with production in 1920 being 82 per cent lower than in 1916; the population of Moscow fell by 44.5 per cent, and that of Petrograd by 57.5 per cent. The class base of the Bolshevik party, which had only amounted to about two million work-ers, was decimated, and the civil war took the heaviest toll upon the most politically active elements in the industrial class. In these circumstances the party was obliged to play a conciliatory role, particularly with regard to the peasantry, which amounted to 82 per cent of the population and had by force of numbers been largely instrumental in carrying through the revol-ution but with its political perspectives confined mainly to achieving a redistribution of the landlord-owned estates.

Different economic policies were applied in the post-revolutionary period, each producing characteristic effects upon the landscape. For three years following the revolution, the strategy of 'war communism' was adopted and practised during a period of extreme disruption, further de-cline in production and widespread starvation. The remaining feudal estates were parcelled out among the peasantry, some nationalisation was carried through, and some coercion was successful in forcing peasants to surrender foodstuffs for the support of towns and the Red Army, but in general the Bolsheviks were obliged to compromise, conciliate and fre-quently to retreat.

The introduction of the New Economic Policy in 1921 embodied many concessions to the vast and discontented peasant majority, and lasted until

1928. Private enterprise in the Soviet economy increased and some industries were denationalised; the enforcement of peasant deliveries to the state was partially lifted and food requisitioning squads disbanded. This retreat from socialism was a means of buying time for the regime, a period of political consolidation and economic recovery. While the NEP was running, a series of bitter factional struggles were being acted out within the party.

As Stalin was securing a web of support among the new bureaucracy, a Right Opposition faction associated with Bukharin and Tomsky favoured further concessions to the peasantry, arguing that industry should concentrate on the manufacture of consumer goods which would be made available to the peasants who would thereby be stimulated to increase their production in order to make more purchases; the main threat to the regime, they argued, came from the capitalist powers, which should not be antagonised. This policy was originally in accord with Stalin's doctrine of 'socialism in one country' which suggested that, given stability, socialism could slowly be built within an isolated Soviet unit. The Left Opposition, centred on Trotsky, asserted that the rate of industrialisation was too slow, that the establishment of heavy and armaments industries was essential to the defence of socialism, that party policy was strengthening the wealthy peasant class, and that the only hope for socialist survival lay in exporting the revolution to an advanced industrial state.

Initially Stalin favoured the Right Opposition group, and in a series of purges the Left was effectively annihilated, but in 1928 its predictions were vindicated when the peasantry withheld food deliveries to the state. Subsequent Soviet development can be traced to a far-reaching policy reversal in which the Stalin group, by this time strongly entrenched in power, turned upon the Right and introduced the policies of the Left, but with more ruthlessness and force than the Left had ever envisaged. In the countryside this involved the enforced collectivisation of the land, and in the Soviet Union as a whole it involved the introduction of omnipotent five-year planning and a sacrifice of liberty and standards of living as producer goods production proceeded at a faster rate than consumer goods production.

Collectivisation, which transformed the Russian rural landscape, can only be understood in a political context, and though it did not significantly affect levels of agricultural production, it broke the power of the peasantry and made cheap food available to support the expanding urban industrial labour force. While heavy industrial production expanded rapidly and the Soviet Union experienced a rate of industrial expansion which had never been equalled, the production of consumer goods remained static. The resurgence of consumer goods production under the last plan and its unprecedented overtaking of producer goods under the current plan again reflect political considerations—a response to popular discontent within the Soviet Union, probably influenced by events in Czechoslovakia in 1968 and the food riots in Poland in late 1970.

Planning in contemporary Russia equally reflects political influences: industrial location policy is formulated with regard to ideological considerations, lessons of Soviet experience, policies in vogue and the relative power of vested interests. In general, and within certain limits, Marxist–Leninist ideology is invoked only to support the ambitions of various interest groups, of which the opposed reformers and neo-Stalinists are the most important.

Any attempt to explain the geography of post-revolutionary Russia which lacks a considerable emphasis on the role of political factors is bound to founder. Geographers in general, and regional and economic geographers in particular, have tended to misjudge the importance of political considerations, and this is indicative of the inadequacy of political geography as well as that of analysis in other branches of geography.[40]

PART 2

Political regions and time

With the exception of inhospitable polar regions and a few scattered areas where colonial relationships survive, the land surface of the earth is now divided up into a political patchwork of sovereign states. In area after area previous forms of political region have yielded to the sovereign state, though the processes of political-geographical evolution have varied remarkably. 'Ideas about boundaries', writes Jones, 'are related to their geographical and historical *milieu*.'[1] The same applies to the political regions contained within these boundaries. Particular forms of political region are related to particular stages in social and political organisation, with changes in the level of a group's development leading to a reappraisal of its political-geographical circumstance.

2.1 Territory in different forms

Recently, writers such as Morris[2] and Ardrey[3] have suggested that insights into human territorial relationships can be derived from studies of animal behaviour. An animal territory is a well-defined area which is regarded by a pair or a group of animals as being an exclusive preserve. Occasionally aggression is directed at all intruders, but more often it is confined to other members of the same species. The mere possession of a territory appears to give the occupant a distinct psychological advantage over the intruder, which almost invariably retreats. The animal territory often exists within a larger home range, an area with which the animal is familiar and within which it forages for food.

Territoriality is evident at many levels in the vertebrate animal kingdom, and arguably among some invertebrates. Some migratory grazing animals do not appear to exhibit territorial behaviour, while in some others, such as the sea lion, struggles for territory are related to the establishment of individual dominance. The baboon is often a migratory animal, and territoriality is the prerogative of the dominant male;[4] a small but inviolable territory is established around him wherever he sits, and other members of the troop intrude at their peril. In most cases where territoriality is evident, it has a distinct survival value. Often the possession of territory is an essential prerequisite for breeding, so the number of breeding pairs becomes adjusted to the territory available, while the struggle to establish territories involves the selection of the strongest males for breeding. Combination in the defence of territory may lead to a strengthening of group bonds in, for example, wolf packs and monkey troops.

It may be tempting to draw analogies between the territory with its focal nesting site, its space and its inviolable periphery, and the sovereign state with its capital, area and boundaries, or between the chorusing of the robin or the howler monkey troop around the margins of their territories and the patrolling of frontier guards between boundary markers. Ethology is a young but expanding science, and may soon provide clearer interpretations of the territorial bases of human behaviour; at present it is not known whether territoriality, which may apply to the home, or even the motor car, can be extended to apply to the state. Loosely based territorial arguments have given spurious justification for the inevitability of warfare and the impracticability of egalitarianism.

Archaeological and anthropological evidence suggests that until recently in the life of the species, men existed as hunters and women as collectors and gatherers. The functional human and geographical units were the clan or extended family, and the clan territory, within which the group pursued a nomadic existence. Though certain sites and features probably had a ritual significance, the strengthening of the association between a group and a particular place would not come until the adoption of a sedentary mode of life, the result of discovery and development in agriculture. After a period of permanent occupancy and an amalgamation of neighbouring groups, the territory will begin to bear the stamp of its occupants. Kirk[5] has detected the existence of cultural if not political regions within the sparsely populated Megalithic Scotland of about 2000 BC, and Muir[6] has attempted to reconstruct the internal political divisions of Pictish Scotland and demonstrated the retention of some of these divisions in subsequent political phases.

The Bushmen of the Kalahari retain clan territories. They are a hunting and collecting culture, precariously surviving in a hostile environment bypassed by more advanced cultures. Their clans have around fifty members, populations which are strictly controlled by the changing food and water resources of the clan territory, while the territory itself is clearly established and neighbouring territories are avoided. Within their territories, the clans migrate between the waterholes which are the central places of the Bushman world, though the territory has no permanent

settlement, single central focus or capital. De Blij[7] correlates growing political sophistication with increases in the importance of central places and
the centralisation of political power. The Australian Aborigines are intermediate between the clan and tribal stages; at times of plenty, separate
groups come together, to fragment in times of hardship. Among the Aborigines, waterholes as central places have a special significance which is not
only economic but also spiritual, since they are considered to be the abodes
of ancestors.

Sociopolitical amalgamation superseded clan forms by tribal organisation in all but the most hostile environments. This transition produced
much more extensive political regions, with populations of tens or even
hundreds of thousands. It was usually accompanied by increased centralisation and remoteness of power, while the physiographical central place
was generally replaced by a permanent political focus differing in function
from other settlements. The limits of tribal territories have frequently been
described as being of a zonal frontier nature, though this is very much of a
generalisation. Often, as with some East African tribal territories, intervening areas constituted a political no-man's-land, claimed by neither bordering tribe, but finer delimitation also occurred—the Vedda of Ceylon
have fixed boundaries patrolled by sentries.[8] Both zonal frontiers and
linear boundaries surrounded the Aborigine territories; where the border
passed through an area of economic significance it was carefully defined
and jealously guarded, though where the borderland was unproductive,
delimitation was neglected.[9] Prescott has shown that the limits of tribal territories in the Niger–Benue area of Africa varied along their length, being
related to physiographical and human characteristics and to the changing
balances of power between the separated peoples.[10]

The modern nation state has been regarded, perhaps wrongly, as the ultimate sociopolitical spatial form. The transition from the tribal territory
to the sovereign nation state has not been accomplished without the intervention of intermediate stages. At the time of its colonisation by Europeans, Africa exhibited many of the political-geographical characteristics
of dark-age Europe; in some places tribal territories held sway, in others
they had been superseded by patterns of kingdom and empire, as the more
successful tribes conquered neighbouring groups and brought them under
their control. A thousand years ago, Europe and Africa were comparable
in terms of levels of political-geographical evolution. In the former, however, new stages of political development followed on the growth of universal institutions, a notion of state sovereignty and ideas about the
territorial rights of nations. The arrested situation in Africa is characterised in Prescott's description of the Sokoto–Gando empire.

In the provinces of Zaria, Bida, Kontagora, Nassarawa, Kano and Muri, the
Fulani subjugated the indigenous tribes. In other areas such as Bauchi and western
Adamawa, enclaves of pagan groups retained their independence on hilltop settle-

ments. Finally, in Libtako and eastern Adamawa, only the main towns on the principal trade routes were subject to Fulani authority.[11]

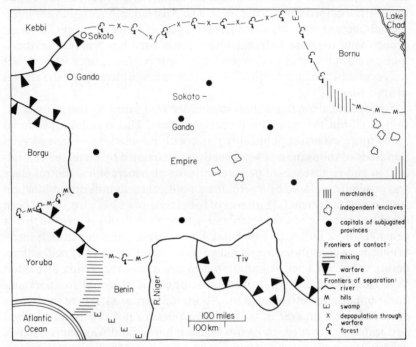

Figure 2.1. The limits of tribal states, territories and empires in nineteenth-century West Africa (based on ref. 10, p. 51)

Much of the coherence of tribal societies derives from the belief in a common lineage; this ethnic simplicity is lost when an expansionist tribe establishes dominance over neighbouring groups and coercion may be necessary to retain the captured territory. The nations of Europe developed within the kingdoms and empires of medieval Europe; they did not evolve directly from tribal groupings, and in western Europe, at least, states preceded nations.[12]

The expansion of political authority beyond tribal limits was usually a response both to economic and to political factors. To quote de Blij, 'In many of the tribal states in Africa that achieved prosperity, it was the felicitous location of the tribal headquarters that provided the impetus'.[13] The growth of far-reaching trading connections gave these central places an influence beyond the tribal confines and encouraged military operations to secure trade routes. Probably the earliest political regions to exhibit a range of state-like characteristics appeared in the valleys of the Tigris, Euphrates and Nile around 5000 BC, where fluctuating patterns of commercialism and empire were superimposed on a system of statelets. These original civilisations were typified by a more developed organisation of people and territory; it is arguable that the roots of this organisation can be traced in the need for wider cooperation and control in the introduction and operation of irrigation schemes. Certainly the semi-arid riverine environments, like those of other early civilisations in the Indus and Chinese valleys, were capable of yielding highly and supporting relatively dense agricultural populations after the application of irrigation and flood control.

The mere production of an agricultural surplus is a great stimulus to political expansion; subsistence farming does not release population for specialist occupations in government, administration, trading or armed service, while an agricultural surplus may support these activities and provide the wherewithal for a flourishing commercialism. While the Mayan, Aztec and Inca empires of the Americas may be viewed from theocratic or militaristic perspectives, ultimately they were based on the surplus production of the humble peasant. Political expansion, commerce and the division of labour in turn required and generated extending networks of communications and new, larger and more specialised urban settlements. Towns grew as the administrative, religious, commercial and industrial focuses of statelets and miniature empires and new phases of conquest, trading expansion and the diffusion of innovations brought the establishment of new towns and further extensions of communications arteries.

2.2 Development in Europe

Though state-like political regions appeared at various times in most parts of Asia, many parts of Africa and some parts of the Americas, the now ubiquitous sovereign state is essentially a product of European evolution. Why this should be so has not been established, and reductionist approaches which stress environmental determinism, and particularly those which suggest European ethnic superiority, should be avoided; historical accident coupled with exceedingly complicated patterns of cultural diffusion and environmental opportunity must have been influential. The Roman Empire, the closest approach to a mono-polar power system, did not lead directly to the appearance of modern states in Europe; neither did the establishment of tribal territories and tribal kingship. Rather, the modern states were preceded by phases of premature consolidation and of fragmentation. The tribal kingdoms which emerged from the collapse of the Roman Empire were retarded in their development, beset and frequently overrun in the dark ages by waves of invasion from less politically advanced peoples such as the Vikings, Huns and Magyars.

Fluctuation in the relative strengths and fortunes of ruling elites initiated waves of expansion and consolidation, contraction and fragmentation, and in the medieval period some kingdoms more extensive than their tribal predecessors were established. However, rather than their being modern states, definable in terms of centrally organised territory, they frequently only found unity under a nominal claim of kingship. Central authority in the medieval period was based less upon the purposeful organisation of territory than upon the establishment of networks of personal loyalty and obligation between the ruler and the nobility. Internal and external instability prevailed, and rules of intranational and international legitimacy which could serve as norms for the stabilisation of systems of authority remained to be developed. Dukes, earls and barons fought each other and combined to oppose kings, and many of them held lands in several kingdoms, while the right to rule territory was based on might, intrigue and fortuitous marriage. Medieval Germany, for example, was characterised by extreme political fragmentation under the veneer of unity which the nominal Reich provided, and imperial authority was unable to maintain effective centralised control as real power radiated outward from a number of regional nodes. Statelets formed as cities exerted control over the tributary areas which supplied them with food; bishops reigned supreme over their bishoprics, and barons over their baronies. Though most of Europe experienced a measure of unity under the umbrella of the Roman Catholic Church, and Latin provided a *lingua franca* for the educated classes, nationalism had no meaning for the mass of ordinary people who found identity in terms of a series of parochialisms; Normans were Normans and Bretons were Bretons, neither were Englishmen or Frenchmen.

The modern state was moulded by both universalist and particularist forces, analgous to Gottman's circulation and iconography discussed in part 5. Though universalism of the scope provided in Europe by the Roman Empire or the pre-Reformation Catholic Church has not been replicated, sufficient remained in the seventeenth century for the concept of state sovereignty—a doctrine of particularism—to gain general acceptance among European statesmen. The roots of state sovereignty are to be found in the Treaty of Westphalia of 1648, when the Holy Roman Emperor conferred sovereign independence on princes who remained formally within the Empire. Sovereignty involves the recognition by the sovereign of the exclusive rights of other sovereigns to govern within their respective states, and of the inviolable nature of the territory of other states. The general acceptance of the doctrine brought a new order and permanence to the international relations and political units of Europe. When in the eighteenth and nineteenth centuries nationalism became a powerful force, the sovereign state which was roughly coextensive with a national distribution added a moral justification to its legal *raison d'être*. Sovereignty, however, was unable to guarantee the integrity of the nonnational state. The topic of nationalism is reserved for a full consideration in part 5, and it is possible to define the modern state without reference to nationalism; according to L. Oppenheim, a state '. . . is in existence when a people is settled in a territory under its own sovereign government'.[14]

The European concept of the state, which by virtue of its sovereignty can recognise no superior authority, and the largely European doctrine of nationalism were exported to the remainder of the world and superimposed directly upon existing forms of politico-territorial organisation. The transformation occurred without the prolonged indigenous evolution evident in Europe, and in consequence, in many parts of the post-colonial world, states and tribal divisions are involved in an uneasy coexistence, with the state competing for loyalty with the tribe. Elsewhere, post-colonial states such as Ceylon which can look back to an earlier unified political existence have resented the 'new state' tag and claim that they have reverted to a sovereignty which was temporarily compromised by colonialism.[15]

People, politics and territory exist in a dynamic equilibrium. Different types of political region have been adopted at different times in different places; occasionally different forms have existed contemporaneously within the same space, for example tribal territories within British African colonies. In the latter part of the twentieth century, various parts of the world have converged in adopting the sovereign state form of political region. One need not suppose that this convergence is permanent, and great variety has been shown in the stages by which this convergence has been reached, as demonstrated in figure 2.2. Two tendencies become apparent: those of politico-territorial integration, and of disintegration. On the broad scale, the former has predominated, and the trend towards increasing political sophistication and socioeconomic complexity has been paralleled by the adoption of larger political regions.

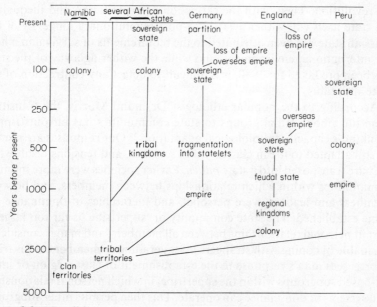

Figure 2.2. Possible stages in the development of political regions. The figure shows the variation in stages by which selected political regions have evolved. Note the use of a logarithmic time scale.

2.3 The shape of things to come

In the earlier years of this century there was fairly general support for the view that the sovereign nation state form of political region represented a culmination of political-geographical processes. Certain more recent developments have encouraged speculation as to whether the sovereign nation state is an ephemeral rather than an ultimate form. These include, firstly, the formation of supranational organisations, membership of which may even, as in the case of the European Economic Community, require a partial surrender of state sovereignty. Secondly, the greater powers have on several occasions shown a readiness to disregard the sovereignty of lesser powers; the American handling of affairs in south-east Asia and the Russian interventions in Eastern Europe suggest a devaluation of the doctrine of state sovereignty.

Because of its wide and varied influences, the state has been of interest to workers in several disciplines, and their predictions are relevant to any attempt to foresee possible political-geographical changes. To Marx and his followers, the state is a device for maintaining the rule of one class over another: '. . . the state as a special apparatus for coercing people arose only wherever and whenever there appeared a division of society into classes, that is, a division into groups of people some of whom are permanently in a position to appropriate the labour of others . . .' .[16] In the course of an inevitable proletarian revolution, the state apparatus will be seized by the toilers and used to crush the last vestiges of oppression and counter-revolution. Then, with the extinction of exploitation and inequality, the state itself will wither away. The post-revolutionary longevity of the Russian state has been attributed to the requirements of survival in a hostile international environment, and while the withering away of the state has been predicted for 1980, it is difficult to detect any contraction of the state apparatus.

According to the popular ethologist Desmond Morris, the transition from life among tribal groups to state communities has far outstripped mankind's capacity for biological adaptation.[17] Our responses are seen to be still adapted to life in clan or tribal societies, and tensions result when they are transposed into a state *milieu*. Earlier societies were more intimate communities within which relationships between members, and between members and leaders, were personal, and hierarchies of dominance became established. The state community or 'supertribe' is far too large to permit personal relationships between all members, and man is considered incapable of coping with strangers masquerading as members of his tribe. Morris sees man's response in the establishment of class, region or interest-based subgroups within the supertribe, in which personal relationships and systems of dominance can operate. This then permits other subgroups such as servants or coloured immigrants to be treated in an impersonal and consequently inhuman way. The breakdown of personal relationships within the supertribe allows the emergence of extra-dominant superleaders or supertyrants. Such leaders realise that the most potent way of maintaining the supertribe intact involves the manipulation of an out-group threat from another supertribe, and no force is seen to unite the supertribe more strongly than war.

Rather than stress an unnatural largeness of modern states, Herz saw the sovereign state as being subject to a precarious survival in the face of growing supranationalist pressures.[18] To Herz, security has been a primary consideration in the formation of political regions. The territorial state came to the fore when the introduction of gunpowder and large mercenary armies rendered the local fortresses of feudal magnates obsolete. The perimeter of security then expanded from the castle walls to the limits of the developing territorial state, whose boundaries then became sacrosanct under the doctrine of state sovereignty. The process involved the establishment, in Europe, of defensible political units, internally pacified and sheltered within a hard outer shell of frontier defences. The continuity of these units was buttressed by the general acceptance of a concept of legitimacy, whereby dynasties recognised each other as rightful sovereigns, with a threat to one constituting a latent threat to all. Nationalism provided a further guarantee where the state was a national state.

The security of the territorial state was seen by Herz to be vested in the sovereign and defensive impenetrability of its boundaries. But recent developments in weaponry have allowed the bombs and missiles of an aggressor to bypass the hard outer shell and strike direct at the population of the soft interior of the state. Various forms of airborne propaganda can permeate the outer defences of the state and may be used in attempts to subvert a civilian population. In some ways industrialisation has weakened the territorial state, which becomes dependent upon foreign sources of raw materials and vulnerable to economic blockade. Few if any modern states have sufficiently large domestic markets to support competitive industries which fully maximise economies of scale in production.

The main elements in the pre-1939 political system were the great powers, lesser powers and colonies. The post-war period has seen the emergence of two, and now perhaps three superpowers. Kristof has pointed out that, while many pre-war international problems concerned disputes over inter-state boundaries, in the post-war period ideology has become the main source of tension, with superpowers acting as ideological heartlands confronting each other across an ideological frontier zone, a grey area of equivocal loyalties and undefined allegiances.[19] He writes, 'On the fringes of the ideological ecumene of our divided world unintegrated elements occupy shifting frontier zones. These zones are not the cause of international instability; they reflect the unsettledness of the contemporary human society.'[20]

To Meinig, the dominant theme in international affairs was a competition for influence and control within a Eurasian 'rimland' which girdles a

Soviet 'heartland'.[21] The rimland is composed of states whose orientations may fluctuate between the continental or pro-Russian and maritime or pro-Western. Whebell suggests that future flashpoints in world conflict are likely to centre on numerous areas inhabited by stateless national minorities scattered along the margins of the Soviet sphere. The Kurds, the Macedonians, the Kashmiris and the Azerbaijanis of Iran are among the peoples whose nationalism may be manipulated to create severe international tensions.[22] Sino-Soviet relations in particular are jeopardised by persistent minority unrest in Sinkiang. This is the only part of China where ethnic Chinese are in a minority, and the indigenous peoples of Sinkiang look across the neighbouring Russian border for support in their attempts to resist Chinese hegemony.[23] It is arguable that developments in nuclear warfare have prevented direct warfare between the superpowers. Superpower rivalry now involves the probing of sensitive areas within the spheres of influence of rivals, but since nobody knows where the real brink lies, experiments in brinkmanship still leave open the possibility of nuclear conflict.

Though sovereignty, as a source of state security, may be on the decline, there is nothing to suggest the dawning of an era of internationalism or world government. Sovereign states are ensuring their survival through membership of supranational organisations which are themselves exclusive. Competition is not being eliminated from the international scene; rather, the scales upon which it operates are being transposed.

The yardstick of national interest is as paramount as ever in determining state policies. These are invariably framed in relation to short-term national interests rather than the long-term interests of mankind as a whole. State sovereignty has been an impassable obstacle to the formation of global policies; since states are sovereign, it follows that they cannot be subject to legal restraint, and consequently international law is not, in the final analysis, binding on states. On this rock the League of Nations foundered and the United Nations was emasculated.

Mankind is desperately in need of a global approach to disarmament, food distribution, resource development, conservation and pollution control, and marine exploitation, but such policies, to be effective, can only be formulated and implemented by a world authority which is unfettered by the constraints of individual state sovereignty. We have no reason to suppose that the tendency towards the formation of larger economic and defensive blocs represents a significant step towards world government.

2.4 Theoretical approaches

Historical research in political geography has broadly tended to follow two complementary patterns. Firstly, there is what might be termed a historical atlas approach, involving attempts to reconstruct political regions as they existed at particular points in time. This approach is not attracting great attention at present, though challenging research problems do exist.

Carter has used connectivity analysis and measures of accessibility in an investigation of the extent and capital location of medieval Serbia,[24] and Muir reconstructed the extents of medieval Scottish counties from information contained in the original land charters.[25] Secondly, there has been a search for common processes in the appearance and development of political regions, and for frameworks for their analysis.

There have been three distinctive political-geographical approaches to the question of the growth of states: Ratzel's organic view, the core area concept, and Jones's unified field theory. Ratzel's impact on political geography has already been discussed; up to his death in 1904 he was interested in the relationship between space and the state. The state was viewed as a form of organism governed by Darwinistic laws, its success and security directly related to its ability to acquire space at the expense of competing neighbours.[26] In order to stabilise their international relations and avoid undue conflict, governments have been concerned with the clear delimitation of state boundaries, but to Ratzel, rigid boundaries were anathema to the state which, deprived of its ability to expand, must decline. He thought that the energy for expansion came through cultural advance and population pressure, and consequently the size of a state could be one measure of the cultural level of its population. He saw the ground for state expansion being prepared by contact and diffusion beyond existing state limits by commercial and missionary activities. Political annexation follows with the success of the annexation depending upon the ability of the state to absorb and win the allegiance of the captured population.

Few biologists would be convinced that the characteristics of organisms, such as growth, reproduction, movement and exchange, are duplicated by states. The supposedly common characteristic to which Ratzel paid most attention—growth—is a completely different process in the state and the organism. Ratzel suggested that the directions of state expansion are affected by attempts to acquire better rather than poorer land and by the cultural preferences of the people concerned. Though the real organism may grow in size, its form is genetically determined before birth and that of the state is not. No matter how successful or competitive we are, we cannot develop a third arm! When actual cases are studied it becomes apparent that the acquisition of territory very frequently occurs along lines of least resistance, or through historical accidents such as dynastic marriage or fortuitous inheritance. With its emphasis on necessities of competition and conquest, Ratzel's approach must be seen, particularly in a nuclear age, as a doctrine of despair in human morality and good sense.

The core area concept is rather more productive. As defined by Whittlesey, the core area is both 'the area in which or about which a state originates'[27] and '. . . it is more richly endowed by nature than the rest of the State'.[28] The role of core areas in the growth of states is extremely variable, and only some states have shown a pattern of growth which can be reconciled with a core area concept. Simply stated, the idea is that the core area, being particularly well-endowed in geographical resources such as fertility or nodality, from an early date supports relatively high population densities at higher cultural and economic levels than those of surrounding regions. The commercial ascendancy and the ability to support armies allow the rulers of the core area to extend political control over adjacent areas, and so the state expands with the accretion of territory around its core. Advocates of the core area concept would describe states which have developed through the expansion of control from a core area as 'organic', and those which have not as 'arbitrary' and, by implication, somehow less viable political units. A fuller critique of the concept appears in part 3.

Certain states have grown by processes similar to those outlined above; Russia provides a classic example. The core area of the state is the Moscow basin which, while not being endowed with exceptional fertility or mineral resources, had extreme nodality in respect of the early waterway-based system of communications. Five centuries of intermittent expansion placed the hitherto insignificant Grand Duchy of Moscow at the heart of the world's largest state. If too rigidly applied, the core area concept can lead to excesses in geographical determinism and the neglect of chance and human factors. France and Russia are frequently quoted as examples of states which have grown from geographically favoured core areas. In the case of Russia, the extension of Muscovite control owed as much to human factors—the devious skills of Ivan III (1462–1515) and his successors—as to geographical factors, while the emergent French state only became centred on the Paris basin when the kingship passed to the Count of Paris in 987.

Difficulties also arise in identifying and measuring the extents of core areas, and the proponents of the concept have relied solely on subjective methods of detection. A core area origin may loosely apply to a number of European states; of twenty-five studied by Pounds and Ball, fifteen were considered to have grown directly by the accretion of territory around a core area.[29] In other parts of the world, the majority of states have either appeared overnight with the granting of sovereign independence to colonies whose areas were frequently arbitrarily defined, or else derived from complex origins which do not accord with the continuity of growth implicit in the core-area concept.

An alternative approach was provided by Jones in the form of his 'unified field theory'.[30] Here, the appearance of a politically organised area is seen as the product of a series of interconnected stages; an initial *idea* is developed to produce a political *decision*, which in turn precipitates *movement* affecting an area or *field* within which a political *area* ultimately materialises. The underlined stages have been compared to interconnected lake basins or to hubs of activity, with the dominant direction of flow from idea to area, though interaction in the reverse direction is also envisaged.

The application of the theory is well illustrated in Jones's own example concerning Liberia; my application of the theory to the recent emergence of Bangladesh reveals some of its strengths and its limitations.[31]

	Liberia	Bangladesh
Idea	Abolition of slavery	Discrimination against the people of East Pakistan by the regime centred on West Pakistan
Decision	Colonisation: humanitarian societies seek a home for repatriated slaves	Sheikh Mujibur Rahman's six-point programme for equality and autonomy
Movement	Transportation of freed slaves to West Africa	Military action by Pakistan army; flight of refugees into India; intervention by Indian army
Field	Territory purchased for settlement	East Pakistan
Area	State of Liberia	Independent state of Bangladesh

The theory provides a useful framework for analysis of this and many other problems in political geography. With regard to the example quoted, it should be remembered that rather than there being one decisive decision, a complex series of decisions was involved. They included the millions of individual decisions to vote for the Awami League, the Indian decision for armed intervention and the decision to proclaim an independent Bangladesh in December 1971. Wider relationships were also involved; Bangladesh was not possible without Indian intervention, and this was itself conditional upon Chinese military abstention. The charismatic leadership of Sheikh Mujib was another highly significant and unique variable. The theory can only be applied working backwards from a political-geographical reality; millions of political ideas are current in society, and only a miniscule proportion of them culminate in the appearance of a political region.

Of the three approaches reviewed, that of Jones appears to be the most universally applicable, though flexibility must be used in its application. Any political-geographical theory must be adapted to the particular rather than *vice versa*. Early historical geographers have been scorned by some historians because of their simplistic invocation of geographical determinism to explain complicated historical developments, and political geographers too have been prone to this tendency.

PART 3

Political regions and structure

Here attention is focused on the morphology of the state, its form and internal structures, while recognising that each state is a complex relationship between people, territory and government. The control of sovereign territory, precisely bounded and administered from a state capital, is a factor common to all states, though variation is found in the effectiveness of this control within and between states, and in the disposition of political-geographical sub-regions. There is great variability in the size and shape of states, while capitals, core areas and boundaries differ in their nature and origins. Though morphological approaches no longer dominate political geography, studies of the morphology of states still have a significant role to play, and advances in morphological analysis are essential to the overall development of the subject.

3.1 Sovereign territory and its components

The elements of statehood are population, territory, sovereignty and government, and the state derives its political-geographical personality from the interplay of these variables within the wider environment of the international system. States, as the fundamental regions of political geography, differ from the regions studied by economic or urban geographers in that they are disjoint area or patch sets; only their boundaries intersect, and there is no overlapping of regions. The territory of the state is united under the umbrella of state sovereignty which applies as rigidly to the most remote portion of the state as to its core. State sovereignty terminates at the state boundaries, which represent interfaces between the sovereign territory of neighbouring units, or at the limits of claimed territorial waters and, in some cases, beyond, where sovereignty can be claimed over the surface of a continental shelf but not over its overlying waters. The interfaces between sovereignties extend downwards as radial planes from the centre of the earth, defining rights over subterranean matter. Difficulties arise when this 'cone wedge' concept is applied to the problem of defining sovereign limits above the territory of the state. Legislation concerning state sovereignty over air space dates from 1919, when an international convention in Paris produced agreements on the rights of innocent passage for non-military aircraft and the rights of states to institute prohibited zones which could not be overflown. The doctrine of *usque ad coelum* involving the upward extension of state sovereignty to an unlimited height is unworkable, and though the space treaty of 1967 propounded the first code of space law, the question of the upper limit of state sovereignty has not been resolved, and figures of 300 miles and a more realistic 50 miles have been suggested. Most governments will concede that state sovereignty may be claimed up to the operational ceiling of conventional aircraft and that, beyond this limit, outer space and celestial bodies are immune from sovereign claims or militarisation and subject to international law in accordance to international law and articles I–IV of the space treaty.[1]

The acceptance of world patterns of sovereignty is not total, partly because of the existence of conflicting territorial claims and the non-recognition of some governments and states by others, and partly because of the incomplete nature of international law and the equivocal attitudes of governments towards it. At present, the greatest source of contention concerns the breadth of territorial waters which may be claimed, though other maritime disputes and land-based claims are current.

Burghardt has listed four modes by which claims to sovereignty over territory can gain international legal recognition.[2] They are: *occupation*, the establishment of control over unadministered territory; *prescription*, the maintenance of effective control for a sufficient period of time; *cession*, or transfer by treaty; and *accretion*, the growth of sovereign territory through acts of nature. Though conquest is outside of international law, there are numerous examples to prove the feasibility of this method of extending the state area.

With the retreat of territorial imperialism, most states today express, partially express, or have generated a close relationship between a human group and a piece of territory. Burghardt symbolises this 'man–land pair bonding' as a multidimensional structure.[3] At the centre is effective control, which is normally based on uncontested administration, binding the area to a particular population. A horizontal dimension is formed by territorial integrity, a group's perception of the portion of space which it deems to be its own. History provides a vertical dimension extending the man–land ties through time and creating a sense of immutability, and the relative strength of the entire structure depends upon the degree of cultural similarity present in the population.

Though the state is united under sovereignty and government, interplay between political man and the land creates a polit-ical-geographical subdivision of state territory into sub-regions which vary in form and function. Frequently the state territory includes a single capital and one or more core areas, and is defined by a set of bound-aries which may or may not also define the 'effective state area'. The pres-ence of distinctive frontier zones adjacent to certain boundaries will depend upon the pattern of colonisation within the state and relationships with neighbours, while former patterns of colonisation or conflict may also be preserved in the landscape. Exceptionally the state may include or be punctured by an exclave, posess a territorial corridor, or be temporarily divided.

3.2 The state capital

The capital is the place within a state where political authority is concen-trated. Normally, it will contain the seat of the state assembly, the resi-dence of the head of state, ministries and government departments, and the embassies of foreign governments. The capital is usually prominent in the iconography of its state, reflecting its history and the culture of its popula-tion, and containing a disproportionately large number of national sym-bols. In some African and South American states, spectacular development has been concentrated in the capital at the expense of the provinces; the construction of showpiece capitals is partly representative of the process of nation-building through the accumulation of national symbols and partly a political projection of a view of the state as it is hoped one day to appear.

According to Jefferson's 'law of the primate city', 'A country's leading city is always disproportionately large and exceptionally expressive of national capacity and feeling'.[4] There are too many exceptions to this rule for it to be regarded as a law, though where there is a deviation from the choice of the largest city as state capital, special political decisions and strategies are involved. In a few states, the capital function is divided; in Bolivia, for example, La Paz is the actual capital and seat of the govern-ment, while Sucre is the legal capital and seat of the judiciary. In federal states such as the USA and Australia, the capital is usually located in terri-tory independent of any constituent state, such as the District of Columbia and Australian Capital Territory.

Various political-geographical classifications of capitals have been attempted. Spate has demonstrated the futility of making a distinction be-tween 'natural' capitals, which have evolved to reach capital status, and 'artificial' capitals, custom-built to serve the capital function: '. . . it may be more natural, more appropriate, to build a new city than to take over a going concern with its own vested interests'.[5] Instead, Spate emphasised the complexity of variables which have influenced the choice of capitals and advocated the study of their historical functions.

De Blij advocated a morphological approach as being the most fruitful, with capitals viewed in terms of their position in relation to the state territory and core areas.[6] His classification included 'permanent' capitals, such as London, Paris and Rome, which have retained their preeminence through successive stages in the politico-territorial evolution of their state; 'introduced' capitals, such as Madrid, Islamabad and Brasilia, established to replace former foci in order to perform new and different functions; and 'divided' capitals, a category to include the rare cases where the capital function is divided, as in Bolivia or South Africa, where an arrangement was introduced which focused government in Pretoria and the legislature in Cape Town.

Rather than attempt to allocate each capital to a particular category, it is more realistic to regard the capital in terms of its function within the state and to recognise that the choice or rejection of a capital may be influenced by several groups of factors. These factors are more amenable to classification than the capitals themselves, and the following appear to be the most significant.

1. *The traditional factor.* Some capitals have retained their function through successive stages in the political history of their states, and have with the passage of time developed a comprehensive range of national symbols; their apparently inalienable right to remain as capital has become imprinted on the minds of people. The importance of the traditional factor is exemplified in the case of London, where the capital function was consolidated after the Norman invasion of 1066. The town dominated the economic life of medieval England, and this economic predominance attracted increasing political functions as administration and international relations became increasingly complex. In due course, the prestige of London deriving from its capital status assisted in attracting to the city the headquarters of most of the country's leading companies. Competition for highly priced sites and the strain on communications within the city has led recent governments to attempt the dispersion of government agencies and industries to less central locations. Restrictions on building in London and development area incentives have been used to dislodge industries, while agencies such as the Royal Mint (Llantrisant), the Stationery Office (Norwich) and the Inland Revenue (Washington, Co. Durham) have been relocated. At various times it has been suggested that a new capital should be constructed, either at a geographically more central place or in an area with a severe unemployment problem, but the general perception of London as a historic national cultural and political focus is too entrenched for such suggestions to be seriously considered. The traditional factor is strongly associated with other ancient European capitals such as Paris, Athens and Rome.

2. *The factor of historical imitation.* Spate has noted the power of tradition as a possible influence on the relocation of a capital. The return of the

Russian capital from the Tsarist focus of Petrograd (Leningrad) to the historical focus of Moscow was largely motivated by defensive considerations, but it also 'symbolised a Russia turning back to its vital springs in the indeterminate marches of Europe and Asia'.[7] Factors of historical imitation were also involved in the replacement of the British colonial capital at Calcutta by Delhi, the seventeenth-century political focus of India, and in the choice of Ankara, centrally located in a region of essentially Turkish culture, to replace Constantinople in 1923, following the final dismemberment of Turkey's European empire.

3. *The dominant nation factor*. In certain multinational states, the chosen capital is the national focus of the dominant national group, while other nationalities look towards other cultural foci. Such is the case in the Soviet Union, where Moscow is the focus of Great Slav nationalism, while Ukrainians are orientated towards Kiev, White Russians towards Minsk and the peoples of the Caucasus and Soviet Central Asia towards national centres such as Yerevan, Samarkand and Ashkhabad. Belgrade, the capital of Yugoslavia, is essentially a Serbian focus, becoming capital of the multinational state because of its short existence as capital of independent Serbia and the leading role played by Serbs in organising the South Slav state, though Croats identify with Zagreb and other groups look towards Ljubljana and Sarajevo.

4. *The head link factor*. In certain circumstances, administrative policy may emphasise the international connections of the state. It was normal for the administrative headquarters of colonies to be located in leading seaports, the main points of contact with their imperial masters. In the post-colonial era, newly independent states have inherited capitals which are central in respect of international trade but eccentric in relation to their administrative and cultural hinterlands. This may urge the choice of a new capital in a more central location, and the example of Calcutta and Delhi has been noted. Each of the twelve West African coastal states between and including Nigeria and Mauritania has a coastal head link capital. The replacement of Moscow by the completely new Russian capital of St Petersburg, built on the mudflats of the Neva estuary in territory newly won from Sweden, was a fundamental aspect of Peter the Great's strategy of modernising and revitalising Russia through exposure to West European influences. Dublin was the main point of contact between Ireland and its Anglo-Norman masters, and the continuing significance of the head link factor is indicated by the retention of Dublin as capital despite its existence as an enclave of cosmopolitan influences in an otherwise rural and conservative Irish cultural *milieu*.

5. *The forward capital factor*. The notion that in particular geographical and political circumstances a capital location may be chosen in a forward position, near to the most actively advancing or retreating margin of the

state, was developed by Cornish[8] and broadened by Spate.[9] Examples include Islamabad, located in the northern frontier area of Pakistan, overlooking territory contested with India, which superseded Karachi as capital; Brasilia, chosen to direct attention towards the underdeveloped interior of Brazil; and also, in some senses, St Petersburg.

6. *The political compromise factor.* Certain capitals have been chosen by governments anxious to avoid allegations of bias in the choice of one of two or more powerful rival aspirants. Canberra, the Australian capital, provides an excellent example; with a population of 146 000, Canberra was chosen to escape involvement in the intense rivalry which exists between Sydney (pop. 2 780 000) and Melbourne (pop. 2 425 000). The Australian constitution demanded the selection of a capital site at least 100 miles from Sydney, and the Canberra city plan was adopted following a competition in 1911. Construction was delayed by the 1914–18 war, and the city did not become the seat of the Australian government until 1927. Canberra is situated in an independent Capital Territory of 940 square miles which is planned and developed by a national commission. Ottawa, the Canadian capital since 1867, is located in an intermediate position between the English and French-speaking spheres, and before its creation on a small village site, alternative sessions of parliament were held in Toronto and Quebec. Washington has likewise developed from a small centre located between northern and southern cultural spheres. Bonn has been adopted as the unofficial capital of West Germany until a solution regarding the status of West Berlin can find acceptance. The instances of divided capital functions mentioned above also reflect the factor of political compromise.

7. *The central location factor.* Other things being equal, the more central the location of the capital, the easier the task of administration, through distance minimisation, and the more intimate the appearance of government. Even in a state as small as the United Kingdom, government from eccentrically located London is felt, by some Scots and northern English, to be remote and unmindful of local circumstances. A capital is an administrative focus for both people and territory, and a location which is central in respect of one need not be central in respect of the other, as in the case of Australia where population is concentrated in the southern coastal margins of the continent. It is possible to discover both the population and geographical centres of gravity, and it would seem reasonable that the theoretically ideal capital location should be biased in favour of the former, though to exactly what degree it is impossible to say, and circumstances will vary from case to case.* An index of eccentricity can be calculated to express the degree by which the actual capital (A) of a state deviates in its location from a selected centre of gravity (C). The index is calculated as the distance from C to A, divided by the average length of at least eight equally spaced radials (r) measured from C to the state boundary, the result being

* The calculation of these centres of gravity is discussed in section 3.7 below.

multiplied by 100.

$$I = \frac{\text{distance CA}}{\bar{r}} \times 100$$

An index of 100 would show a capital location which was no better than random in terms of its centrality, and one of more than 100, one which was worse than random. (See also sections 3.7, 8.4 and 8.5.)

The choice of Ankara was influenced by the consideration of the question of centrality, while the capital of Malawi was switched in 1964 from Zomba to the more centrally located Lilongwe. Madrid was selected as capital of Spain in an attempt to impose strong centralised rule upon the divergent and separatist cultural provinces which composed the kingdom of Spain.

Rarely can the selection or retention of a capital be explained by reference to only one group of factors; for example, Moscow reflects the factors of tradition, historical imitation, national dominance and, within European Russia, central location. Prague has at various times reflected the traditional, forward, central and, more recently, dominant nation factors. The list of factors presented above is not complete, though it is suggested that, rather than attempt to slot capital cities into predetermined classifications, the student should analyse each case both in terms of its uniqueness and in respect of a range of frequently occurring and combining factors.

Case studies

The statement that each capital owes its status to some factors which are common to other capitals, and to some which are unique, is exemplified in the case of Belmopan, inaugurated as capital of British Honduras in 1970. 'Since the paramount criterion was safety from hurricanes, the major cities, all located on the coast, were automatically eliminated from consideration. This spared British Honduras the unpleasant and divisive experience of major cities becoming bitter rivals for capital status.'[10] The previous capital, Belize, which already experienced hypercentralism, a factor favouring the removal of its capital function, was devastated by Hurricane Hattie in 1961, and many government documents were lost. The new capital was built on a former village site which offered nodality in terms of communications, an invigorating climate, and relative freedom from flooding and hurricanes. Though conceived as a national centre which would symbolise and intensify the nationhood of British Honduras and stimulate the development of the interior, like other planned capitals such as Brasilia and Canberra, Belmopan was slow to generate popular enthusiasm. 'Although many years will pass before the full flower of Belmopan's destiny will be realised, a stance of cautious optimism seems warranted.'[11]

As Best points out, for eighty years (1885–1965) Botswana or, as it was then known, Bechuanaland had the dubious distinction of being the only territory whose administrative capital lay beyond its borders.[12] Mafeking was selected for the comforts which it could offer its Resident Commissioners rather than for its administrative suitability. In 1960 a committee was appointed to advise on possible sites for relocated administrative headquarters, and nine possible sites were selected. Candidates were rejected on the grounds of peripheral location, water shortage, the possibility of inter-tribal rivalries where tribal lands were involved, strong pro-South African sentiment, or lack of rail connections. The only surviving candidate was Gaberone village, which could offer adequate water and accessibility in respect of six of the eight major tribes, and had existing administrative functions. British authorisation for the transfer of functions from Mafeking to Gaberone came in 1961, Botswana itself becoming independent within the Commonwealth in 1966. A planned showpiece capital was built adjacent to the existing village, but with a population of only 13 000 in 1968, Gaberone was smaller than some neighbouring villages. Difficulties were encountered in attracting industries which would diversify the functions of the capital, and in 1968 it was necessary to offer protection and tax incentives to pioneer industries locating in the town. Though the suitability of the site as a capital location is not in question, the economic viability of the centre, like that of other new capitals, remains to be proven.[13]

Bucharest, in contrast, is a well-established capital which has expanded with the growth and extension of its administrative hinterland and has developed a leading economic function. Originating as a medieval fortress designed to protect Wallachia against Turkish advance, during the Turkish occupation Bucharest was one of the few Balkan cities to prosper, having a population of around 122 000 in 1860. Turkish withdrawal from areas north of the Danube came in 1828, and during the Russian occupation Bucharest became the self-governing capital of Wallachia. The unification of Moldavia and Wallachia in 1860 expanded the capital's administrative sphere of influence, and Bucharest became a fully independent capital with the removal of Turkish suzerainty in 1878. After 1918, the national unification of Romania was completed with the addition of the Banat, Bessarabia, Bucovina and Transylvania to the Moldavian and Wallachian nucleus. At each stage in the enlargement of the state, Bucharest was the only serious contender for the capital function, and Hungarian pressures following the cession of Transylvania to Romania strengthened the case for the strong centralisation of government in Bucharest. Since the inter-war period industrialisation has taken place, stimulated by the town's role as a major market, its extensive labour catchment and its existence as a route focus with easy access to the river Danube and the Mediterranean. In contrast to the two preceding examples, Bucharest's problems do not concern the attraction of economic functions but the avoidance of industrial hyperconcentration, a problem shared with many long-established capitals, though Romania contains several locations suitable for the redirection of industry.[14]

3.3 Core areas

The significance of core areas in the historical development of certain states has already been noted, though core areas pose a number of problems and possibilities relating to the functional and morphological approaches to political geography. Two of America's leading students appear unable to agree upon the nature and significance of such areas; according to De Blij, 'Every adequately functioning state system includes . . . a core area',[15] while Hartshorne thought 'A core area is neither sufficient nor essential to the evolution of a nation or state'.[16] The literature on core areas amounts to a maze of contradictions, within which two basic problems can be discerned: firstly the question of identifying and of measuring the spatial extent of the core area, and secondly the problem of deciding upon which functional criteria core areas are based.

When Pounds and Ball decided that, of twenty-five European states studied, fifteen had distinct core areas, four had peripheral or external cores and five lacked core areas, they concentrated upon the role of the core as a nucleus for subsequent state expansion and used a methodology based upon historical survey.[17] However, Philbrick, in his definition of core areas in North America,[18] and Zaidi, in his choice of the core of West Pakistan, both considered core areas as areas of contemporary economic leadership.[19] The term 'core area' has been used to embrace past and present areas of political dominance, areas of intense national or cultural consciousness and areas of economic leadership. The picture is obviously confused, and the following points and recommendations on terminology may help to clarify and classify the functional aspects of core areas.

1. The idea of state growth from a small core or cell was discussed by Ratzel[20] and developed by Whittlesey.[21] The expansion of control from a nuclear area clearly influenced the growth patterns of a number of states, France and Russia for example. In some cases, such as that of Muscovite Russia, the limits of the state advanced with the extension of political control from the core; in others, such as early medieval England, more effective control was exported from the core area over territory which was enclosed by preexisting boundaries. Here we are dealing with what might be termed 'germinal core areas'.

2. An area which has not played a germinal role may still be associated with an intensity of national sentiment and contain a large proportion of national symbols. Almost invariably such an area will include the state capital which provides practical expression to the area's highly developed political consciousness. The Budapest area provides an example of what

might be termed a 'national core area'.

3. Within each state is an area which, to a greater or lesser extent, is in a leading economic position. In some states, economic activities may be highly concentrated, as in the Irish Republic where economic affairs are dominated by the Dublin area, while in other cases, such as India, the dominance of a single economic region is much less marked. The leading economic region of a state may be termed its 'economic core area' and defined without recourse to any but economic criteria. Zaidi defined the economic core area of West Pakistan by mapping levels of agricultural productivity, the intensity of market potential, the magnitude of manufacturing and the degree of urbanisation.[22]

4. Some states include areas where, for historical and cultural reasons, separatist sentiments are strongly felt, usually by a national minority. These feelings may be equally associated with all parts of the minority homeland, as in Scotland or Brittany, or they may be focused on a particular cultural centre which has played a leading role in separatist iconography, such as Kiev in the Ukraine or Zagreb in Croatia. Only where the latter is the case could the term 'separatist core area' be used.

5. In some cases the development of the state has been associated with the transference of political, economic or psychological leadership from one area to another, or with one germinal core area being superseded by another. Pounds notes that political control in China has migrated between northern and southern core areas.[23] An area which has formerly served as a core area may be termed a 'relict' germinal, political, economic or separatist core area.

6. Subsidiary areas may be associated with germinal, national, economic or separatist functions, and can be described as 'secondary' germinal, national, economic or separatist core areas.

The germinal, national and economic functions seldom occur in isolation, but usually appear in combination; the London and Paris areas combine all three roles. The above classification is a means of differentiating core areas in terms of their function, or combination of functions, in terms of their past or present and primary or secondary status, while a separate category is reserved for separatist core areas.

Burghardt has also criticised the vague and arbitrary nature of the core area concept, though his efforts towards systematisation produced a rather different classification of cores from the one presented above.[25] He recognised 'nuclear' cores, similar to our germinal core; 'original' cores, the original areas of greatest political and economic importance which had not, however, played a germinal role; and 'contemporary' cores, current areas of political and economic significance. He then noted the elements of relative location and scale, which could equally be integrated with our own

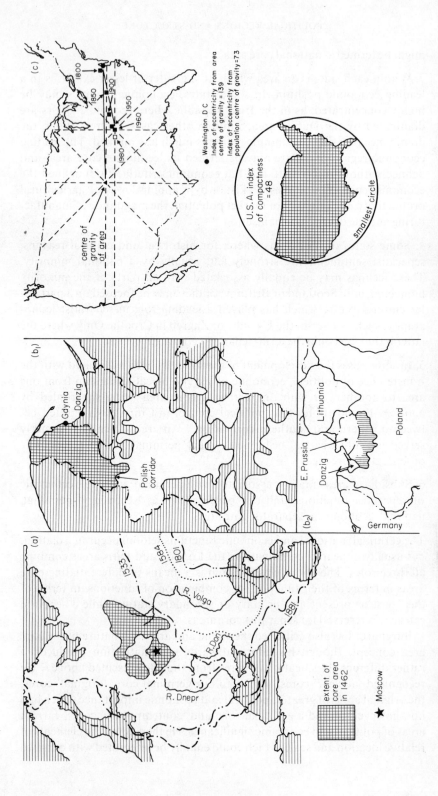

(c)

1800
1850
1900
1950
1960
1980

● Washington D C
■ Index of eccentricity from area centre of gravity=139
□ Index of eccentricity from population centre of gravity=73

centre of gravity of area

U.S.A. index of compactness = 48

smallest circle

(b₁)

Gdynia
Danzig

Polish corridor

(b₂)

Lithuania

E. Prussia

Danzig

Poland

Germany

(a)

1533
1584
1801

R. Volga

R. Don

1891

R. Dnepr

Moscow

extent of core area in 1462

★ Moscow

classification. He was therefore able to produce three distinct but interwoven classifications of core areas.

A. *Chronological*   1. Historically orientated   a. Nuclear
                                                    b. Original but non-nuclear
                                                    c. Ephemeral
                     2. Contemporary

B. *Location with respect to the state area*   1. Central
                                               2. Peripheral or eccentric
                                               3. External

C. *Scale*   1. World
             2. Continental
             3. Primary national
             4. Secondary

With core areas classified in terms of function, the problem of their spatial extent remains. From the very nature of cores as centres for the dissemination of political or economic influences, it follows that their limits will be transitional, not linear. The original limits of germinal cores, such as the fifteenth-century Grand Duchy of Moscow, may be mapped by recourse to historical sources, while various economic criteria such as those of Zaidi may be used to demarcate an economic core, though it is unlikely that a universally applicable economic measure exists. The political aspects of core areas rest partly on psychological associations, the relative spatial intensities of which might prove exceedingly difficult to delimit.

Though core areas have usually been considered on the state level, the

---

Figure 3.1.   Aspects of the structure of some states.

(a) The growth of the Russian core area. Dates and contours represent stages in the expansion of control from the Moscow core area.

(b) The Polish corridor. (b_1) The post-First World War boundaries of the divided state of Poland are shown, along with a simplified version of the ethnic distribution. Mainly German-occupied areas have horizontal shading; mainly Polish, unshaded; mainly Kassube, cross-hatching. (b_2) Post-war boundaries: solid lines; Polish boundary proposals to the Paris Peace Conference: broken lines. Plebiscite area is shaded.

(c) The shape of the USA. The geographical centre of gravity is shown by the triangle; successive population centres of gravity by squares; the capital by the circle. Note the westward migration of the population centre of gravity as a result of westward colonisation and settlement. Broken lines show the radials used in the calculation of indices of capital eccentricity, as outlined in the text.

The figure below includes the index of compactness, calculated according to the Cole method, as described in the text.

Calculations do not include Alaska or insular possessions. See ref. 24.

concept may be transposed to embrace global ideological cores—the USA and the Soviet Union, mentioned by Kristof,[26] and now including China—or scaled down to include intra-state core areas. Whebell argues that a core area concept is applicable to the study of lower levels of politico-territorial organisation where local core areas may exert pressure for the amendment or retention of local government areas.[27] Within its city region, the regional city is not incomparable to the core area within its state, and in fact a continuum of control and influence may be discerned, ranging from the regional city, or even below, through the state core area to the global ideological core.

3.4 Effective state area

Continuous patterns of state sovereignty overlie relatively discontinuous patterns of effective governmental control and effective human occupancy. Though sovereignty is indivisible, within each state are areas which vary in the degree to which they are integrated into the functioning state system. A prime objective of any government is the establishment of effective control over the entire territory of its state. As shown by Whittlesey, effective central authority is a force for uniformity, stamping controlled landscapes with standardised symbols of state control, ranging from post offices to planned towns and state-sponsored developments.[28] However, the establishment of such control is a gradual process which many areas have resisted because of the recent nature of colonisation, the lack of environmental incentives, the intransigent nature of populations, or a combination of these factors. Where central authority is too weak and remote to impose effective control, unintegrated areas exist, either totally beyond the pale[29] of state control, or subject to special arrangements between the government and indigenous elements. The rulers of medieval Hungary and Russia granted lands and freedom to the haiduks and Cossacks in return for the guardianship of the margins of their realms against Turkish incursion. Similar freedoms were given by the early medieval kings of England to the lords of the Welsh and Northumbrian marches, until such time as effective central control could be imposed.

The concept of effective state area is a valuable but underdeveloped one. Its origins lie in Whittlesey's notion of an 'ecumene' and James's 'effective national territory', while the concept was more recently employed by Zaidi, introducing the term 'effective state area'. All the writers viewed the integrated portion of state territory in economic and functional terms; the ecumene is 'the portion of the state that supports the densest and most extended population and has the closest mesh of transportation lines'.[30] The effective national territory was defined as 'only that part of total territory which actually contributes to the economic support of the citizens of the country'.[31] The effective state area of West Pakistan was defined as that part of total state territory which had a minimum population density of 25 people per square mile and lay within 10 miles of a railway station or a road passable by motor traffic.[32]

The economic contributions of particular areas to the state economy, and the degree to which they are connected to the state transport network, are obviously of prime importance in any discussion of effective state area, though they do not express directly the effectiveness of central authority. The paramount consideration concerns the degree to which the laws and directives of the central authority are observed and enforced in everyday life, a much harder phenomenon to measure. Also significant are the availability of state services and the level of participation in state political activities by the populations of the areas concerned. Areas beyond the effective state area are frequently associated with the lack of many normal state services, military rather than civil forms of policing, and a lack of the forms of security and stability normally provided by the state. Settlement patterns are likely to be defensively nucleated rather than dispersed, and banditry dominant over other forms of crime; '. . . "modernisation", that is to say the combination of economic development, efficient communications and public administration, deprives any kind of banditry . . . of the conditions under which it flourishes'.[33] With these points in mind, the possession of territory unintegrated into the effective state area is a characteristic of the developing rather than the developed or 'ecumenical' state.

Areas of varying degrees of integration occur between the unintegrated and core area extremes, and Zaidi subdivided the effective state area of West Pakistan into the minimally effective area, lying within 10 miles of a railway station or a road passable by motor traffic and with a population density of at least 25 per square mile, the intensively effective area, containing a minimum density of 100 per square mile and within 5 miles of the communications, a sub-core around Karachi, the most densely populated part of the state, and the core area, defined in relation to a number of variables, as mentioned above.[34] The following table resulted.

Limit of functional effectiveness	Percentage of total area of e.s.a.	Percentage of total population of e.s.a.
core area	2.7	10.4
sub-core	1.0	5.2
intensively effective area	68.9	74.8
minimally effective area	27.4	9.6

The extra-ecumenical area covered 55 per cent of the area of West Pakistan but contained only 2 per cent of the cropped area and provided economic support for only 7.7 per cent of the population.

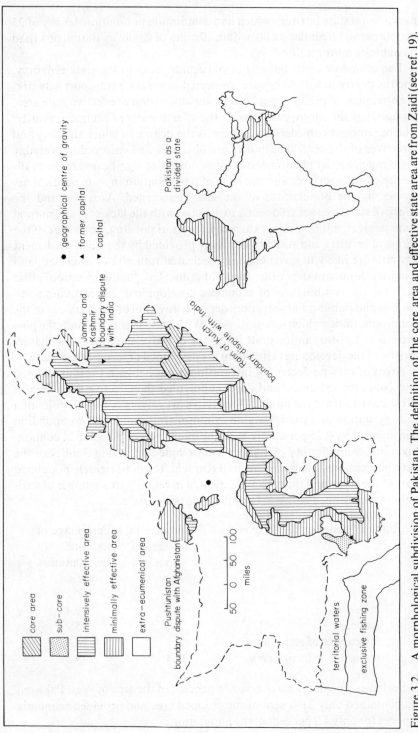

Figure 3.2. A morphological subdivision of Pakistan. The definition of the core area and effective state area are from Zaidi (see ref. 19).

Since political geography is concerned with the triangular relationship between people, state and territory, it is surprising that more has not been written on spatial variations in the functional effectiveness of state control. The possession of extra-ecumenical territory is a characteristic of the developing state and may reflect an early stage in the extension of effective central authority, as in several African and south-east Asian states, or the possession of very extensive areas of environmentally hostile territory, as in the cases of Canada, the Soviet Union and Brazil. Within the extra-ecumenical territory may be found centres existing as enclaves of effective state territory, the nodes from which effective control will permeate. The effective colonisation of Canada west of the Great Lakes developed from a 'string of beads' settlement pattern of towns located along the transcontinental railway, while in contemporary Siberia extensive areas of extra-ecumenical and minimally effective territory are gradually becoming more fully integrated into the state system as effective control and development radiate outwards from settlements along the trans-Siberian railways, which represent expanding pockets of more intensively effective territory.

Total state territory is therefore likely to include areas of varying effectiveness. Territorial effectiveness concerns the relationship between a particular area and a functioning state system and should be measured according to legal, economic, administrative and accessibility factors involved in this relationship. As with the core area concept, it is doubtful whether a universally applicable measure of effectiveness can be obtained, though generic approaches would be of the utmost value.

3.5 Exclaves

An exclave is a portion of a state which is entirely surrounded by the territory of a neighbouring state.* Exclaves were exceedingly numerous in medieval Europe, which was not clearly divided into exclusive sovereignties, but covered in overlapping and impermanent lordships. Kings were frequently tenants of estates beyond their kingdoms while inheritance and ecclesiastical and marital arrangements endowed kingdoms with lands beyond their limits. The consolidation of states developed with the adoption of sovereignty and nationality as bases of statehood. The territorially consolidated state is more easily defended and administered, and it is likely to be more expressive of national distributions. Exclaves were characteristic of an earlier form of political system, and the few which survive are anachronisms and, with the modern exception of Berlin, of minor political-geographical importance. Here, 'what calls for explanation is rather their survival today than their existence in the Middle Ages'.[35] In the case of the four European survivals, historical accident explains their persist-

* The terms 'exclave' and 'enclave' are sometimes confusing. Llivia is an exclave *of* Spain, and an enclave *within* France. An enclave state such as Lesotho is entirely surrounded by the territory of one other state.

ence, and the Spanish exclave of Llivia, surrounded by France, provides an example. 'The treaty of the Pyrenees allocated to France 33 villages in the Cerdagne to link her territories in Conflent with those in Val Carol. Though lying directly in the way, Llivia could not be included in the 33 because it had the status not of a village but of a town.'[36] Such exclaves as Llivia, Campione (Switzerland in Italy), Büsingen (Germany in Switzerland) and Baarle (Belgium in Holland) are not important in themselves, but, because of the inconvenience and special arrangements which must be made for their administration, they highlight any difficulties in international relations between the mother and host state and demonstrate the advantages of uninterrupted territory.

Robinson has categorised a number of political-geographical phenomena related to normal exclaves: quasi-exclaves, which for various reasons no longer function as exclaves; virtual exclaves, which, though not legally exclaves, are treated as such by the host country of which they are a part (the example being certain ecclesiastical sites in Italy, treated by the Italian authorities as part of the Vatican City state); temporary exclaves, where the division of territory is avowedly temporary; and pene-exclaves. Though not physically detached from the mother country, pene-exclaves can only be approached conveniently by wheeled vehicles through the territory of a neighbouring state. An example is the Drumully pene-exclave of the Irish Republic, formed when Northern Irish county boundaries were elevated to international status, and only accessible by road and rail across Northern Irish territory.

Exclaves cause inconvenience both to the mother and to the host countries; access is a matter for negotiation, and the enforcement of customs controls is made burdensome, while the populations of exclaves are isolated from the nearest markets for their produce and from sources of supply and employment. In some cases these disadvantages are offset; the laxity of customs controls around Llivia made the town a favoured shopping centre for surrounding French villages, while the relatively flexible Belgian gaming laws attract Netherlanders to Baarle.[37] On the whole, the topic of exclaves belongs to the detail of political geography, the towering exception being the case of West Berlin. (While technically a case could be made for considering Alaska as an exclave of the USA, and Bangladesh as a former exclave of Pakistan, others pointing to the possibility of maritime connections with their mother countries would consider these as examples of fragmented states.)

Case studies

In 1943, representatives of the UK, USA and USSR agreed that the defeat of Nazi Germany would be followed by a fourfold division of the country into separate Allied occupation zones. Berlin, as the seat of the Allied Control Council (Kommandatura), was excluded from the division and was itself divided into four occupation zones, and was considered the probable capital for a future united Germany. With the intensification of the cold war, the Kommandatura became inoperable, the city council dissolved, and a seperate council was installed in the Russian zone. The western occupation zones of Berlin constituted an enclave within the Russian occupation zone of Germany, and the vulnerability of this anomalous location became apparent in 1948 as the Soviet Union instigated a blockade. The only negotiated rights of access to West Berlin consisted of three twenty-mile wide air lanes which were used in a massive daily airlift of 6000 tons of supplies to the beleaguered exclave until the blockade was lifted in May 1949. The failure of the blockade led to attempts to seal off the Russian zone, while the merger of the Western occupation zones of Germany provided a pretext for the creation of a seperate East German state. Though the Western zones became the Federal Republic of Germany, the Allied occupying powers were unable to accept the designation of West Berlin as the twelfth province and capital of the republic, since this would have compromised the status of Berlin as a fifth district and united zone of occupation. The city was awarded proportional representation in the Bonn parliament, though Berlin representatives could not be given voting rights and Bonn legislation did not automatically apply in West Berlin.

For a time, rights of transit between East and West Berlin remained, though the labour-deficient East was losing up to 1000 refugees to the West each day. The manpower crisis led to the construction of the Berlin Wall in August 1961, as a result of which the 52 000 East Berliners who worked in the West were obliged to find new employment. Shortly afterwards, permits for visits to the West were refused, and the isolation of the West Berlin exclave became complete.

Robinson noted that the special significance of exclaves derives from their 'illustrating the relations of states in difficult geographical circumstances and in illuminating the importance of uninterrupted territory to present-day states'.[38] For more than twenty years, West Berlin felt and reflected each crisis in East–West relations. Though the economy of the exclave required artificial support at enormous cost to the Western powers, the city was preserved as a showpiece for Western democracy, and any retreat from Berlin would have undermined Western prestige among allied and uncommitted states. To the Eastern powers, West Berlin represented an ideological threat from which the socialist populations were to be insulated, but also a pressure point, sensitive to any force they might choose to exert. An amelioration of relations between the FRG and the Eastern bloc, in the context of a more general détente, led in 1971 to the conclusion of a four-power agreement on West Berlin which regularised Western road, rail and waterway access to the exclave and provided for an improvement of communications with the West and visits to the East by West Berliners. In autumn 1971 an exchange of secondary exclaves scattered around the city resulted in five areas amounting to 15.6 hectares being transferred to the GDR and three areas amounting to 17.1 hectares being transferred to West Berlin.[39]

In 1953, long before the construction of the Berlin Wall, Robinson studied the political geography of West Berlin.[40] The transition from state capital to exclave was a sudden one, and with the hardening of East–West relations the city lost an urban field which had covered most of eastern Germany, resulting in a traumatic loss of its service and manufacturing functions. In 1952 the exclave was sustained by 3409 million marks' worth of imports, while receiving only 2083 million marks for the export of goods and services, the vast deficit being met by subsidies from the West. All industries suffered from war damage or dismantlement by the Red Army, and distance friction in importing raw materials and exporting manufactures, coupled with the periodic interruption of traffic by the Eastern powers. The economic survival of the exclave was ensured only by the subsidies and the provision of a series of trading preferences.

It also became necessary to duplicate a number of schools, hospitals and power plants separated from their service areas by the intra-city boundary, though the exclave was self-sufficient in water, available from shallow wells within its boundaries. Most sewerage spreading grounds, however, lay in East Berlin, and the West paid one million marks per annum for the use of these facilities.

Subsequent to Robinson's survey, many changes became entrenched. The old city core lies in East Berlin, and a new core has developed in West Berlin, while the economic and administrative functions of the city have declined as a result of its exclave relationship with the FRG. Planners in the two separated halves of the city are no longer able to coordinate their activities, and with the redevelopment and redesignation of urban areas and the duplication of municipal facilities the reunification of the city would present severe difficulties.[41] Though the 1971 agreement has done much to defuse the political instability of the situation, the economic viability of a central place seperated from its urban field and fifty miles removed from nearest sources of supply and export outlets remains in question.

Serious academic studies of pene-exclaves are extremely rare. An example is Minghi's study of Point Roberts, a pene-exclave formed by the USA–Canadian boundary which, following the 49th parallel, cuts across the tip of a peninsula that juts southwards across the boundary from the Fraser lowlands.[43] Point Roberts, though part of the USA, lacks direct land access to it except through Canadian territory. By a technicality the area is a pene-exclave rather than an exclave, since US territorial waters extend beyond the peninsula, though Point Roberts itself lacks adequate mooring facilities.

Because of its peculiarities of location and political status, the inhabitants of Point Roberts are obliged to pay inflated prices for goods and services from and within the rest of the USA, but these economic disadvantages are partially offset by positional advantages, and the two-

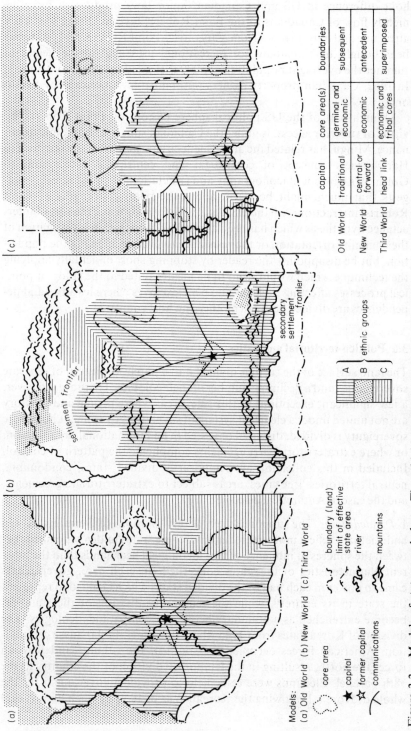

Figure 3.3. Models of state morphology. These highly generalised models illustrate some of the typical aspects of state morphology in the old, new and third worlds. Note the close coincidence of state and ethnic boundaries in the old-world model and the lack of such correspondence in the third-world model. Partly influenced by ref. 42.

Models:
(a) Old World (b) New World (c) Third World

core area
capital
former capital
communications

boundary (land)
limit of effective state area
river
mountains

A
B ethnic groups
C

settlement frontier
secondary settlement frontier

	capital	core area(s)	boundaries
Old World	traditional	germinal and economic	subsequent
New World	central or forward	economic	antecedent
Third World	head link	economic and tribal cores	superimposed

hour difference in US and Canadian liquor laws produces a lucrative nightly flow of Canadians to the Point Roberts taverns. Being scenically attractive and only 35 miles from Vancouver, Point Roberts real estate has been bought by Canadians for recreational uses, and in the height of summer the overnight population of 3000 is swelled by 4000 day-trippers. In 1962, Canadian property owners outnumbered Americans by five to one.

Though part of the US political sphere of control, Point Roberts, by virtue of superior access, is under the Canadian sphere of economic dominance. Minghi has related the ambivalent circumstances of the territory to Hartshorne's concept of centrifugal and centripetal forces and to Gottman's concept of iconography and circulation. He most sensibly suggests that much might be learnt about the relative strengths of Point Roberts' interaction with the USA and with Canada using the sort of interactance hypothesis which has been applied by Mackay[44] in investigation of the changing orientation or the resistance to change affecting the population, but he disappoints the reader by stopping short of actually applying the technique which would seem to be ideally suited to the study of political processes affecting exclaves and pene-exclaves where loyalties and dependences are divided between mother and host countries.

3.6 Politico-territorial anomalies

The land surface of the earth is divided into a patch set pattern of separate sovereignties and a declining number of their colonies. There are, however, a few significant exceptions to this rule, areas where people and territory are not united under a clear-cut system of sovereign government but where sovereignty is divided, disputed or vested in an international organisation, or where extraterritorial arrangements complicate the pattern of control. Included in this collection are temporarily divided states, condominia, neutral territories, free cities, areas subject to extraterritorial agreements, and the case of Antarctica, discussed in part 6.

1. *Divided states*. The supposedly temporary divisions of Germany, Korea and Vietnam reflect more the location of these states under watersheds between the spheres of influence of two ideological heartlands than the inherent characteristics of the states concerned. In each case, governments came to power in each half of the divided states which claimed to represent the state in its entirety, while the temporary division of the state has become entrenched as a boundary between incompatible ideologies. The division of Korea dates from 1945 when, following the Japanese capitulation, American forces occupied the south of the isthmus and Russian forces the north, resulting in the temporary division of the country at the 38th parallel. Elections were to be held to provide a government for the whole of Korea. Following the Korean War of 1950–1, when an invasion

of the south from the north was repulsed, a cease-fire line was negotiated in 1953 which runs in the general area of the 38th parallel. The 'temporary' division of Vietnam along the 17th parallel results from the Geneva conference of 1954 which followed the defeat of French colonial forces at Dien Bien Phu by the Viet Minh. Again, provisions were made for elections which would unite the country under a single government, but the division became entrenched when the southern regime refused to participate in proposed elections, claiming that elections held in the north would not be free.

The German case can be used to exemplify the political-geographical problems which may face the divided and the reunited state. At the Potsdam agreement of 1945, Germany was temporarily divided into Soviet, American, British and French occupation zones, while German territory east of the Odra–Nisa line was awarded by the Russians to Poland. In 1949, the worsening of East–West relations, coupled with British and French difficulties in the management of their occupation zones, resulted in the merger of Western occupation zones into the Federal German Republic, while the Russian occupation zone became the German Democratic Republic.

The inter-war period had witnessed the economic development of eastern German territories, and modern light industries,. particularly motor vehicles, strategic war industries, synthetic and pharmaceutical industries were installed to counterbalance the longer-established heavy industries of the Ruhr. The industrial infrastructure of pre-war Germany involved a harmonious equilibrium between the heavy industries of the west and the light industries of the east, the two areas being linked by a national transport system basically orientated along a west-to-east axis.

The post-war division of Germany caused imbalance in the industrial economies of each separated half and a reorientation in each towards alternative sources of raw material supply, with the East becoming dependent upon Polish sources of coal and Soviet petroleum while the West was obliged to develop light and pharmacutical industries of its own without access to the excellent lignite, water and chemical resources of the East. The West German transport system was reorientated along a north–south axis, while towns on each side of the introduced boundary declined as their urban fields were bisected and their locations became strategically unstable and unattractive to investment.

The reunification of Germany no longer seems a possibility, and a united Germany, following a quarter of a century of separate development, would face political and economic problems perhaps as severe as those caused by the original division. It is unlikely that industries developed in the East, in relation to Comecon markets and raw materials, and successful within a state-planned economy, would be able to prosper in a free-enterprise milieu in competition with similar industries developed in the West. A united Germany would also destroy the rough parity of power which exists between Britain, France and the Federal Republic within the EEC, and would be unpopular within the organisation as a whole.

2. *Condominia*. In a condominium, sovereignty is exercised jointly by two states. The New Hebrides is in such a position, administered according to the Anglo-French agreements of 1906, 1914 and 1922. Both the United Kingdom and France are represented by High Commissioners; though there is a joint development plan, each administration provides schools and medical services, and both Australian decimal currency and New Hebrides francs are in circulation. Each administration also provides its national courts, so the accused is offered a choice of jurisdiction. Canton and Enderbury in the Gilbert and Ellice islands were claimed by both the United Kingdom and the USA in the late 1930s. In 1939, a fifty-year condominium was negotiated, but with the closure of the Canton airport, both islands are now conveniently uninhabited, so problems of administration do not arise. Condominia belong to the trivia of political geography, but their study reveals the extreme complications which can result from the division of sovereignty, a doctrine based on exclusiveness.

3. *Free cities, ports and zones*. Free cities, in this century, have only been created in exceptional circumstances. In the case of Danzig, mentioned below, the designation of an autonomous city under a League of Nations High Commissioner was a compromise response to the Polish need for a Baltic port and the almost exclusively German population of the obvious port choice. Fiume (now Rijeka in Yugoslavia) had a short existence as a free city between 1919 and 1924; allotted to Yugoslavia, the largely Italian-populated town was seized by Italian irregulars in 1919, and existed as a free city until its incorporation into Italy five years later. It was returned to Yugoslavia in 1945. Trieste, nearby, as a Yugoslav outlet with an Italian population surrounded by a Slovene countryside, was in a similar position. Claimed by both Yugoslavia and Italy at the end of the 1939–45 war, the city, port and surroundings of Trieste were subject to British and American military government as the Free Territory of Trieste until a division of territory in 1954 awarded the city to Italy, as a free port, and the surroundings to Yugoslavia. (A stretch of 24 kilometres was defined as a 'line of demarcation' rather than a frontier, and several small pockets of land along this line, around 1250 acres, were absorbed by Yugoslavia, though claimed by Italy. In February 1974 Yugoslav authorities erected signposts of the Yugoslav type in the disputed areas, resulting in an Italian protest and a strong Belgrade rejoinder.)

In free ports, no duties are charged on imports handled, and since it is almost impossible to prevent the seepage of goods from such ports into surrounding areas, free ports are rare and associated with very small countries with low tariffs; Hong Kong is an example. Much more common are free zones within important entrepôts, to which entry and exit can be controlled, and where goods in transit can be on and off-loaded without incurring the tariff charges of the state in question, though the free zone is part of the sovereign territory of that state.

4. *Extraterritoriality*. This concerns rights awarded to one state in the territory of another, and extraterritoriality found its greatest expression in China following the opium wars, when European powers forced rights of commercial exploitation and the maintenance of their own armed forces onto the defeated Chinese. After the German defeat of 1918, ownership of the Saar coalfield was leased to France until 1935, when a plebiscite of Saarlanders was held, resulting in an overwhelming vote for a return to Germany. Most current extraterritorial rights concern provisions made for the trading activities of landlocked states; for example, a provision of the Treaty of Versailles made a free zone available in Hamburg for goods in transit to and from Czechoslovakia, while Paraguay used bonded-warehouse facilities in Buenos Aires and Montevideo.

5. *Neutral zones and demilitarised areas*. Neutral zones of various types exist; neutrality may be adopted by a state as a deliberate policy, as by Switzerland in 1815, in which case a compromise of state sovereignty does not seem to be involved, or neutrality may be forced upon a state, as upon Austria in 1955 as a condition of the Allied peace treaty. Alternatively, neutrality may be applied only to a portion of a state; for example, Norway has agreed not to militarise Spitzbergen. A supposedly demilitarised zone lies astride the 'temporary' boundary between North and South Vietnam. A different form of neutral zone exists between Kuwait and Saudi Arabia, arising from the inability of the parties to agree on a final boundary delimitation, and within this zone joint sovereignty is operated, with exploration rights ceded to respective oil companies.

3.7 The size, shape and location of the state

Each state is unique in terms of its location and shape, while great variation is found in the size of states. In discussions concerning the location and area of states it is difficult to penetrate beyond the geographically obvious. It is obvious that from its shape, size and location on the globe, the state will derive its particular climatic characteristics which, in conjunction with its geology, will in turn produce its soils and vegetation, its control over a particular set of subterranean resources, and proximity to a particular set of neighbours. It is equally obvious that locations vary in terms of their strategic significance; Poland has suffered from its location between powerful and avaricious neighbours, the English Channel has allowed the British in the past to avoid undesirable involvement in Continental affairs, while Panama would be a most insignificant state were it not bisected by the Panama Canal. Unless generalisations concerning the locations of states can be organised into some form of geopolitical framework, it seems unlikely that much of value will result.

The variation in the size of states is so extreme that the difference between the smallest and the larger becomes more qualitative than quantitative. In terms of size, the Soviet Union (8.65 million square miles) is the largest, followed by China (3.70 million square miles), Canada (3.56 million square miles), the USA (3.55 million square miles), Brazil (3.29 million square miles) and Australia (2.97 million square miles). The smallest state is the Vatican City (108.7 acres, 44 hectares), and other microstates include Monaco (467 acres, 189 hectares), San Marino (24.1 square miles), Liechtenstein (61.8 square miles) and Andorra (190 square miles). The statehood of the microstates must be in question: Monaco was placed under the protection of France in 1861 and is involved in a series of conventions of neighbourhood and assistance; San Marino since 1862 has had a customs union and treaty of friendship and cooperation with Italy; Liechtenstein is in customs union with Switzerland, and is represented diplomatically by the Swiss; while Andorra is a co-principality, with its sovereignty exercised jointly by the French President and the Bishop of Urgel. In addition to the compromised sovereignty of most microstates, there is the question of whether a certain minimal size should be a prerequisite for full statehood. Microstates are disadvantaged by their dependence on the goodwill of their more powerful encircling neighbours, upon which they rely for essential imports and exports, and often employment. However, their peculiarities of size, location and political status have sometimes been exploited as a basis for tourism, occasionally for smuggling, and particularly in the case of Monaco for gambling. However, other microstates which have attempted to emulate the Monagasque success have been made aware of the disapproval of their neighbour and the incomplete nature of their sovereignty.

Size, though an element of state power, is only one of a number of such elements, while the possession of extensive unintegrated or economically negative areas may result in a drain on state resources from the costs of administration and communications construction. There are numerous historical examples of very small states which have wielded great power; at the turn of the century Great Britain, with an area then of around 116 000 square miles, controlled an empire of 900 million square miles. Today Kuwait, with an area of only 9375 square miles, ranks as the world's seventh oil producing state. Formerly, extreme size presented problems to effective administration, but today there is no limit to the range of instant telephone communication between the capital and the furthest corner of the state. In the extreme case of the Soviet Union, difficulties arise from the fact that the administrator in Moscow is separated by eleven time zones from his counterpart in Uelen on the Bering Straits and is eight time zones apart from officials in Vladivostok. Though it has been pointed out that most large states have adopted federal constitutions, that of the largest state is federal only in form, not in function; the Soviet Union is administered by the most centralised system of decision-making the world has known, and decisions made in Moscow are instantly enforceable in the Soviet far east. There seems to be no upper limit upon the size of state which it is now possible to administer from a single capital, though the devolution of power to component regions might be expected to produce more popular government. In the Soviet Union regionalism is seen as potentially disruptive, and contacts between provincial decision-makers working for different ministries are limited. Awareness of local conditions diminishes with distance from the capital, and consequently the more remote the region concerned, the more numerous become consultations between local officials and central ministerial decision-makers.[45]

In the analysis of the shape of states, descriptive methods have been replaced by a variety of more efficient mathematical techniques. There are a number of shape indices available which can provide particular shapes with index numbers, allowing them to be compared and also frequently showing their deviation from the most compact shape form, the circle. Boyce and Clark devised a shape index based on the formula

$$\sum_1^n \left| \left(\frac{ri}{\sum_1^n} \times 100 - \frac{100}{n} \right) \right|$$

where r represents the radials extending outwards from a central node, and n is the number of radials used.[46]

The central node is conveniently the geographical centre of gravity of the shape concerned, and the number of radials used should be at least eight, with greater accuracy resulting the more radials are employed; the radials themselves should be equally spaced. The calculation of the geographical centre of gravity is outlined below; then, 'Measure the distance from the center to the outside edges of the shape along equally spaced radials. Compute the percentage of each radial distance with respect to the sum of all radials, and subtract each percentage from the percentage each radial would be expected to have based on a circle'.[47] The summation of the resultant figures gives the index.

When this method is employed, the indices range from 0 for the circle, to approximately 12 for the square, to 175 as measured from the centre of a straight line. For all but hollow, highly fragmented shapes, or shapes with bulbed elongations, this method is suitable.

The method can also be used to measure compactness of shape in terms of deviation from the zero index of the circle, though here Haggett's shape index is more convenient[48]

$$\text{shape index} = (1.27\,A)\,/\,L^2$$

where A is the area of the shape in square kilometres, and L is the length of its longest axis. This produces an index of 1.00 for the circle, ranging towards 0 with progressive elongation. An equally simple measure of compactness was suggested by Cole,[49] whereby the area of the shape concerned is divided by the area of the smallest circle which will enclose it, and the result multiplied by 100. Here the index decreases with decreasing compactness from 100 for the circle, 83 for the hexagon, 64 for the square, to 43 for the equilateral triangle. According to this measure, France has an index of 57.5, Mexico one of 22, and Chile one of 5. One further alternative is to relate deviation from the most compact form to the percentage of shape area which will not be included in an inscribed circle.

It has generally been assumed that the ideal shape of the model state would be circular, with a centrally located capital, and that where a number of contiguous states are involved, then the hexagonal shape provides the closest approach to the circle without creating voids or overlaps between neighbouring units. The advantages of compactness would include distance minimisation in internal administration, and ease of defence against both external attack and internal separatism. The difficulties arise in discerning the degree to which peculiarities of shape alone cause administrative and defensive difficulties and interfere with the functioning of the state system. Pounds quotes Chile and Norway as examples of states with unfortunate shapes, pointing out that neither has railways running its entire length, and states that Chile was obliged to relax tariff regulations in its most northerly and southerly provinces.[50] However, it is impossible to determine the exact contribution of shape, as opposed to terrain and other possible factors, in causing such difficulties.

Questions concerning shape are often related to centres of gravity. In political geography two such centres are of particular interest: the geographical, or mean centre of a shape, normally a state or other political region; and the population mean centre of gravity of such a region. To discover the mean centre, the area concerned should be covered with a grid of squares; the finer the grid, the greater the accuracy. A dot is then placed in the centre of each square, each dot then having an x and a y coordinate. Then, using the x and y coordinates of each dot, it is possible to find the mean x coordinate and the mean y coordinate, and the mean centre is at the intersection of these. Thus

$$\bar{x}_{cm} = \frac{\sum x_i}{n} \qquad \bar{y}_{cm} = \frac{\sum y_i}{n}$$

where $\bar{x}_{cm}$ and $\bar{y}_{cm}$ are the x and y coordinates of the mean centre, x_i the x coordinate of each location, y_i the y coordinate of each location, and n the total number of locations. A more rapid method simply involves cutting out the exact shape of the area in question, on stiff card of even thickness, and balancing it on a pencil point; the mean centre then lies at the location where the shape will balance.

The statistical procedure for discovering the population centre of gravity is similar but more complicated, since each dot must be given a weighting according to the population of its grid square. The formula is modified to include a weighting value.

$$\bar{x}_{cm} = \frac{\sum(x_i P_i)}{\sum P_i} \qquad \bar{y}_{cm} = \frac{\sum(y_i P_i)}{\sum P_i}$$

where P_i is the weighting of each location.

Where census data are collected on a grid-of-squares basis, the weighting of each dot is available, but where enumeration districts are irregular, then guesswork must be used to estimate the population of each grid square, and the exercise becomes exceedingly time-consuming. The significance of these centres of gravity to the problem of selecting theoretically ideal capital locations has already been noted.[51]

The difficulty of isolating the impact of variables such as size, shape and location upon the functioning of the state systems has led political geographers to concentrate on extreme cases such as the micro, the fragmented and the landlocked state where the effects of peculiarities of form and location are more readily discernible.

Some states have survived the special difficulties caused by fragmented form, while others such as the Caribbean Federation have not. The problems facing the governments of fragmented states are those of maintaining close political and economic ties, and of sustaining a state idea superior to the separate insular identities which each component island may be expected to generate. It can be argued that the apparently expansionist policies launched by the post-independence Indonesian government, involving territorial claims on land and at sea, were motivated by fears of secession and designed to unite the culturally diverse Indonesians against out-group threats, real or imagined, thereby creating an all-Indonesian outlook.

With the arrival of independence for Papua–New Guinea, there are few apparent centripetal tendencies, and the secession of the island of Bougainville, with its exceedingly rich copper mines and considerable oil potential, seems likely. The Bougainville population identifies, ethnically and politically, with the British Solomon islanders, while the powerful Bougainville separatist movement has influenced separatism in the islands of New Britain and New Ireland. In the Dodecanese islands, tourism, bringing both development and contact with tourists, has affected outlooks and perceptions of change. The populations of smaller, less-developed islands feel aggrieved at their apparent neglect by the central government, while being sufficiently small to suppress the political and social diversity which has grown up between the village communities of the larger islands.[52] Writing on the collapse of the Caribbean Federation, described in part 5, which reached its latest stage with Anguilla's unilateral declaration of independence from the associated state of St Kitts–Nevis–Anguilla, Clarke states

The associated states comprise groupings of two or more islands whose links were determined in the past more by the Colonial Office's desire for tidy administrative units than by the existence of close ties of sentiment. Many of the forces which bedevilled attempts to federate the West Indies now operate *within* the associated states; insularity, isolation, and parochialism persist on a reduced scale. Furthermore, the smaller partners' fear of domination by the larger is characteristic of many of the associated states as it was of the former federation. All these factors, but especially fear of domination, played a vital part in the initial estrangement of Anguilla from St Kitts.[53]

The difficulty of proceeding beyond the geographically obvious in the search for meaningful generalisations about state location has already been mentioned. Location is a paramount factor affecting the political geography of states and their interactions, but unless research is carried out in the form of painstaking small-area studies there are distinct dangers that oversimplification and crude environmental determinism will result. A more systematic analysis of the connection between state location and state behaviour was attempted by Bradshaw, who wrote, 'The essence of the location approach to the explanation of state behaviour lies in the fact that the geographical location of a state bequeathes upon it certain sets of spatial relationships *vis-à-vis* other states', and, 'So many of the potential activities and potential characteristics of a state may be largely attributed to the state's location, that location may become a useful focus for explaining the state's general pattern of behaviour'.[54]

An examination of the traditional approaches to state location reveals a considerable superficiality, and Bradshaw attempted to refine analysis and suggested useful improvements through an examination of the question of relative location. This firstly involved reference to transport technology and the effect of improvements in systems of transport. An example given concerns the circumstances of the Atlantic Alliance and the Soviet Union; in the late 1940s and early 1950s the Soviet Union had the capability of overrunning Western Europe with its land forces, but may have been deterred by the threat of retaliation by US air power, having no capabilities for attacking the USA. The subsequent development of Soviet bomber and missile capabilities transformed this relationship, particularly affecting the relative location of the USA. Secondly, the distribution of power and changes in this distribution should be considered, since both affect the relative location of states, an example being the termination of Nepal's existence as an isolated state located within a power vacuum following the growth of Chinese and Indian power and the development in each of greater interest in their frontier zones. Perception is a third element to be considered, and is discussed more fully in part 4. Political decision-making is undertaking in terms of politicians' perceptions of relative location. President de Gaulle's perception of relative location was revealed in his statement, 'Great Britain is an island; France, the cape of a continent; America another world'; this description of Britain probably accorded with the images held by the majority of British people, though most leading British politicians of the period were prepared to accept neither the insularity of Britain in relation to Europe nor the remoteness of the USA.

Another source of refinement to the locational approach might involve the investigation of other similarities between states with similar locations. Holt and Turner investigated three states with supposedly similar locations, Britain, Japan and Ceylon, all islands offshore from continents, and claimed to detect certain similarities of inputs to policy making and policies.[55] Such approaches are potentially valuable, but extreme care is necessary if inaccurate assessments and the temptation to invoke nonexistent forms of environmental determinism are to be avoided.

Russett has investigated state location from the viewpoint of relative proximity. The measure of distance employed was straight-line great circle distances between capitals.

A matrix of the distance from each state's capital to that of every other country was constructed. . . . All the values were then standardised by dividing each by the largest distance in the matrix (New Zealand to Spain, almost 12 400 miles) and subtracting the dividend from one. This simultaneously converted them to a range of zero to one and changed the distances into proximities, with the shortest distance in the entire table. . . becoming 0.998. Unities were inserted in the diagonal, making the proximity from each country to itself equal to 1.0.[56]

Russett was correct in noting that the results of a factor analysis of the matrix, producing grouping of states into 'Europe', 'Western Hemisphere', 'Asia' and 'Africa', would not surprise the school geographer, but the organisation of data concerning contiguous regions into a factor matrix was useful for the purpose of systematic comparison with other criteria, such as regions of sociocultural homogeneity, and so on. Perhaps most surprising was the grouping of Iran, Israel and all the Arab states except Yemen with Europe rather than North Africa or Asia.

3.8 The landlocked state and access to the sea

Just as the study of exclaves and islands reveals the advantages to the state of uninterrupted area, the study of landlocked states accentuates the importance of direct access to the sea. If the European microstates are to be included, twenty-six states, about one-fifth of the total, are landlocked, twelve of these occurring in Africa. In attempting to develop theories about landlocked states, East looked for common factors other than their lack of sea frontage, and detected fairly common denominators of weakness and buffer-state status.[57] He based a model on a hypothetical circular continent, and suggested that the existence of one centrally located landlocked state would be advantageous to the surrounding maritime states, avoiding the embarassing convergence of the boundaries of powerful neighbours at the centre of the continent. In a similar position was Arcadia, a weak and backward landlocked state which served as a buffer between the more powerful city states of ancient Greece. Luxembourg, Austria, Czechoslovakia, Afghanistan and Mongolia were among contemporary examples quoted by East, and Dale considered that the African landlocked states which gained independence after the publication of East's article were also lacking in cohesion and strength, though these characteristics were shared with coastal neighbours.[58]

Naturally, not all landlocked states need be weak or buffer states, nor all weak or buffer states landlocked. Hapsburg Austria was the focus of an exceedingly powerful continental empire, and though the empire subsequently gained coastal outlets, its internal self-sufficiency was always far more important than its external trade. Though the capture of a Baltic foothold was a primary policy objective of Peter the Great (1689–1725), the Russian empire to which he acceded was powerful despite being effectively landlocked by icy seas to the north and by Turkish control of the Black Sea outlet to the Mediterranean. Indeed, Mackinder's heartland thesis emphasises the strategical advantage to Russia of the relative lack of maritime connections which might be exploited by hostile naval powers.

East studied landlocked states in terms of their relative weakness and their relationship with neighbouring states. Using GNP as a crude measure of relative strength, the median GNP value for coastal states ($1800 million, 1969 or nearest available previous estimate) is exceeded by only three landlocked states, and is greater than the upper quartile value of landlocked state GNP ($1080 million). When landlocked states are studied in terms of their relationship with neighbouring powers, the following groups emerge.

1. The African group of weak landlocked states, which are mostly surrounded by relatively weak neighbours.
2. Those which originated specifically as buffer states and which clearly retain this role. Despite East's analysis, Laos is the only absolutely clear-cut example, though Afghanistan and Nepal approach the description, and Austria, originally a frontier buffer province of the Holy Roman Empire, has reverted to this condition after several centuries of greatness.
3. Landlocked states which have become dominated by more powerful neighbours, either through coercion or voluntary association. Examples include Mongolia, Czechoslovakia, Hungary, Luxembourg and Lesotho.
4. Landlocked states located between more powerful neighbours, but within which the buffer function, if it existed, has become dormant. In this group, Switzerland, Bolivia and Paraguay might be included.
5. The European microstates, living fossils of the medieval period.

The common concern of landlocked states involves the securing of access to the sea. It has long been argued that access to the sea and the international usage of navigable waterways accessible to ocean-going vessels is a natural right involving facilities provided by God for the use of men. At the Barcelona Conference of 1921, thirty-two states signed and ratified the Convention of Freedom of Transit, undertaking to assist the movement of goods across their territories, free of tax and subject only to reasonable charges. Some non-signatory states concluded bilateral agreements with neighbouring states which provided for similar rights. In 1958, a United Nations conference of landlocked states was convened preliminary to the Conference on the Law of the Sea, and the rights of landlocked states to innocent passage were reaffirmed. By 1964, a number of new independent landlocked states had been created in Africa, and a further United Nations conference was convened which produced a convention embodying the principles of the Barcelona Conference but protecting the sovereignty of the transit state at the expense of that of the landlocked state by permitting restrictions on the transit of undesirable aliens and goods which might cause a medical, moral or security threat to the transit state.[59]

Political approaches to the problem of access to the sea have varied through time. Some landlocked states have navigable river access to the sea, and the notion of such rivers as international highways provided by a supernatural power dates back to the eighteenth century, and formed the basis of the 1795 claim of us rights to use the Spanish-controlled section of the Mississippi, and the us claims of 1823 and 1853 of international rights on the St Lawrence and Amazon respectively. The question of the use of international rivers is not peculiar to landlocked states, but applies also to the trading practices of all states and the use of alternative outlets by coastal states, such as the West German use of outlets in the Netherlands or the Peruvian use of the Amazon.

In the later nineteenth and early twentieth centuries there was considerable support for the awarding of territorial primary corridors as a means of extending the sovereign territory of the landlocked state to some convenient coastal location, or secondary corridors to international rivers, providing alternative outlets for certain coastal states. Mississippi and Alabama were awarded territorial corridors to the Gulf Coast through Florida territory purchased from Spain in 1819. Under the Austrian and Hungarian *Ausgleich* of 1867, the Hungarian boundaries were drawn in such a way as to provide Hungary with a land corridor to the Adriatic Sea. In 1885, at the Berlin Conference, the German South-West African colony was awarded a land corridor to the Zambezi international river, which survives as the Caprivi strip extension of Namibia, and between 1913 and 1919 Bulgaria possessed a corridor to the Aegean. International support for territorial corridors reached a climax in 1918 when the thirteenth of President Wilson's Fourteen Points for World Peace was accepted, involving the award of a land corridor to the Baltic to a newly recreated Polish state. Even at this time, President Wilson's principle of free and secure access to the sea was not considered to be universally applicable in the award of land corridors to landlocked states, since the defeated Austrians and the independent Czechs and Hungarians became landlocked in the wholesale dismemberment of the Austro-Hungarian Empire. Marshal Foch identified the Polish corridor which divided Germany into two portions as 'the root of the next war', and events proved him to be partly correct.[60] The troubles which ensued from the granting of the Polish corridor probably did much to prejudice politicians against future such territorial awards, and subsequently the problems of landlocked states tended to be settled according to the principle of the Barcelona Convention and bilateral agreement, though Iraq obtained a land connection with the Persian Gulf in 1922, and in the same year Columbia obtained the Leticia secondary corridor from Peru, providing access to the Amazon. As recently as 1938, abortive Jewish and British plans for the partition of Palestine into Jewish and Arab states envisaged territorial corridors connecting mandated Arab territory with the Mediterranean, and in the stormy growth of the Israeli state, an Israeli land corridor to the Gulf of Aqaba port of Eilat was won.[61]

The contemporary landlocked state, not traversed by an international river, must rely upon the goodwill of its coastal neighbours in upholding the spirit and provisions of the conventions of 1921, 1958 and 1964. In several recent instances these rights have been withheld or restricted, while the transit state which observes the spirit of the agreements experiences a limited compromise of its sovereignty and a measure of inconvenience. In general, bilateral negotiations providing for the use by the landlocked state of communications, port and bonded warehouse facilities in the transit state will cause less disruption than the annexation or cession of territory for corridors, though a stricter application and observation of the rights of landlocked states is to be desired.

Case studies

The Polish corridor was very much a product of a particular European emotional and political climate. The original Polish state, after centuries of power and influence, disappeared in the late eighteenth century in a series of partitions between Prussia, Austria and Russia. Poles were among the most ardent participants in the Central European nationalist movements, and during the 1914–18 war, the creation of a Polish nation state was forcefully canvassed by expatriate Polish leaders, and was acceptable to the Allied powers, appealing both to President Wilson's idealistic approach to the concept of national self-determination and to the more pragmatic objectives of Western European politicians anxious to see the dismantlement of the powerful Central European empires. The defeat of the German and Austro-Hungarian alliance and the weakness of revolutionary Russia provided the necessary condition for a Polish recreation.

President Wilson's principles concerning the rights of nations to free and secure access to the sea were one-sidedly applied to the Polish case, but not to others, despite the fact that the Swiss had shown that the ability to prosper was not conditional on the possession of a territorial corridor. An ethnic justification for the Polish corridor was provided by the presence in the corridor area of pockets of Slavonic Kassube and Polish population, interspersed among German-speaking areas (see figure 3.1b). Danzig (Gdansk), at the terminus of the corridor, was the natural Baltic outlet for Polish trade, but with a population which was 99 per cent German. This contradiction of the ethnic principle was approached by the creation of a Free City of Danzig, in customs union with Poland and autonomous under a High Commissioner appointed by the League of Nations.

The effect of the Polish corridor was the separation of East Prussia from the rest of Germany, and though Germany had guaranteed rights on trans-corridor railways, the settlement was unacceptable to the German point of view and a potential source of war. In 1920 Polish armies assaulted Russia, taking advantage of the temporary weakness of the revolutionary state. Workers in Danzig sympathetic to the socialist cause refused to cooperate in the unloading of Polish arms shipments, and the Poles retaliated by con-structing the port of Gdynia on Polish territory adjacent to Danzig. Polish trade was then channelled through Gdynia at the expense of Danzig, and in 1938 the value of Gdynia's trade was three times that of Danzig's. As a consequence extreme unemployment was experienced in Danzig and many Danzigers became ardent supporters of Nazi Germany, while the divisive nature of the Polish corridor and the plight of Danzig provided pretexts for the German invasion of Poland. The ultimate solution to the problem, fol-lowing the Russo-German partition of the country, came in 1945 with the westward Russian advance against invading Germans resulting in the Russian recovery of the territory taken by Poland in 1920–1, and the com-pensation of Poland with German territory in the west, causing the disap-pearance of the Polish corridor.

While the Polish corridor exemplifies the weakness of the corridor solution to the problems of landlocked states, the experiences of several of the recently independent African states reveal the inadequacies of the rights-of-transit solution as it exists at present. Disputes over the usage of routes and ports which did not arise during the colonial era have appeared with the fragmentation of African empires into sovereign units.

Mali was formed in 1959 from the union of Soudan and Senegal, with Soudan as the weaker component, dependent on railway connections with the Senegalese port of Dakar for the export of groundnuts. In 1960 a clash of interests concerning foreign policy caused the severance of the union; Soudan retained the name of Mali, and the Senegalese closed the rail outlet to Dakar. Mali was therefore obliged to explore new trade outlets and de-veloped road communications to Bobo Dibulasso in Upper Volta, which had rail connections to the Ivory Coast outlet of Abidjan. This outlet proved successful and was retained after the reopening of the Senegal–Mali border in 1963.[62]

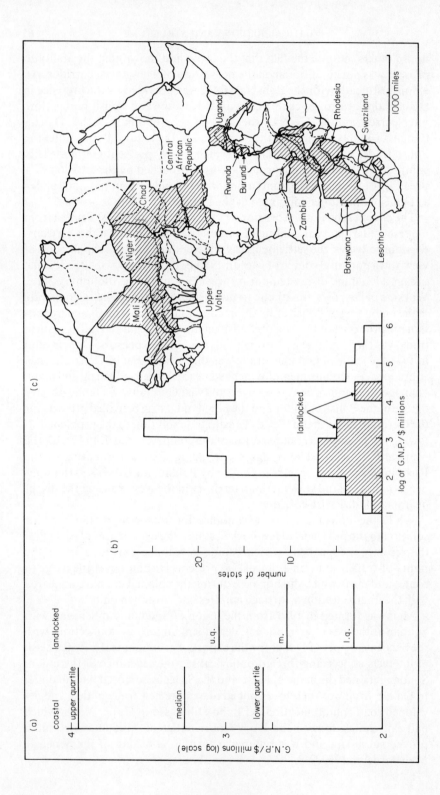

The enclave state of Lesotho, entirely surrounded by South Africa, is in a less favourable position still, being unable to explore alternative outlets should its neighbour prove uncooperative. As a weak and landlocked state, Lesotho is inevitably dependent on the goodwill of its sole neighbour. 'Lesotho is theoretically at least South Africa's political and economic hostage. Though Lesotho's independence is a political reality, in economic terms it can be argued that it is little more effective than those of the projected self-governing Bantustans of South Africa.'[63] Since the Customs Agreement of December 1969—under the terms of which South Africa collects all customs dues from Lesotho, Botswana and Swaziland and repays a proportionate share for lost revenue to each—the question of access to and use of port facilities has not arisen directly, though any system of sanctions imposed on South Africa by the international community would obviously affect Lesotho equally. At the time of writing Lesotho has no negotiated air corridor over South African territory, and on occasions the South African authorities have seized individuals in transit to Lesotho.

Harsh necessities of access to the sea have produced cooperation between unlikely black African and white supremacist partners. The natural opposition of the black government of Malawi to the white regimes in South Africa and (at the time) Portuguese Moçambique was sacrificed for a £5.4 million loan from South Africa to finance the 101 kilometre Nacala railway extension connecting the Malawi rail system with the Moçambique rail link to the port of Nacala, opened in 1970. Previously Malawi had been served by a railway to the Moçambique port of Beira, but this connection was periodically disrupted by flooding and no alternative direct road link exists.[64] Until February 1973, black Zambia and white-dominated Rhodesia were unlikely bedfellows, cohabiting on the basis of the Zambian need for the use of Rhodesian railways in the transport of copper to Beira and the Rhodesian earnings of £25 million *per annum* deriving from transit revenue. However, a series of guerilla attacks on Rhodesian homesteads from across the Zambian border led to the Rhodesian closure of the border to all but the lucrative copper shipments. The Zambians replied by halting the delivery of copper shipments for transit, which can be redirected through Zaïre to the Angolan port of Lobito, while other exports can be taken by road to the Tanzanian port of Dar es Salaam. The

Figure 3.4.   Economic aspects of landlocked states. (a) and (b) are based on published estimates of GNP for 111 coastal and 26 landlocked states. Note the use of logarithmic scales for the plotting of GNP in $ millions (1969, or nearest previous estimate) and the relative positions of the median values for coastal and landlocked states in (a). (c) shows landlocked states in Africa and their relationship to railways and to relevant roads (pecked lines).

completion of the Tanzam railway to Tanzania in 1975 may be expected to produce more positive support for black African policies in Zambia, and the Rhodesian strategy obviously misfired.[65]

The above examples serve to show the dependence of the landlocked state on its neighbours, testified both by the compromise of the political independence of states such as Lesotho and Malawi, and the survival of white supremacy in Rhodesia despite international sanctions, owing to the connivance of the South African and Portuguese neighbours. Rhodesia must be the only state to profit from its landlocked status, being immune to the sort of blockade which might be mounted against a coastal state.

3.9 Conclusion

In structural terms, there is no such thing as the typical state; each state has certain characteristics, such as sovereign territory and a capital, which are common to other states, and each has unique qualities, such as shape and the disposition of political-geographical subregions within its boundaries. Whebell suggests that models can be used to symbolise forms of states characteristic of three macro-regions.[66] The Old World state model is ethnically based and includes a number of cultural core areas which have come together as population expansion has replaced intervening frontiers of separation with frontiers of contact. The modern economic state may incorporate ethnic minority territories too small to function effectively in isolation, along with other areas where distinctiveness has developed through relative isolation.

The New World model is based on spatial economic systems, and cultural differences are only incidental. Economic core areas originated as scattered enclaves of coastal European settlement and were expanded along communications corridors leading to the interior. States are separated by geometrical boundaries drawn through frontiers of separation, while indigenous populations were frequently displaced into extra-ecumenical territory in the course of European penetration. Capitals are either coastal metropolises or forward capitals (figure 3.3).

In the Third World model, developed ethnic patterns of Old World type are overlaid by the economic patterns of urbanisation and communications of New World type. Both ethnic and economic core areas exist, with the capital as a coastal economic focus. Political boundaries are superimposed upon the indigenous cultural systems, and are unlikely to reflect their characteristics. The models outlined were intended primarily as teaching aids and are acceptable only as the loosest generalisations, though they do evidence a certain tendency towards grouping of some political-geographical phenomena in global macro-regions. This morphological survey is incomplete without mention of frontiers and boundaries and associated landscapes; however, the topic merits special attention, and is considered in part 6.

PART 4

Political process, perception and decision-making

This part is designed to introduce the concept of political process as an agent for landscape change, in recognition that political process is itself influenced by characteristics of the political landscape. In part 5 political processes which are effective mainly within a state system are studied, and in part 7 attention is focused on processes active at the international level. In the context of states as subsystems within the international system, the rigid separation of factors internal and external to the state is not possible, and the framework adopted here is partly influenced by convenience.* Two processes in particular, perception and decision-making, apply equally at the internal and external levels, and since they are closely interrelated, they are considered here together.

4.1 Political process

Much as the geomorphologist is concerned with the creation of new landscapes through the action of processes of erosion and deposition on existing landscapes, the political geographer is interested in the processes of change affecting political geographical patterns and relationships, as evinced in place, area and landscape. Process in political geography has been defined as 'the succession of events, actions, or operations that man employs to establish, maintain, or to change a political system', the latter being composed of political processes and geographical space.[1] A dissection of political process reveals that in the immediate sense landscape change results from transactions—specific decisions made often, but not always, through a formal political structure of government. Examples of political transactions which would affect existing landscapes include decisions to repatriate aliens, to erect tariff barriers against certain imports

* An introduction to some systems approaches is provided in the appendix.

to stimulate home production, or to impose an *apartheid* policy. In a broader sense, it is clear that transactions are influenced by societal forces, the enduring values, fears, customs and aspirations current in a society, possibly including such phenomena as nationalism or imperialism, capitalism or socialism, religion or atheism.

Other variables will influence the nature of transactions. Firstly, while political decision makers usually form transactions to accord with their perception of the national interest, this perception will vary from time to time and from person to person, while none of these perceptions will exactly replicate reality. Secondly, the political system will vary between the more open extreme where foreign influences permeate relatively freely, as in the case of modern Switzerland, and the more closed extreme as exemplified by the USSR of the 1930s or mainland China in the 1960s.

Therefore political process—acting through transactions themselves influenced by societal forces, perception, or 'locational perspective', and the open–closed nature of the political system—is brought to bear on areas. Initially transactions affect more limited political action areas to which they immediately relate, though broader landscape change may follow.

The ideas outlined above were presented in full by Cohen and Rosenthal, and Figure 4.1 represents an attempt to simplify some of the main points of their argument.[2] Prominent in their thesis is the concept of a law–landscape thread, and the significance of this approach was anticipated by Whittlesey[3] in his study of the impress of central authority upon landscape in which he outlined the considerable and varied ways by which political authorities instigate landscape change through legislation concerning security, territorial integration, law, economic and social policies and colonial activity. In some cases the effect of law on landscape will be direct and obvious, as for instance in the Ugandan decision to expel Asians with British passports. In other cases the relationship may be more subtle; for example, one outcome of the Icelandic decision to extend fishing limits may be a movement towards greater economic diversity in British east-coast fishing ports such as Hull and Aberdeen.

The landscape-changing transactions vary in their nature and objectives through time and from one political community to another, as do the environmental factors that influence them. Whittlesey, describing what he termed the 'earth impress on political thought', wrote, 'The political structure erected by every group of people is, ideally, a device for facilitating the economic and social life of the community. It is most successful when it neatly fits the conditions of the natural environment in the area where it functions.'[4] Groups with different appreciations of the environment will enact differing sets of transactions. The British, as a nation active in world trade, have tended to support an 'open seas' policy favouring minimal claims to territorial waters, while several developing states with restricted trading fleets but expanding fishing fleets favour extreme claims to territorial waters. The constitution of the USA, at the time of its introduction,

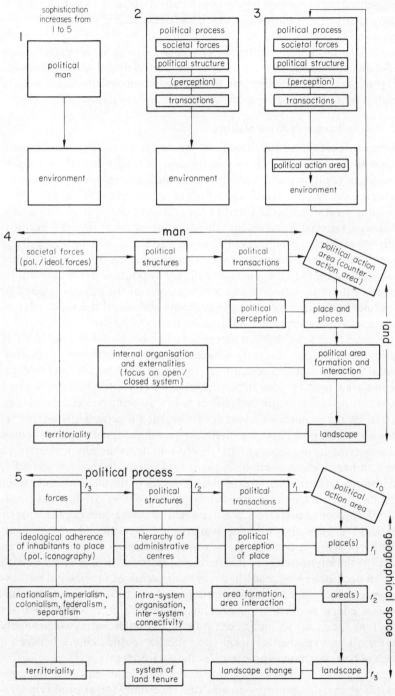

Figure 4.1. The Cohen and Rosenthal model, simplified by the present author in stages 1, 2 and 3, with sophistication increasing from 1 to 5. Based on ref. 1.

represented the maximum degree of centralisation acceptable to an aggregate of distinctive communities which had developed in different environments and directions, though with necessary amendments the constitution
was sufficiently flexible to form the legal basis of a well-integrated state. As
an organisational basis for the study of the interrelationship between political process and the environment, the Cohen–Rosenthal model succeeds in
developing and systematising earlier, more loosely presented ideas.

4.2 Perception and decision-making

Studies in perception are based on the fundamental fact that human
decisions are not formed in total knowledge of reality but rely upon perceptions of reality which are always incomplete and frequently grossly inaccurate. As reality exerts its influence upon decisions made, these
decisions must often be adjusted to take account of unperceived factors.
Assuming rational government, then the closer to reality the political
decision maker's perceptions, the more successful will be the policies
adopted. In terms of an international society in which the main actors are
sovereign states, then the main determinant of political behaviour will be
perceived national interests, and a comparison of the policies applied to
particular states by successive governments will reveal the wide range of
variation in the perception of national interest which exists.

On the broad scale, human perceptions can be related to appraisals of
the environment on a spectrum between the opposed extremes of environmental determinism and possibilism. In an approach which links ecological and behavioural studies to political science, H. H. and M. Sprout noted
that environmental factors only affect policy by being perceived and considered by decision-makers, and they discerned five fairly distinctive relationship theories.[5] These are, firstly, environmental determinism, which
in its extreme form accords all powers to initiate to the physical environment and casts human actions in the role of passive responses; secondly,
environmentalism, which stresses the influences of the environment rather
than its strict control of human behaviour; thirdly, environmental possibilism, which interprets man as a free agent choosing between the wide or
restricted range of choices made available by his particular environment;
fourthly, cognitive behaviourism, which emphasises the fact that man
reacts to the environment as it is perceived rather than as it really is, with
human decisions being made in the light of perceived factors and past experience, while unperceived limitations and opportunities exert no immediate effect; and fifthly, environmental probabilism, which does not
deny man the ability to initiate, but anticipates that decisions will probably
conform to a hypothetical norm and reflect a sensible choice between a
range of best alternatives presented by the environment.

One might attempt to locate the attitudes of decision-makers at different
points on the determinism–possibilism spectrum; for example, in pre-
industrial Britain and Tsarist Russia decision-making was probably

greatly influenced by perceived environmental limitations, while in the Britain of the Industrial Revolution or post-revolutionary Russia, it was probably more influenced by the search for opportunities. Present knowledge would suggest that a combination of the fourth and fifth approaches listed would generally be most appropriate.

Boulding has developed an approach to perception in political science which is relevant to political geography, and which links the internal and external levels of enquiry.[6] He identifies the most important images (perceptions) in these contexts as being those which a political community has of itself, and those which it has of other political bodies in the international system. The national image is a historical image formed mainly by the individual in childhood within the family group; it is normally a folk image based on a selective view of the nation, emphasising past successes and past injustices, and it is reinforced by national historians and by the national political elite. Members of this elite have themselves inherited the image, but in the course of their political activities they seek to emphasise certain aspects of it in order to strengthen their positions, increase national coherence and mobilise popular opinion behind their policies. Three main groups of factors make national images effective in international relations. They are, firstly, the geographical dimension, involving the territorial nature of nationalism, with nations thinking of themselves as occupying, or having the right or need to occupy, territory of a particular spatial form and contents; secondly, the hostility *versus* friendliness factor, with other nations tending to be regarded in relation to a scale of hostility and friendliness. Attitudes towards outsiders may change over time, and the extremes on the scale are represented by stable friendliness and stable hostility. Thirdly, there is the strength *versus* weakness factor, which introduces the importance of relative power in international relations, with policies being conditioned by perceptions of the strength of the nation relative to the power of allies and of potential enemies.

Since the pursuit of individual national interests encourages the competitive rather than the cooperative aspects of state behaviour, conflict is inherent in the international system, and may exist at an intranational level when different groups within the state, such as national minorities, pursue different objectives. Real incompatibility exists when two nations or subgroups have irreconcilable images of the future, such as common claims to ownership of a particular piece of territory. Illusory incompatibility exists from the inadequate exploration of the possibilities for cooperation. An excellent example of incompatible images was provided by Koch, North and Zinnes, concerning the irreconcilable claims mounted by Bulgaria, Serbia and Greece in 1912 to ownership of the whole or parts of Macedonia.[7] Boulding pointed out that the national image is the last great stronghold of unsophistication, but that future stability must depend upon the refinement of national images leading to more rational international behaviour.

Variables such as the hostility–friendliness one can be roughly represented in terms of a matrix (figure 4.2) in which the degree of hostility or friendship felt by the nations in the rows towards those in the columns is shown. According to the weighting used, the greater the hostility, the higher the negative value; the greater the friendliness, the higher the positive value.

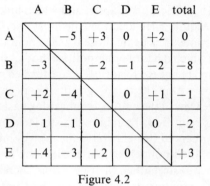

	A	B	C	D	E	total
A		−5	+3	0	+2	0
B	−3		−2	−1	−2	−8
C	+2	−4		0	+1	−1
D	−1	−1	0		0	−2
E	+4	−3	+2	0		+3

Figure 4.2

Since attitudes tend to be reciprocated, the matrix should generally be reasonably symmetrical; in the example shown, B is a 'paranoid' nation, generating hostility and receiving it in return, and E is a 'friendly' nation, offering friendship but reciprocating B's hostility.[8] The obvious difficulty in the application of this model to real-life situations involves the choice of appropriate weightings on friendliness and hostility.

FitzGerald neatly points out that 'The perceived environment (as opposed to the so-called "real" environment) may be regarded as a subsystem operating in the existing "real" as a result of the decisions which are made'.[9] Questions relating to perception intervene in political geography in almost innumerable ways; an attempt to represent the role of perception in policy formation is given in figure 4.1. Perceptions change, and many decisions relevant to political geography were made on the basis of a considerable discrepancy between the perceived and the real environment; a frequently quoted example concerns the Russian sale of Alaska to the USA in 1867, the decision being influenced by Russian doubts about their ability to organise and administer the territory, which would have been nullified had they had knowledge about the gold resources of the territory or foresight concerning its oil reserves, the uses of petroleum and the pattern of geostrategic relations which would develop in the twentieth century. Before the ages of discovery and colonialism, the human world consisted of a series of rather closed systems, and decisions concerning matters such as trade, defence and conquest were made in relation to the limited knowledge of known worlds. FitzGerald has attempted to reconstruct an Athenian's-eye view of the Greek colonies (figure 4.3a), and they form the centre of a very circumscribed Mediterranean world; space has been transformed so that distance, instead of increasing linearly, increases logarithmically.

An important source of subjectivity in geography derives from the use of

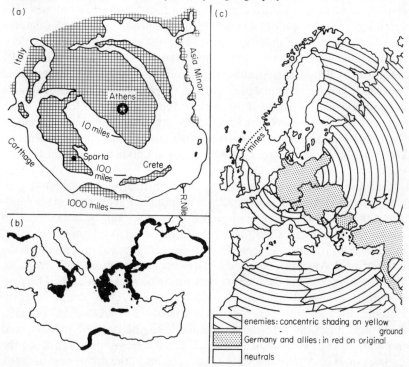

Figure 4.3.   Perception and politics in maps.

(a) FitzGerald's Athenian's-eye view of the Greek world (560 BC). A logarithmic transformation of distance centred on Athens. Greek area of influence is shaded (see ref. 9).

(b) Greek colonies *circa* 550 BC.

(c) A map from a German atlas of the second world war, designed to exaggerate the encirclement of Germany in the first world war. This is achieved by the use of a projection which exaggerates area away from the centre of the map and the employment of the unusual concentric ring shading. Enemies are coloured yellow, symbolic of cowardice; Germany and allies red, symbolic of courage (see ref. 10).

maps. Every map represents selectivity in the inclusion of information; in some cases the map may be relatively comprehensive, as with the British Ordnance Survey maps, in other cases only one sort of spatial relationship is represented, as in dot distribution population maps. In most cases the selectivity is rational and purposeful, and the vast majority of maps are designed to inform, though a minority are designed to give misleading support for particular political viewpoints. Optical effects may be employed to encourage a misinterpretation of data, significant information may be omitted, or captions may be phrased in emotive language, all without actually falsifying fact. Such techniques are still in use, both in the East and in the West, though this art of deception was most widely practised in Nazi Germany and was a stock in trade of the geopoliticians; figure 4.3c is included as an example from a German war atlas of 1941 and emphasises the supposed encirclement of Germany by hostile powers in 1914 through the use of concentric ring shading. The psychological connotations of colour may also be exploited, and in the same atlas the rosy pink conventionally employed by British cartographers to colour the British Empire is replaced by a sickly yellow, symbolic of cowardice.[10] Speier has quoted the case of a geopolitical map used to illustrate the repatriation of Germans from Latvia, and though the German minority constituted only 3.7 per cent of the Latvian population, the thirteen large symbols used to represent the German population covered the whole area of Latvia and gave the illusion of a country populated by Germans.[11]

Decision-making is an important element in all branches of human geography, and is particularly important in political geography since landscape change as an outcome of political processes can be traced back to conscious human decisions. The use of decision-making theory in international relations was pioneered by Snyder, and is based on a model of the international system in which the states behave as actors in a situation, their behaviour being decided by decision-makers within each. The process of decision-making was subdivided into spheres of competence, including the activities of decision-makers in producing policies, communication and information available to the decision-makers, and motivation, the psychological and subjective factors which influence the decision-makers.[12] The approach takes account of the differences between the perceived or psychological environment, which conditions the decisions reached, and the real or operative environment, which determines the limits of possible actions, feedback from which will affect subsequent decisions.

The nature of decisions reached will be partly dependent upon the decision-makers' perceptions of reality, but it will also be affected by the form of decision-making which is currently favoured. Most of the decisions which concern political geographers are made by formal bodies, taking the UK as an example, at the intranational level; many decisions affecting local government are made by sub-committees of county councils, in consultation with permanent council employees, and are forwarded for formal ratification to the full council. At the national level, most important decisions are reached by Cabinet discussion, frequently involving consultation with leading civil servants from appropriate ministries, and the decision may be presented for parliamentary approval in the form of a bill. These systems of decision-making are far different from those operated in, for example, a military dictatorship. The most important forms of decision-making are independent discretion and free will, in which a dictator has the power to initiate and to overrule all counter-proposals; cooperative interdependence, in which a number of decision-makers participate with the objective of producing the best solution to a given problem; and conflict interdependence, in which individual decision-makers are primarily concerned with protecting and furthering their own particular vested interests, and the ultimate decision is likely to represent political compromise and relative power.

Authoritative geographical studies of decision-making are as yet in short supply, and in political geography they are virtually nonexistent. One of the best examples of a geographical application is Hamilton's study of decision-making in the Soviet Union.[13] The decision to launch the virgin lands scheme of the mid-1950s, involving the ploughing up of hitherto unfarmed lands on the southern steppe margins in the Ukraine, Siberia and Kazakhstan, resulted from a conflict interdependence process. The Soviet Union faced a critical shortage of wheat and animal foodstuffs, but there were strong political objections to their importation from the west, while Khrushchev, during his visit to the USA, and a number of Soviet agricultural delegations to that country had been impressed by the system of converting maize into pork practised in the mid-west. The introduction of maize to the Soviet Union would necessitate the displacement of wheat to unfarmed semi-arid regions. The suggestion to plough up the virgin lands for wheat farming was supported by Siberian representatives who were anxious that Siberia should be seen to make an active contribution to the Soviet economy, but was opposed by Kazakh delegates on the grounds of cost and probably unarticulated fears that further large-scale Slav settlement would be involved, which might undermine the national basis of the Kazakh Republic. In the event Khrushchev overruled the Kazakhs, but the partial failure of the virgin lands scheme probably played a part in his downfall.

A simplified matrix framework for the systematic interrelating of geographical and policy factors was devised by Koch and his associates (figure 4.4). The variables included were resources, physical entities which have some positive or negative value for a state, and the geographical form in which they occur such as a natural harbour or cultivable land; their arrangement with respect to each other, such as the location and configuration of a harbour or the proximity of coal to iron; their boundaries, which determine the allocation of resources and their division between groups of people; the value which a state attaches to resources and to their allocation; the relationship of the resources to the policy conditions or goals of the interested parties; the choices of alternative available in respect of these goals, and the instruments, strategies and weapons available to the interested parties in furthering their policies. While the matrix indicates the possible interactions between geographical elements and other aspects of policy and conflict, it does not postulate relationships.[14]

In the early stages of the development of political geography, several writers were tempted to approach the aspect of the subject concerned with the effect of geography upon politics from the standpoint of environmental determinism, blandly stating that the political behaviour and characteristics of state X were a response to environmental attributes A, B and C. Frequently such statements were made without consideration of the political structures, personalities or conditions affecting the states concerned, and fortunately work of this type is seldom encountered today. A more promising if as yet poorly explored alternative approach would involve attempts to assess the ways in which geographical factors are considered during the policy-making process.

Bradshaw has devised a model which attempts to incorporate the geographical factors in political decision-making. Two important elements of the decision-making process are perceptions of the *milieu* or total environment and values. The decision-maker selects from the *milieu* the information which is acceptable and seems relevant, with the geographical environment constituting a large and important part of the *milieu*. Once perceived, the abstracted information will be interpreted

	Geographical elements: form of resources	relation of a particular resource to other resources	boundaries (allocations for human beings)	Human evaluations: perceptions of positive or negative value, benefit or injury, gain or loss	Goals–means: policy condition	choice of alternative	instrument
Geographical elements: form of resources							
relation of a particular resource to other resources							
boundaries (allocations for human beings)							
Human evaluations: perceptions of positive or negative value, benefit or injury, gain or loss							
Goals–means: policy condition							
choice of alternative							
instrument							

Figure 4.4

and assessed according to the decision-maker's values.[15]

One of the fundamental elements in the geographical environment is distance, often expressed in terms of relative location, and a major problem in analysis concerns the choice of an appropriate measure of distance. Linear distance will seldom be found to be acceptable. For example, to Chamberlain in 1938, Czechoslovakia, no further from London than the Orkney Islands, was 'a faraway land', populated by 'people of whom we know nothing'; the distant British imperial possessions, one expects, were perceived to be in some senses much closer than Czechoslovakia. Probably different measures of 'real' distance need to be developed to apply to different perceptions and situations.

Game theory has developed in political science to link decision-making to theoretical international conflict situations. Some of the less complex games models are based on a pay-off matrix in which the strategies of one player are represented in rows and those of the other in columns (figure 4.5). In a 'zero-sum-game', all gains and losses are equal, so one player's gain is the other player's loss. The simplest forms of zero-sumgame are those in which players base their strategy on the 'minimax' concept, and each aims for the greatest gain but will accept the smallest if this seems to be the most that he can obtain. A stable 'saddle-point' solution results when the players opt respectively for the maximisation of the minimum (maximin) and minimisation of the maximum (minimax). In games without a minimax there is a resort in randomised or 'mixed' strategies in which each player plays a few of his strategies at random and each side obtains the best it can over the long run.

In international relations pure conflict is replaced by cooperation as well as conflict, for example cooperation to avoid mutual annihilation in a nuclear war, and here variable-sum-games are more appropriate (see

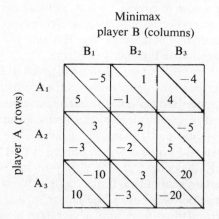

Figure 4.5. A_1, A_2, A_3 and B_1, B_2, B_3 denote different strategies of players A and B. Payoffs to A are shown in the bottom left-hand corner of each cell, and payoffs to B in the top right-hand corner of each cell. Minimax outcome is at cell (A_1, B_2).

figure 4.6). One of the best known of these is 'Prisoner's Dilemma', according to which deadlock exists as two nations are unable to cooperate because of mutual distrust. It applies, for example, to a situation in which each side is anxious to disarm but reluctant to do so unilaterally. In figure 4.6a, the economic advantage of being disarmed and saving investment is 5, but the disadvantage of being the only disarmed state is -10. The storyline of Prisoner's Dilemma concerns a situation in which two prisoners charged with the same crime are each kept in isolation. The governor offers freedom to the first prisoner to confess; the remaining prisoner is to be hanged. If both confess at once, each receives a prison sentence.

A second variable-sum-game is known as 'Chicken', in which two dri-

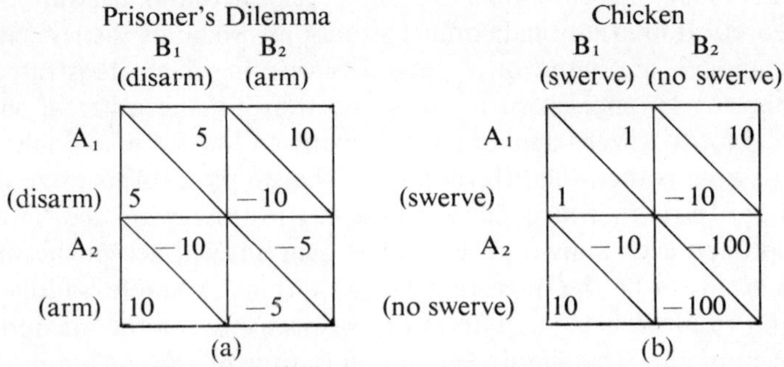

Figure 4.6.   (a) Minimax outcome is (A_1, B_1): the states disarm together. (b) Minimax outcome is (A_1, B_1): both swerve together. From ref. 16.

vers drive towards each other at speed; the one who swerves is branded a coward, the one who does not becomes a hero. If neither swerves, both are killed, but if both swerve, disgrace is avoided. In contrast to Prisoner's Dilemma, the penalty for two non-cooperators is more severe than that suffered by a single non-cooperator. It is analogous to a situation in which one nuclear power is able to convince another of its determination not to 'swerve', and the latter power's only choice is to cooperate to avoid its own destruction along with that of its adversary. The 'rational' incentive not to cooperate is stronger than in Prisoner's Dilemma.

Models such as these are limited in their predictive value, though numerous refinements are possible, culminating in the construction of exceedingly complex computerised games. Considering commercially produced games, students will discover some of the strengths and weaknesses of game simulation by playing 'Diplomacy', a political-geographical game based on a hypothetical European war beginning in 1901. The outcome of the game is largely dependent on the ability of individual players to deceive, though certain geopolitical factors do tend to emerge, such as the British dependence upon sea power, the nature of Belgium as an international battlefield and the vulnerability of Germany to assault from more than one direction. Game theory has been applied with success to decision-making in some branches of human geography, though its potential value in political geography has not been investigated to any appreciable degree. For a decision-making process to be of interest to political geographers, the decision should be taken in account of geographical factors, or once operative should be reconsidered in the light of intervention by unperceived geographical factors, or should produce geographical results.

In the geographical investigation of decision-making, it should be remembered that, while decisions studied are affected by the perceptions of decision-makers, different perceptions can also be brought to bear on the nature of decision-making. Allison has shown how the process of US decision-making during the Cuban missile crisis can be interpreted as, firstly, rational policy, carried out by a unified national decision-making system pursuing goals in a controlled and rational manner; or, from the perspective of policy as an organisational process, seeing the decision-making in terms of large and semi-autonomous departments in the US national security establishment which make habitual responses, distribute policy problems between themselves and operate each according to its nature, in account of its interests and from its own perspectives; or, from the perspective of policy as bureaucratic politics, where government action is interpreted in terms of bargaining between key personalities in the decision-making elite. Though each approach is different, a plausible analysis can be based on each.[17]

Case study

Some of the least sophisticated images prevalent are those concerning national character. Though perceived national character is much less influential than previously in the formation of foreign policy, perceptions of national character are still effective in influencing decisions which have geographical relevance; for example, the German reputation for industrious effeciency has been important in attracting foreign concerns to locate enterprises in Germany.

In spring 1974 my students and I carried out a survey of perceptions of certain foreign nationalities held by a sample of the townspeople of Cambridge. In studies such as this it is important that the sampling techniques employed should not bias the results; therefore, rather than asking people to ascribe characteristics selected from a list to different nationalities, we simply asked them to give two characteristics which they associated with five nations selected from the EEC membership. It was then found that all descriptions of national character could be summarised under seventy synonyms, 'indolent', 'idle' and 'lazy', for example, all being included under 'lazy'. As different nations scored highly on different synonyms, national stereotypes began to emerge, though since certain common descriptions such as 'friendly' were much more likely to be chosen than esoteric descriptions such as 'regimentalised', one could not look for deviations from a null model which would predict equal scoring on each synonym. The synonyms were arranged into categories of 'pro' for favourable descriptions, 'neutral', and 'anti' for unfavourable descriptions. There was little to suggest xenophobia, and in fact the favourable descriptions (35 per cent) slightly outnumbered the unfavourable (33 per cent)—see table 4.1.

Table 4.1

Nation	Pro	Neutral	Anti
French	22	41	36
German	55	20	26
Irish	21	30	49
Dutch	68	24	8
Italian	14	42	44

Percentages are rounded off, so not all total 100

Though national stereotypes clearly emerged, that of the French was the least defined, the highest individual scores being 8 per cent on 'arrogant' and 9 per cent on 'romantic'. That of the Germans emerged with much greater clarity, with the highest of all scores, 21 per cent, on 'industrious'. The dynamic nature of national stereotypes was demonstrated, and the old stereotype of Germans as militant and ruthless has been replaced by one which emphasises diligence and resourcefulness; this becomes clear when the combined score on the synonyms of 'industrious', 'intelligent', 'efficient', 'sensible' and 'purposeful', amounting to 35 per cent of all descriptions of Germans, is compared to the combined score on 'aggressive', 'cruel', 'domineering', 'humourless' and 'tough', which amounted to only 14 per cent.

The Irish stereotype is interesting because it suggests that people's perceptions of the Irish are more influenced by the tasteless comedians now in vogue than by media reports of violence in Northern Ireland. The combined score on the 'Irishman joke' characteristics of 'lazy', 'stupid' and 'drunken' amounted to 30 per cent; that on 'aggressive', 'violent' and 'bad-tempered' was only 9 per cent. The stereotype of the smaller and perhaps less familiar Dutch nation was one of overwhelming favourability, which might reflect the lack of serious rivalry between the British and the Dutch over the recent historical period. Italians will obviously not be flattered by the majority of descriptions, though the high 'anti' score was not clustered on particular synonyms; the Italians had a remarkable score of 20 per cent on the neutral description of 'volatile'.

The study was solely one of perception, and did not purport to demonstrate the existence or nonexistence of national character, though it did reveal strong preferences and distinctive stereotypes.[18]

PART 5

Political process and the state

5.1 The state

It is possible to view the world in political terms as an international system composed of a number of subsystems or actors, of which the most important are the sovereign states. Though in the post-war period there has been a reaction against approaches that focus exclusively on states and their interactions, it must be recognised that the contemporary international system is subsystem-dominant. It has been established practice in political geography to divide subject matter between the categories of that which is internal to the state and that which is external to it, thus according a paramount position to the state level of investigation. In political science, traditional ethnocentric approaches have been attacked by a number of modern theorists who emphasise the importance of non-governmental political interactions at intra and extra-state levels.

Nation-states no longer provide the only source of authority in the nation-state systems. International organisations and regional groupings, by their existence and actions, provide new forms of authority. . . . Nations today are not sovereign, in the meaningful sense of that term, and are not self-contained, and are not impermeable.[1]

However, as Singer remarks,

. . . even as the alleged trend toward the demise of the territorial state sets in during this century the countervailing trend is definitely still with us, no matter how erratic the fluctuations in its strength. To put it another way, national governments remain the most important mediating agency between individuals at home and others abroad.[2]

It was earlier stated that 'a state is in existence when a *people* is settled in a *territory* under its own *sovereign government*'. The state is a form of political organisation of people and territory, and it is obvious that without a population there could be no state, or for that matter no government either. It will be apparent that some political scientists use the terms 'state', 'nation' and 'state population' as if they were interchangeable, but here it is considered necessary to reserve the term 'nation' to describe a group with certain unifying characteristics as described below, in which case the population of a state need not constitute a nation or the spatial distribution of a nation correspond with the boundaries of a state. The state territory consists of that area which is contained within the state boundaries and over which the state government exercises control or is considered to do so by other sovereign governments. The politico-territorial influences of the state do not terminate at the state boundaries; beyond these boundaries is its contiguous environment, which extends outwards to merge into the regional environment, which perhaps loosely corresponds to the continent within which the state is located. Boulding has developed the concept of a 'loss of strength gradient',[3] and Singer describes a similar concept in stating that 'The distance out from a nation's (state's) boundaries at which its influence matches that of the global system itself might very well mark a line of system–nation equilibrium, within which we find the individual nation's (state's) zone of dominance'.[4] While all states are active in international relations in a variety of ways and with different levels of effectiveness and involvement, and some of the more powerful are able to influence considerably events in contiguous or non-contiguous spheres of influence, the actual territory of the state is that area over which its government exerts internal sovereignty.

Sovereignty is the outstanding characteristic of the state, setting it apart from other political or arguably political organisations which involve interactions between people, areas or places, and the exercise of power, rule and authority, as may take place for example within tribal territories, schools or family groups. In the states of eighteenth and nineteenth-century Europe, sovereignty was vested in the monarch, as expressed in Louis XIV's declaration 'L'état c'est moi'. Today it is more difficult to identify exactly where sovereignty resides. Kitzinger investigated three candidates, the law, the parliament and the people, and revealed a maze of interdependencies, controls and shifting balances of forces, 'operating in different ways in different sectors, a gigantic multi-dimensional jigsaw puzzle of interlocking directorates'.[5] The government, which may exist in a wide variety of forms, claims the right to exercise internal sovereignty within the boundaries of the state and sovereignty in international relations, involving the right to conclude international agreements on behalf of the state population which are binding upon the population. The output functions of government are rule-making, rule application and rule adjudication. In state societies the use of legitimate force is the particular prerogative of the government, and at this point Weber's widely accepted definition may be introduced: 'a state is a human community that (successfully) claims the monopoly of the legitimate use of physical force within a given territory'.[6] If we adopt Almond's suggestion of prefixing 'legitimate'

with 'more or less', then the definition becomes more satisfactory in including totalitarian political systems where the degree of legitimacy may
be in doubt and revolutionary systems where the basis of legitimacy may
be in process of change, but we must exclude from a definition of a state
non-sovereign political organisations which can be classed along with the
state as political systems.[7]

A political-geographical approach to the state will involve the investigation of the spatial causes and effects of the relationship between people,
territory and sovereign government. The state can be studied in terms of its
morphological political-geographical characteristics and components, as
has been attempted in part 3, but such an approach is far from complete,
and the political geographer will also find it necessary to emphasise the
functional relationships involving people, territory and sovereign government. Such an approach was suggested by Hartshorne and has subsequently been developed by other writers, but as yet remains backward and
overdependent upon a few rather loose generalisations, while geographers
have not explained the spatial significance of a range of theoretical and
empirical studies carried out by political scientists working in the same or
similar fields.

State populations consist of a series of intertwined and overlapping subgroups which may variously be defined by reference to class, nationality,
regionalism, political alliegance and aspiration, kinship, work, and a host
of other criteria. In no state is the relationship between the state, its territory and the various elements in the population a completely harmonious
one, and a majority of empirical studies in political geography reflect the
journalistic adage that 'good news is no news': they have been concerned
with incompatibility, real or illusory, such as may exist for example when a
national distribution does not coincide to a desired degree with a state territory, when a minority group seeks to secede from a state, or when conflicting communities find difficulty in coexisting within a state.

Many of the questions posed by political-geographical analysis at the
state level concern the efficiency and acceptability of the state as a political
and spatial *milieu* for its population as a whole; subgroups in its population; populations, subgroups and governments in neighbouring states; and
the degree to which the state in its existing form is acceptable to its own
government. In the exercise of internal sovereignty, governments will normally attempt to include rather than exclude cultural subgroups and geographical subregions, and pursue policies of integration and unification,
seeking to emphasise and develop centripetal rather than centrifugal tendencies and to create new opportunities for further cultural and spatial
integration, while providing facilities for devolution and diversity only on
terms which are compatible with the governmental images and values relating to the state. One can expect to find spatial variation within each state
in the degree of popular support for and resistance to such policies. The
interplay between the state and its cultural and ethnic divisions forms the

theme for the remaining sections of this part.

5.2 Idea and raison d'être of the state: centripetal and centrifugal forces

A vital aspect of political process concerns the relationship between populations or sub-populations and their state. It has been suggested that in
order to survive and flourish, the state must continually justify itself to its
inhabitants. Preston James encapsulated this concept in the phrase 'state
idea' which describes a set of distinctive purposes to which the bulk of a
population subscribe, a complex of shared traditions, experiences and objectives.[8] The state idea will vary in potency from time to time and place to
place. A strongly developed state idea will continue to present new positive
goals to the population of the state.

At the present time, the UK in general may be said to have a moderately
strong state idea, though the continued existence of the state as an insti-
tution is questioned by certain socialist and anarchist groups, and of the
UK in its present form by an important section of the population of
Northern Ireland and by smaller minorities of the populations of Scotland
and Wales. The British state idea was probably at its strongest during the
middle years of the 1939–45 war when there was the closest association of
popular aspirations and avowed state aims, despite the partial suspension
of democratic procedures. Many post-colonial states have only found consensus in terms of negative state ideas of opposition to colonialism and
neocolonialism, and some have not developed a state idea sufficient to
override the various divergent tribe ideas.

Closely analagous to the state idea is Hartshorne's notion of the *raison
d'être* of states.[9] Originally noted by Ratzel[10] as the 'political idea' of the
state, the *raison d'être* concept was developed by Hartshorne as a part of
his 'functional approach' to political geography. At any time, the state is
seen as existing in a dynamic equilibrium between the centripetal forces
which bind it together and work for its survival, and the centrifugal forces
which threaten to tear it apart. For the state to continue to exist, the centripetal forces must exceed the centrifugal. The basic centripetal force is the
elusive *raison d'être*, which may vary in its intensity from loyalty to a popular leader or fear of outsiders, characteristic perhaps of Alfred the Great's
England, to a fully fledged nationalism working within a united and democratic state. According to Hartshorne, political-geographical investigation
should begin with the isolation of the state's *raison d'être* and proceed to
determine the areas to which it applies, which need not be coextensive with
the state. The terms '*raison d'être*' and 'state idea' are not always completely interchangeable; for example, the *raison d'être* of South Africa is
white supremacy, though the state lacks a state idea to which the bulk of its
population can subscribe.

Objective techniques of investigation are difficult to apply to problems
of state idea and *raison d'être*, and quantitative analysis cannot readily be

employed either to isolate the state idea or to measure accurately the intensity with which it is held. State ideas are dynamic, while different versions of the state idea may be held by different sections of a population. Arguably, the Irish Republic contains one of the most nationalistic populations, yet a variety of state ideas are held be different sections of the population; supporters of the Official IRA look to a united Ireland of radical social reform and scorn the existing government and the state idea associated with it. Other Irishmen value a Roman Catholic Ireland in which religion is institutionalised in the state, while others, no less nationalistic, see the strong links with Rome as a restraint on the development of a more dynamic and prosperous Ireland.

There is a fundamental flaw in the assumption that the survival of the state depends upon the existence and constant revitalisation of a state idea; the political map of the world is studded with examples of states held intact by repressive and autocratic regimes virtually devoid of popular support whose permanency is (regrettably) not in question. It is true that at any point in time the state represents a stage in a dynamic equilibrium between centripetal and centrifugal forces. While Hartshorne's functional approach offers a broad framework for functional political-geographical analysis at the state level, it does not itself provide the tools for detailed enquiry, and says nothing about the roles and attitudes of the individual in the state population.

Societal forces may, with variation in time and place, tend towards territorial integration of fragmentation. Gottman has described a dynamic equilibrium within political societies between groups of societal forces which reinforce the status quo, the *iconography* of a people, and those which favour the establishment of broader relationships, described by the French word *circulation*.[11] The latter includes all forms of movement of people, goods and ideas, and with its emphasis on diffusion and new contacts, *circulation* is a force for innovation and the development of new relationships: it threatens the established order and brings fluidity and instability to international affairs. The counter-force of iconography embraces the values of the past and is resistant to change. The 'spirit' of a nation signified, to Gottman, a psychological attitude resulting from a combination of past events and beliefs deeply rooted in the minds of its members. A national iconography is a compendium of national symbols, history and legend, literature and an established social system.

The interplay between counter-forces of iconography and *circulation* was clearly evident in Britain when the country was poised on the brink of EEC membership. Iconography was represented by xenophobia, anxieties that the 'British way of life' might become submerged in some 'Euroculture', and fear of the consequences of a partial sacrifice of sovereignty. *Circulation* found expression in arguments based on the needs for new and larger markets for British industry, the development of more productive orientations and friendships, and a decline in British insularity. Also, clear divisions in locational perspective were apparent between those decision-makers who perceived Britain as an Atlantic island with strong maritime associations, and those who visualised Britain as an extension of the continent of Europe in an era of European resurgence.

The present pattern of world partition reflects the importance of three societal forces in particular: nationalism, ideology and colonialism. In the social sciences, the individual often presents fewer problems of analysis than the aggregate. Psychologists can divide the individual's drive, into the basic, linked to a biological function, such as a hunger drive, and the social, such as the drives to achieve or assist. While life in a society may be essential for the satisfaction of basic and social drives, it is not clear how individual drives become transposed into group drives and societal forces, though nationalism, a societal force, can articulate individual social drives for identity, belonging, achievement or security. Nationalism is variable in its nature, aims and political-geographical effects, while considerable disagreement exists over the relative importance of forces which create nationalism. Since nationalism is inextricably intertwined with the nation, it is here that investigation must begin.

5.3 Nation, nationalism and nation state

Observers have been unable to agree on the definition of a nation; some have pointed to the presence of shared objective characteristics such as language or ethnic background, while others have seen the choice and consent of the individuals belonging to the nation as being crucial. In fact, nations vary, and a definition based on objective characteristics will include some nations, such as the French, and exclude others, such as the Belgian or Swiss. The geographical significance of the nation is evidenced in the following quotation from Lanyi and McWilliams.

. . . a nation implies a common culture, common symbols, a particular view of the world which is distinct from other world views. What makes a nation different from other cultural groups, however, is that one of the symbols associated with its values and attitudes is a particular piece of territory.[12]

Whereas the term 'state' refers to a particular form of organisation of people and territory, a nation is a form of human group whose members usually share a range of objective cultural characteristics, values and aspirations, and a close political association with a particular piece of territory. Members of a nation are said to have a certain closeness which will 'make them cooperate with each other more willingly than with other people, [and they] desire to be under the same government, and desire that it should be government by themselves or portion of themselves, exclusively'.[13]

Each nation is unique, with the different elements of nationhood varying in combination and importance from case to case. A belief in a common ethnic descent is frequently an important factor, but could not apply to the Swiss nation, which is also linguistically diverse. In some instances, groups can aspire to dual nationhood—most Scots tend to perceive themselves as both Scottish and British, and a similar dualism applies to many American Jews. Sometimes the determination of nationhood is difficult; for instance, does one speak of a Canadian nation or a French-Canadian nation and an Anglo-Canadian nation, and does Ireland encompass a single nation or are there separate Protestant and Catholic nations? In some cases, such as the German, nationhood is defined in cultural rather than territorial terms, while Irish Republican nationalism gives the highest priority to the territorial idea of recovery of the six Ulster counties. In Britain as a whole, religion is of low priority as an element of nationhood, while in Poland it is fundamental. The Dutch nation has been cemented by a long tradition of unity against external threats, a tradition which is lacking in the cases of many African nations. An attempt to illustrate the varied bases of nationhood from nation to nation is given in table 5.1.

While most nations can claim a range of shared objective characteristics, for a nation to exist most of its members must share a sense of belonging and display a measure of nationalism. It is perhaps best then to view the nation in functional terms. Members of a nation will reveal a degree of common purpose over a range of issues and a period of time, and they are conscious of themselves as forming a particular political community.

Nations are larger than tribal groups and are frequently composed of different but intertwined ethnic strands. The processes by which a series of frequently heterogeneous groups become cemented into a nation are variable, and writers disagree over which process should be emphasised. Pounds, while recognising the significance of shared objective characteristics, stresses the importance of a shared tradition of national solidarity in the face of historical sequences of opportunity and threat.

The most articulate nations today have in some measure been molded by pressures. The pressures may not always be an attempt by an outside power to thwart or destroy the nation. It may merely be an experience through which its members have passed . . . but many have passed through an intense emotional experience which has matured them quickly.[14]

Such an interpretation would seem relevant in a number of cases; peaks of English national sentiment seem to have been associated with struggle against an out-group threat, as at the times of the Spanish Armada, the Napoleonic wars and the wars of 1914–18 and 1939–45, and with periods of national expansion such as the industrial revolution and the nineteenth-century colonial phase.

Deutsch prefers to give the central role to the development of the ability to communicate effectively within a group: communicative efficiency.[15] Members of a nation are able to communicate more effectively, and over a wider range of topics, with each other rather than with outsiders. Effective

Table 5.1.   Variability in the elements of nationhood

element of nationhood / nation	language	religion or ideology	belief in common ethnic ancestry	distinctive national culture	recent unity in face of out-group threat	long-standing common tradition
Belgian	×	○	×	○(?)	√	○
Canadian	×	×	×	×	√	×
Chinese	√ (?)	√	√	√	√	√
English	√	○	○(?)	√	√	√
French	√	○	○(?)	√	√	√
Icelandic	√	○	√	√	√	√
Polish	√	√	√	√	√	√
Swiss	×	×	×	√	○	√
all Russian	×	×	×	×	√ (?)	×
Great Russian	√	×	√	√	√	√

√   important unifying factor
○   low or indeterminate importance
×   divisive or potentially divisive factor

communication does not merely imply the sharing of symbols, such as language, style of writing and literature, but also cultural similarities; thus the linguistically diverse Swiss, through their common social customs and traditions, are able to communicate more effectively with each other than the German-speaking Swiss can with Germans.

The growth of nations involves both an intensification of the effectiveness of intra-group communication and an expansion of the area in which this communication takes place. The former process is assisted by the adoption of a common language or dialect and the acceptance of a range of social customs, group symbols and memories. The expansion of the area occurs with improvements in the potential for *circulation*, notably through growth in commerce, urbanisation and communications. Groups which have the capacity to develop effective habits of communication are set apart from each other by communicative barriers which may be of a cultural, political or geographical nature (see figure 5.1).

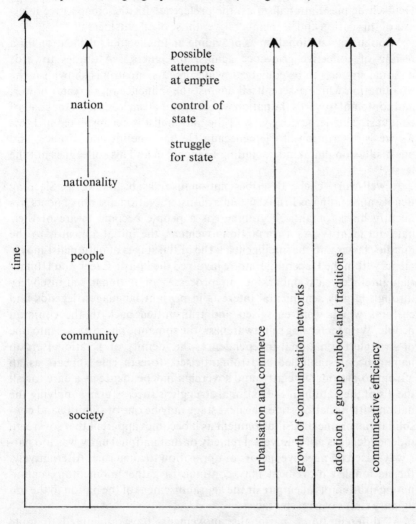

Figure 5.1. Growth of nations, after Deutsch

Deutsch uses the term 'nationality' to describe a group with complementary and effective habits of social communication. In an age of nationalism, such a group may be expected to press for control of its own sovereign nation state, and Deutsch reserves the term 'nation' to describe the nationality in control of its nation state.

Nationalism can be said to be the political expression of nationhood, and the nation state to be the political-geographical expression of nationalism. If the political geographer is interested in process, it is not sufficient for him to study the nation state in morphological terms; he must also be aware of the process of nationalism which brought it into being. Deutsch defines nationalism as 'the preference for the competitive interests of this nation and its members over those of all outsiders'.[16]

Minogue saw nationalism as providing an intellectual justification for a feeling of collective grievance against foreigners.[17] Attitudes towards nationalism tend to be equivocal; widespread sympathy is shown for the small nation which asserts itself against the influence of a greater power, and contempt towards the nation whose nationalism leads it on the road of conquest. The derogatory view of the nationalist is encapsulated in J. M. Keynes's description of Clemenceau: 'He had one illusion, France; and one disillusion, mankind, including Frenchmen and his colleagues not the least'.[18]

A well-worn cliché describes nationalism as beginning as Sleeping Beauty and ending as Frankenstein's monster. Nationalist movements frequently have romantic beginnings as a people become aware of their national identity. As a romantic movement, the initial appeal is to the middle classes and the intelligentsia; the initial stages of nationalist movements within the Hapsburg Empire involved the Polish, Czech and Hungarian intelligentsias embarking on processes of national self-discovery through largely sentimental interests in peasant languages, legends and customs which were eulogised and transmitted back to the common people. With increasing self-awareness, the romantic phase passes into one of struggle for national independence; the identity of a national group having been established and romanticised, foreign rule appears as an affront to national integrity, and sovereign independence as a cure for all the ills of the nation. If the national struggle is successful in supplying the nation with its nation state, the next stage may be one of stability and consolidation, or one of disillusionment as it becomes apparent that sovereign independence is not a universal remedy or that national unity was too narrowly based on negative factors of opposition to alien rule. Alternatively, the nationalist movement may continue to gather momentum, culminating in attempts at empire or the aggrandisement of the nation to the imaginary status of a master race.

At different times, nationalist movements have attempted to unite various types of group around a range of objectives. Minogue[19] has suggested a sixfold classification of forms of nationalism, but it is felt that the following is in some ways more realistic.

1. *Ante-state nationalism*: the nationalism of a nation which develops a strong national consciousness before becoming endowed with its nation state, which is normally only acquired after a period of nationalist struggle. Examples include the nationalism of the Poles and Jews, who now

have nation states, or the Kurds and Macedonians, who do not.

2. *Post-state nationalism*: the nationalism of a nation which has developed, often from the integration of diverse cultural strands, cocooned within an existing state which readily provides the maturing nation with its custom-built nation state. Obvious examples include the English and French cases.

3. *Third world nationalism*: the nationalism of peoples who have come together under a programme of resistance to colonialism, and who need not constitute nations in the traditionally accepted sense of the word. Culturally diverse peoples may or may not generate an ongoing nationalism after the expulsion of the colonial power and so create a nation where none existed previously. In this respect, the Cubans have apparently been successful and the Nigerians so far unsuccessful.

4. *Pan-nationalism*: on certain occasions, groups larger and less integrated than nations have united around a limited range of objectives. Examples include the apparently declining Pan-African movement, which acquired a formal structure in 1963 when the leaders of thirty African states established the Organisation of African Unity, intended to further African political unity and solidarity and economic integration; and the Arab League, formed in 1945 in an attempt to recreate a sense of community among Arab peoples who had been separated by centuries of imperial rule. The Pan-Slavic movement of the late nineteenth and early twentieth centuries was a forceful attempt to articulate the identity and aspirations of Slavs divided among the empires of East and East Central Europe, though it became discredited in the eyes of many Slavs as a vehicle for Tsarist imperialism and intrigue.

5. *Community conflict nationalism*: when civil tension or strife divides communities each of which has a measure of cultural coherence, problems which might more properly be analysed in social or economic contexts are often popularly interpreted as nationalist struggles. In this category might be placed the nationalism of the Black Muslims, Ulster Catholics and Ulster Protestants.

6. *Totalitarian nationalism*: exceptionally in the history of a nation, a party may come to power claiming to embody the will of that nation, and will launch its members on a programme of myth-building, xenophobia and, ultimately, racism. In such a situation—the example is too obvious to need stating—individual rights and public morality are sacrificed at the altar of national interest, as interpreted by the party or dictator.

The categories suggested are not intended to be rigid or exclusive, and a particular nationalism may overlap categories; for example, French-Canadian nationalism includes elements of ante-state and community conflict nationalism in addition to its own unique characteristics.

The political map of the developing world was largely fashioned by colonialism before nationalist movements secured the independence of the colonial units; in Europe, on the other hand, nineteenth and twentieth-century nationalism has largely recast the political map. Frankel writes

Ever since the French Revolution nationalism has been the main spiritual and emotional force cementing all the elements of statehood in nation-states. . . . Wherever the nation-state was a reality, nationalism buttressed and reinforced the state; where it remained an aspiration, nationalism endangered the existing multinational units.[20]

At the core of nationalist thinking is the national territory or nation state; in an age of nationalism, the nation in charge of its state may attempt to include within the state any communities of conationals living across its boundaries. For the stateless nation, acquisition of a state is the prime objective; almost invariably this involves the attempt to create a sovereign unit out of the territory occupied by the nation, though the case of Israel is a rare exception in which the Jewish nation laid claim to a territory which contained only a minute proportion of the nation. According to Pounds

A state is likely to show the greatest stability and permanence when it corresponds closely with a nation. In such instances the state is the political expression of the nation, the mechanism through which the welfare of the nation is safeguarded and its identity preserved.[21]

5.4 National independence, landscape change and political problems

The new condition of national sovereignty produces immediate and far-reaching expression in landscape change. Frequently the more superficial manifestations of this process are the most obvious to the casual observer. Place names associated with the former colonial condition are likely to be changed; thus Leopoldville, the capital of the Belgian Congo, was renamed Kinshasa, while in the Irish Republic the process of renaming villages which in many cases had been named after a British landlord is still continuing (to the considerable confusion of the populace), and the British-style post boxes remain but with green paint over the original red. If religion is an important basis of nationhood, it may be institutionalised with a privileged position in the new constitution, as in the case of Irish Republican Catholicism, and Islam in Pakistan. If all the major public buildings and monuments date from a colonial past, the government may consider it a matter of national pride to erect new specifically national symbols, with a high priority being given to statues of patriots, national sports stadia and national museums. If the new nation state is linguistically diverse, the language of the colonists may be retained as a *lingua franca*, as in the case of India; the Irish Republic presents an exceptional case of a partially moribund language (Gaelic) being resurrected and imposed as the official language. By projects such as these, the newly independent nation adds to its national iconography new sets of national symbols, most prominent among which are the national flag and the national anthem.

Less obvious to the casual onlooker, but in reality much more traumatic, is the fact that the new nation state will find itself existing in a radically different economic *milieu*, and the industries and contacts which flourished under the conditions of the old *milieu* may be ill-adapted to the new circumstance. Before the tidal wave of boundary changes at the end of the 1914–18 war, parts of Poland and the emergent states of Latvia, Estonia and Lithuania had formed part of a Tsarist economic unit stretching from Warsaw to the Pacific, while the single customs union of the Hapsburg empire became divided among seven different national economies. The imperial *milieu* had favoured regional specialisation—Bohemia provided the empire with textiles and glass, and Hungary specialised in agricultural production. Much of Slovakian and Croatian development took place in relation to Hungarian markets, and Slovenian development took place in relation to Austrian outlets. These orientations changed with the creation of Czechoslovak, Yugoslav and Hungarian states, though readjustment was often difficult; thus, for a time, the Voivodina in north-east Yugoslavia was continuing to export wheat to Hungary at the same time as the southern parts of Yugoslavia were importing wheat from abroad. With the coming of independence, the *laissez-faire* patterns of regional specialisation became replaced, in an environment of instability and inter-state tension, by emphasis on national self-sufficiency, with the states protecting their developing strategic industries.

A new nation state having come into being, external relations become the preserve of the national government, which must foster an inner orientation of people and territory to replace regional ties with areas outside the state. Fundamental to this process is the creation of a national system of communications, and the inherited system is unlikely to be suited to the cause of national integration. When Yugoslavia was created in 1918 to accommodate the south-Slav Serbian, Croat and Slovenian nations, it inherited bits and pieces of the Hapsburg imperial railway network which had been constructed to serve the needs of empire and was strongly focused on Vienna and Budapest. Further, the application of the Hapsburg policy of 'divide and rule' had minimised the possibilities for intercommunication between the south Slavs; Bosnia had no link with Serbia or Croatia, and other regions either lacked lines or were separated by unbridged rivers. A national programme of railway construction was therefore necessary to connect the regions of the state with one another and with the capital at Belgrade.[22]

The capital itself may be the leading administrative and commercial centre of the preceding colonial period. Frequently the colonial power selected a 'head link' capital, nodal in respect of communications with the mother country but ill-suited to purposes of national consolidation. Such centres have sometimes been replaced by capitals with a more central location within the state or with strong associations with the national iconography.

When Bangladesh became independent of Pakistan in 1971, it became the eighth largest state in the world, and enormous problems of post-war recovery and realignment were faced; an estimated three million of the civilian population had been killed, two million had been rendered homeless, and ten million returning refugees had to be reaccommodated. As a part of Pakistan, 45 per cent of Bangladesh's imports had come from West Pakistan, while Bangladesh had produced 55 per cent of Pakistan's exports, though only receiving 30 per cent of development investment.[23] The economic prospects of Bangladesh, then, were brighter than those of many other newly independent states, and considerable exploitation of the country's economy had been practised by the Islamabad regime. Further, the crucial role played by India in securing Bangladesh independence, and the establishment of Bangladesh as a non-secular state, offer the possibility of recreating some of the natural economic unity of the Ganges basin, Bangladesh will be able to take advantage of Indian coal, while Calcutta may be able to recover some of its lost hinterland. The reorganisation of the Bangladesh economy began with the nationalisation of jute and other leading industries, insurance companies and export trade, along with a programme of agrarian reform, though in 1974 severe problems of economic readjustment and rising prices were still being faced.

Johnson studied patterns of economic change in newly independent countries, and found that 'many features of the policies, concepts and methods of economic development planning in such countries either do not make economic sense, or else would make economic sense only in certain specific and rather exceptional economic circumstances the actual presence of which no one has felt it necessary to establish by empirical economic research'.[24] The direction of economic development in the cases considered was typically towards industrialisation at all costs and irrespective of local circumstances, with a bias towards strategic or status-symbolic industries; '. . . a steel industry is generally regarded as the *sine qua non* of economic development, even though steel requires a massive investment of capital and the world steel industry has tended to suffer from chronic over-capacity rather than excessive pressure of demand'.[25] Another characteristic tendency noted was the creation of prestigious employment for the national educated middle class, partly through the nationalisation of certain industries.

As well as serving an economic function, national development, involving the expansion of communications and educational infrastructures, dam construction and industrial and agricultural diversification and expansion, is frequently politically motivated. Its success demonstrates the economic viability of the new state, and the creation of a system of national economic interdependence makes secession a less palatable alternative.

The desperate hurry of African leaders for economic development is due not only to the desire for a higher standard of living and the need to fulfill their promises on this front, but also to the sheer political need to hold a unit together. Economic development does this both by showing that the nation works, and by enlarging the penalties of disintegration of the state. The changes in the economy thus affect the psychological attitudes of the population toward the state.[26]

Those in positions of political authority in newly independent states in the developing world have frequently faced the problem of transforming the opposition to rulers which was fermented during the struggle for independence into positive attitudes towards the authority of the state. Utopian attitudes towards independence will have been disappointed, while often the only real basis for national unity, opposition to colonialism, is partly removed with the retreat of the colonial power. In such circumstances, loyalties may turn to more firmly rooted traditional structures of tribalism. 'The problem of integration is essentially one of getting people to shift loyalty from a structure based on tradition to a new artificial entity, the nation-state, whose only justification for authority lies in its constitution.'[27] Political elites, in attempting to create domestic nationalism, may launch campaigns of national revitalisation involving efforts to purge the state of alien symbols and practices, often with the invocation of a mythical golden age of cultural purity. However, the elites themselves are generally greatly removed from the populations which they claim to represent, being modern in culture, intensely nationalistic, and educated to a high level and in the language of the metropolitan country.

The separation of the uneducated 'masses' immersed in their traditional culture and the 'intellectuals' who have a modern education is representative of some disjunctions observable in the social structure of practically all the new states. Almost everywhere, the societies consist of relatively discrete collectives—ethnic, communal, religious, or linguistic—that have little sense of identity with one another or with the national whole.[28]

Though national revitalisation favours the replacement of the European official language with an indigenous one, the cause of nation-building requires a *lingua franca* which is not associated with a single subgroup in the state population. Wallerstein points out that potentially every African state has its Katanga, and in almost all of them the political opposition takes the form of a claim to regionalism and decentralisation. At the same time there is a tendency among elites to confuse opposition to state policies and secession, and this leads to the suppression of opposition parties and the formation of one-party states.[29]

5.5 National character

The most elusive thread in the complex fabric of nationhood is that of national character. Though geographers have tended to disregard the subject, variations in national character can produce concrete geographical manifestations, and may form a significant factor in political-geographical process; '. . . the main alternative to the idea that power accounts for inter-national behaviour seems to have been that the traits of nations are expressed in international actions'.[30] In the 1930s political scientists tended to reject national character as being based on subjective stereotypes of nations; a decade later it was rehabilitated on the basis that different dis-tributions of cultural traits are found from nation to nation, and the con-cept of modal personality was developed. The subsequent history of the concept has been chequered; elusive as it may be, modal personality exists, though correct interpretation and evaluation are extremely difficult.

Firstly, it should be remembered that two different forms of behaviour resulting from national character may be of interest to political geo-graphers: on the one hand, behaviour which reflects national idiosyncra-sies, and on the other, reactions to the perceived national character of others. Secondly, national character in its actual and perceived states is changeable over time; 'In the seventeenth century the English were regarded to be the most turbulent nation in Europe and in the eighteenth the Germans the most romantic and peaceful, but quite justifiably neither reputation holds today'.[31] Nowhere have people's reactions to one another been so coloured by national stereotypes as in East and East Central Europe; thus, at the time of the Hungarian Revolution, when the Poles showed an unprecedented but level-headed sympathy for the Hungarians while the Czech puppet regime supported the Russian invasion, the cliché circulated in Warsaw and Budapest that 'the Hungarians behaved like Poles, the Poles like Czechs and the Czechs like the swine they are'.[32] Thirdly, it is usually difficult to establish in any analysis the degree to which national character, as apart from other influences, has affected specific decisions.

Despite the prevalence of subjective stereotyping, one need not be sur-prised that national character exists; each individual is to a considerable extent moulded by the process of socialisation that he or she has under-gone, and the values, attitudes and patterns of behaviour implanted during socialisation vary from nation to nation as well as from time to time, place to place and class to class. Mehnet has studied the relationship between a communist system and societies in Russia and China.[33] He interpreted Chinese culture and history as producing a nation which would take a pragmatic and materialistic approach to communism, while the Russian experience could be expected to produce a more emotional and messianic approach. The logical and analytical thought process of Marxism had more points of contact with the Russian system of reasoning, but the Chin-ese were prepared to accept a communist outlook and drastic change after the convulsion of their society through its traumatic contacts with the West.

Further studies involving national character should be made at a variety of levels; one might attempt to discern how policy-making may be affected by national characteristics of the decision-makers, or by the perception that decision-makers hold of other nations. In the geographical sphere, it would be interesting to know how foreign investors are influenced by national stereotypes; for example, to what extent has the German reputation for industriousness and efficiency attracted investment for development in West Germany rather than elsewhere? Unfortunately, it is frequently impossible to extricate the national character variable from all the other variables involved in such studies.

At a less ambitions level, it can be demonstrated that national customs and preferences influence national patterns of industrialisation.

It is by no means objective criteria alone that decide what a location is suitable for, since different peoples will develop it differently. . . . The diversity of production of a people is determined by how far they can resist a general levelling. The more they can do so, the less will they specialise one-sidedly in goods for a larger market.[34]

5.6 The multinational state

Not all states are nation states, and no nation state either expresses exactly the spatial distribution of the nation or includes no ethnic minorities. The degree of ethnic differentiation within any state can be calculated and compared with that in any other using an index of ethnic differentiation[35]

$$S = 100 \sum_{i=1}^{k} n_i^2/N^2$$

where n is the size of ethnic group i, N is the total population of the country and k is the number of ethnic groups. The lower the resultant index, the higher is the degree of ethnic differentiation; the state which is completely ethnically homogeneous has an index of 100. In 1930 Czechoslovakia had an index of 33, and in 1961 one of 51, reflecting the expulsion of large numbers of Germans and Hungarians after the Second World War.[36]

While the index records the degree of ethnic differentiation, it does not express the degrees of compatibility or tension existing between the various ethnic groups. The relationship between the national minority and the state can vary from almost complete harmony to widespread antipathy, and a selection of possible relationships is shown in table 5.2.

For the multinational state to achieve and maintain stability, justice to the minority groups must be done and constantly be seen to be done. A series of spatial factors are likely to influence and characterise the state–minority relationship. Firstly, if the minority is dispersed fairly evenly throughout the state (disregarding for the moment segregation within actual settlements), as with the negroes in the USA, then the likelihood of secession is much less than if the minority occupies a particular national territory, as do the Basques in Spain. Secondly, the minority may have a historical homeland which has been absorbed by the larger state, or they may have migrated into the state after its inception, like the Pakistani com-

Table 5.2. Variability in minority/majority relationships

minority \ indicator	language	employment	intermarriage	distribution	segregation in cities	external relations
French-Canadian	×	○	√	×	○	√
Negro in Cuba	√	√	√	√	√	√
Negro in S. Africa*	×	×	×	‡	×	×
Negro in USA	√	×	○	√	○	√
N. Ireland Catholic	√	×	○	√	○	×
Pakistani in Britain	‡	○	○	√	○	√
Scot	√	√	√	×	√	√
Slovak	○	√	√	×	√	√
Soviet Kazak	×	○	○	×	○	○

language: √ same as majority ○ similar to majority × different from majority
employment: √ no discrimination ○ discrimination claimed × discrimination practised
intermarriage with majority: √ not uncommon ○ exceptional × prohibited
distribution: √ interspersed within state × concentrated in national territory
segregation in cities: √ not apparent ○ not formalised but apparent × institutionalised
external relations: √ conationals not significant in neighbouring state ○ a minority in neighbouring state × majority in neighbouring state
* not numerically a minority
‡ complex situation

munities in the United Kingdom or the forced migration of negroes into the USA. Thirdly, if the minority is associated with a particular national territory, that territory may either be surrounded by the state or, as tends to be the case, occupy a peripheral position within the state. The situation gains an added potential for instability when the minority exists as the majority national element in the neighbouring state, and to a lesser degree if the minority also forms an ethnic minority in the neighbouring state.

An example of the former situation involved the Sudeten Germans, whose imagined grievances against the Czechoslovakian government were inflamed by Nazi propoganda to provide Hitler with a pretext for the invasion of Czechoslovakia and annexation of the Sudetenland in 1938; where the national minority forms a minority in more states than one, their nationalism may be directed simultaneously or sporadically against all other parties, as has been the case with the Macedonians, divided between Yugoslavia, Greece and Bulgaria. Alternatively, members of the minority may attempt to unite with their conationals in one of the larger states. Many of the Kazaks of China would appear to favour inclusion within the Russian Kazak Republic. Minority unrest may become a tool of great-power politics, as when Tsarist diplomats intrigued with Poles within the Hapsburg empire.

The non-spatial characteristics of the minority will also affect its relationship with the majority and the state. The minority language may be similar to that of the majority, as with the American negro, whose native languages have been lost, or the Slovaks, who speak a similar language to the Czech majority; or it may be completely different, as with the Uzbeks of the Soviet Union. Where the language is different, the minority may be encouraged to retain its language, but usually a command of the majority tongue is essential for career advancement. Preferential treatment is given to Welsh speakers in certain fields of public employment in Wales, while in the Soviet Union the minority languages are protected in the constitution but have been subject to a Russification of alphabets and a purging of foreign loan words and their replacement by Russian equivalents; the French and Spanish governments have tended to treat their respective Breton and Basque minority languages with mixtures of suspicion and indifference.

The relationship between each ethnic minority and the state is unique, and it would be impossible to develop a set of laws applicable to all relationships. Of considerable value would be an index of irridentism* for use in analytical or comparative surveys, but it is not possible to calculate, for example, an index of linguistic freedom against a measure of ethnic segregation or political oppression. In a few extreme cases the dominant national group constitutes a minority of the state population, as in South Africa, where 3.5 million whites dominate 16 million non-whites. The minority may be numerous in population, as in Northern Ireland, or only a minute element in the population. Again as in Northern Ireland, there may be just one minority group, or a large and lesser minorities as in Canada, where there is a large French-Canadian minority and lesser Eskimo and Red Indian minorities, while the Soviet Union recognises 108 nationalities within its territory. Techniques devised to study the relationship of the 1100 Russian Eskimoes to the Russian state could not be

* Irridentism: the term derives from the *Terra Irridenta*, the Italian-speaking areas of northern Italy claimed by Italian governments after unification.

applied to the Catholic position in Northern Ireland or to the relationship between the 13 million negroes and the dominant whites in South Africa.

The concept of 'relative deprivation' as developed by Runciman may be usefully applied in the analysis of some of the sociopolitical problems of the multinational state; relative deprivation involves discrepancy between a group's perceptions of what should be expected and what is likely to be received, and results in feelings of frustration which may be rationalised by ethnic minorities in the form of nationalism.[37] Bertsch applied the concept to conditions in Yugoslavia, where he considered that the impressive material gains of communist government during the 1950s and early 1960s had encouraged large elements in the population to desert traditional attachments and accept the ideologies of the widely popular Tito regime.[38] However, as difficulties were encountered in the fields of economic development, decentralisation and nationality, the individual became susceptible to nationalist forces which impelled him back to the old ethnic and religious heritages. Frustration was high among Croats who had high expectations about what Croats deserved and what they could achieve but low evaluations of Croat capabilities within the Yugoslav federation. In figure 5.2 the 'collective value position' forms a vertical scale and represents those economic, political and status conditions which both elites and masses within the broader society deem important and strive to realise. Relative deprivation represents the difference between 'value expectations', average economic, political and status values to which the minority believes it is entitled, and 'value capabilities', a composite picture of what the minority perceives to be possible of attainment within the federation. The separatist sentiments of the Croats were paralleled by unitarist interests among the Serb majority, with Serb relative deprivation increasing through the 1960s as a reaction against the decentralisation of power which marked a retreat from the ideal held by many Serbs of Yugoslavia as 'Greater Serbia'. Difficulties and obstacles encountered in the attainment of Serb economic and political objectives were atributed to the subversive activities of other groups.

The attitudes and aspirations of the ethnic minorities vary considerably; the Cuban negro apparently has no separate national aspirations, while according to a 1968 opinion poll 65 per cent of Scots would prefer a greater measure of national autonomy within a British framework, and the Muslims of Eritrea, annexed by Ethiopia in 1962, will be satisfied with nothing less than total separation. The minority attitude is also changeable; in the post-war period, the establishment of reactionary regimes in Albania and Hungary led to a diminution of demands for *enosis** by Albanian and Hungarian minorities in Yugoslavia. The granting of a large measure of federal autonomy to Slovakia and the Russian invasion of Czechoslovakia

* *Enosis*: a Greek term for 'union' which came into more general use after the intensification of Greek Cypriot campaigns for union with Greece in the 1950s and 1960s.

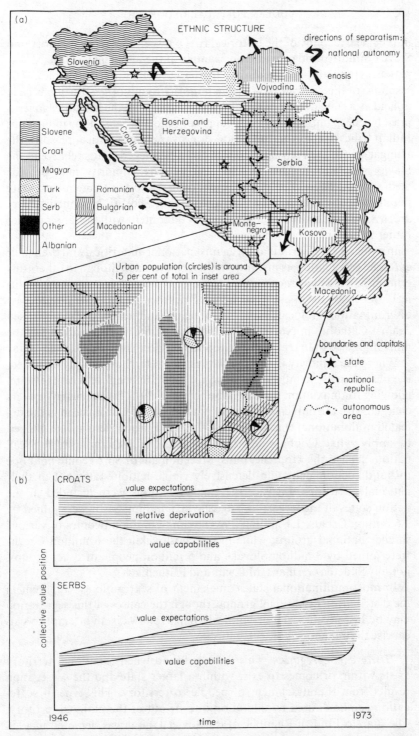

Figure 5.2. Ethnic diversity and relative deprivation in Yugoslavia. (a) Ethnic structure, federal boundaries and separatism in Yugoslavia. The inset shows a simplification of the extreme ethnic diversity of the Kosovo autonomous area. (Inset based on part 6, ref. 23.) (b) The concept of relative deprivation as applied to the Croats and the Serbs (from ref. 38).

in 1968 healed many of the historical rifts between the Czech majority and Slovak minority and provided an example of the importance of shared experiences and out-group threats in the consolidation of peoples. The response of the state may vary from minority to minority; Brazil has been upheld as a state devoid of racial discrimination, yet the Brazilian government has been implicated in campaigns of genocide against the indigenous Indian tribes of the Amazon basin. For a variety of political reasons, the Hungarians of the Hapsburg empire had a privileged status relative to the Slavic populations. Membership of a national minority may provide media for the expression of discontent denied to other elements of a state population; it can be argued that votes for the Scottish Nationalist Party are to a considerable extent influenced by discontent with the larger parties rather than by national sentiment.[39]

In some cases, discrimination against national minorities, and even their enforced segregation, is institutionalised by the state, though in others discrimination may be practised through informal social, economic and political processes, as in the treatment of negroes in the USA or the past discrimination in local authority housing and employment practised against Catholics in Northern Ireland. Again, the discrimination may be more imagined than real, as with the Sudeten Germans in Czechoslovakia.

Where the minority is small and its national territory poorly endowed, the best that its members can hope for is a compromise with the state, allowing for maximum national autonomy. In 1918 the boundary-makers charged with the implementation of national self-determination in the defeated multinational empires of East Central Europe were in fact obliged to apply what Cobban described as 'national determinism'.[40] Small nations such as the Montenegrians, Macedonians or Sorbs could not hope to build economically and defensively viable nation states out of their national territories. Instead, the smaller nations were included in the nation states of the larger. In Yugoslavia, 6 million Serbs were joined by 2.6 million Croats, 1.1 million Slovenes and 2 million peoples of various smaller national groups, while in Czechoslovakia the 6 million Czechs were joined by 3 million Slovaks and 5 million people of other groups, notably Sudeten Germans, Magyars and Ruthenians.

In most multinational states an element of segregation is apparent in the distribution of national groups, though the causes of this segregation may be historical, social or political. What follows is an attempt to categorise the main forms of segregation.

1. *Historical segregation.* This form is found when a national territory exists within or comes to exist within a larger state and the segregation results from the attachment of people to territory. This type of segregation can be diluted by migration into or out of the national territory. The Karelo-Finnish Republic of the Soviet Union was demoted in 1956 to the status of an autonomous republic after Russian immigration had

produced a population which was 70 per cent Russian. A historical form of segregation is apparent in Canada, where defeat of French colonial forces by the British at Quebec in 1759 and Montreal in 1760 placed the British in control of Canada, including the French farming community which had grown up along the St Lawrence river. The cultural integrity of the French settlement area was protected by the Quebec Act of 1774, an early act of religious tolerance which gave the inhabitants of Quebec the right to use the French language, remain Roman Catholic and retain French civil law. A complex of social and political factors then preserved the pattern of cultural segregation; the bureaucratic and aristocratic elites of the French community departed after British domination, and leadership of the French communities passed entirely to the only remaining elite, the clergy. Being opposed to the egalitarianism apparent in the French and American revolutions, the senior French clergy allied themselves with the British, being at the same time anxious to preserve Catholicism; they achieved preservation through a policy of isolation involving the safeguarding of the French language and institutions, facilitated by their control of education in Quebec.

French-Canadian society is traditionally agricultural and conservative, and education has been of a classical type favouring the production of clerics, doctors and lawyers. When land pressure forced the French population into urban occupations, the entrepreneurial skills and command of English necessary for advancement in white-collar occupations were frequently lacking. American firms operating in Quebec have tended to prefer English managers, for ease of communication, and a poorly unionised French work force, which is a product of clerical opposition to all manifestations of socialism. Within Montreal, the world's second largest French-speaking city, there is a correlation between low income and lack of bilingual abilities. 'The French element in the city is most likely to improve its position if it masters the other official language, as the English-speaking cosmopolitan element is certainly that which is gaining access to the higher income levels.'[41] The province of Quebec, however, still has a population of which 80 per cent has French as a first language, a remarkable testimony to the exclusiveness of a national iconography, especially in a state so economically dynamic as Canada.

2. *Community conflict segregation*. This form of segregation is the product of mutual fears and antipathies between groups, and is evident in both urban segregation, as is intensifying in Northern Ireland, and regional segregation. In 1960 Britain gave independence to Cyprus's 500 000 Greek Cypriots and 100 000 Turkish Cypriots, under a constitution which guaranteed Turkish minority rights and allowed for the establishment in the island of equal numbers of Turkish and Greek armed forces. After three years of independence, the Turkish community became suspicious that President Makarios was working for *enosis* with

Greece, and outbreaks of violence resulted in the despatch of a United
Nations peace-keeping mission. The situation deteriorated, and in 1967
the Greeks and Turks agreed to withdraw their forces. The island became
divided by 'green lines' separating the Greek and Turkish communities
and patrolled by United Nations forces; Greeks were debarred from the
Turkish areas, but Turks in civilian clothes were allowed to enter the
Greek areas.[42]*

3. *Socio-economic segregation*. Characteristic of this form of segregation is
the ghetto situation which results from minority migration into towns to
form a poorly paid and underprivileged element in the urban population.
Push and pull factors induce segregation as immigrants are drawn towards
their ethnic kinfolk and pressurised out of other residential zones. Racial-
ism frequently operates as a push factor and is directed against skin colour
rather than specific nationality. A different form is sometimes encountered
in areas which have been affected by political colonisation; when the
Russians colonised Soviet Central Asia in the nineteenth century, they
tended to construct modern planned Russian towns adjacent to the ancient
walled settlements of the indigenous population (though subsequent lack
of population mixing derived largely from the resistance of the native Moslems).

While the study of social segregation according to class or caste pertains
more to the field of social than that of political geography, in certain cases
the segregation of classes within a single ethnic group has been so extreme
as to cause each class to exist almost as a separate nation, though extremes
in social segregation were more characteristic of the period predating
nationalistic movements. The Slavonic population of mid-nineteenth-
century European Russia was rigidly stratified. A rural serf class comprised about 83 per cent of the population, with serfs existing as the chattels
of landlords, almost totally devoid of rights; freedom from bondage could
be obtained by a successful defection to urban employment, and artisans
and industrial workers formed 9 per cent of the population. The nobility,
comprising hardly more than 1 per cent of the population, virtually monopolised the ownership of property and the operation of power, while about
6 per cent of the population was engaged in military occupations. Since
there were virtually no opportunities for upward social mobility, the Slavonic middle class was minute, with much entrepreneurship being practised by aliens who were less bridled by the rigidities of the class system.

In a number of colonial situations the social class division of society corresponded to national divisions. In many African and some Asian colonies, the Europeans formed an upper stratum of top administrators, estate
and farm owners, and the indigenous population the lower labouring stra-

* The recent Turkish invasion of northern Cyprus and resultant refugee movements now make a north and south division of the island, possibly on federal lines,
seem likely.

tum. A vacuum existed in the field of lower-middle-class employment, which was considered beneath the Europeans and was not available to indigenous peoples without advances in education and detribalisation. This vacuum was often filled by an immigrant population, a role frequently taken by Levantines, the Cantonese and Goanese. The Indian merchant class in East Africa are an excellent example, subject now in Kenya and Uganda to expropriation as the African populations develop the capability to assume middle-class occupations.

4. *Institutionalised segregation*. In this form, segregation is an instrument of state policy; the segregation may result from a paternalistic attitude adopted by the government towards a minority, exemplified by the reservation policies practised by US governments towards the Red Indians, or it may be the result of an *apartheid* policy, as is operational in South Africa and developing in Rhodesia. *Apartheid* was given a legal embodiment in South Africa in 1948; non-white peoples are required to live in segregated areas, and mixed marriages are prohibited by law. Further, the non-whites are denied parliamentary representation and the right to form trade unions, while their political parties are outlawed. Currently the *apartheid* policy is moving in the direction of the creation of 'independent' Bantustans for the Bantu peoples as part of a programme of legislation introduced in 1959, and one Bantustan, Transkei, has been operational since 1963.

The Bantustan policy symbolises the South African government's rejection of the notion of a multiracial state and involves the creation of seven or eight highly fragmented Bantu states in the republic and eleven in South-West Africa (Namibia). These states are to be nominally self-governing but in economic union with the republic. The plan is loaded heavily in favour of the whites; no 'states' will be created for the Cape Coloured or Indian minorities, while the Bantu, who form 70 per cent of the population, are being offered 13 per cent of the South African land surface. The Bantustans are best interpreted in a political rather than an economic context, and the authorities hope that they will create an illusion of Bantu independence, reduce the dangerously high level of Bantu in the four major South African cities, and lead to increased industrial dispersion. 'Surely this was not a concession, but an attempt to divide and rule, an inexpensive means of dumping "surplus" blacks (i.e. those whose labour was not required) in backward reserves, thereby creating vast reservoirs of cheap labour for the whites.'[43] It is anticipated that new industries will be established in white towns bordering the Bantustans and that the Bantu, leaving their families behind, will live in segregated satellites where they will be deprived of political rights. The border industry scheme gives the appearance of an attempt to develop the native homelands while providing cheap labour for white industries which are being offered incentives to disperse to the border towns.[44] If some index of the degree of exploitation of the blacks in South Africa is required, in 1969 the whites were earning, on average, twenty times the wage of the blacks.

5. *Expulsion and extermination.* In certain isolated cases, governments have prefered to exterminate or expel rather than accomodate a minority. Cases of extermination are rare, the most notable case being the atrocities committed against European Jews during the 1939–45 war. The Jews of medieval Europe were also intermittently subjected to expulsion; the most recent instance of a policy of expulsion being applied to an ethnic minority involved the Asian population in Uganda, whose role as a dynamic and prosperous element in the community was comparable to that of the Jews of western Europe in the medieval period. There are also rare instances of national minorities being expelled from one part of a state and relocated in another. Between 1941 and 1942 a total of 1.5 million people belonging to the Volga German, Crimean Tartar and five North Caucasian nations were transported from homelands in the south-west of the Soviet Union to other, remoter, parts of the country; Stalin's distrust of certain national leaders resulted in the wholesale removal of nations. Despite Khrushchev's denunciation of these deportations in 1956, the Volga Germans and Crimean Tartars have been politically but not territorially rehabilitated.[45]

Case study

A variety of forms of cultural segregation have been experienced during the history of Northern Ireland. Occasionally, between the Norman conquest and the creation of an Irish Free State, attempts at the extermination of Catholic populations were made by the English and their agents, though on a localised scale and not as part of a broadly conceived policy. Aspects of historical and institutionalised segregation were apparent in the early seventeenth-century plantations of Ulster by Scottish and English Protestants following the flight of the indigenous aristocracy and subjugation of the Catholic population, 'Even today, over 350 years later, the Protestants and self-consciously British sections of the population are found in the more fertile, accessible, low-lying areas, while the Catholic and Irish group are notable in the less prosperous upland zones.'[46] Maps of Ulster towns dating from the seventeenth century, and certain Ulster town charters, reveal instances of institutionalised segregation, with squalid Irish towns developing outside the walls of the Protestant strongholds.[47]

At the end of the eighteenth century the Catholic element probably formed less than 10 per cent of the Belfast population, and the first Catholic chapel did not appear until 1783.[48] In the nineteenth century, however, rural famine and the industrialisation of Belfast brought a considerable Catholic influx; initially relations between the Protestant and Catholic communities may have been relatively cordial, but by 1861 Catholics formed 34 per cent of the Belfast population, and sectarian rioting was reported in the middle of the century. The distribution of Catholics was influenced by the direction of approach to the city (with a wedge of Catholic settlement forming along the Falls Road leading northward to the city centre), by the poverty of the average Catholic, and by the distribution of Catholic churches. But the main factor preventing the dispersion of Catholics into Protestant areas and *vice versa* involved community conflict segregation; at times of sectarian tension and rioting, Protestants have migrated into Protestant strongholds and Catholics into Catholic ones, a process which is intensifying at the present time. Socioeconomic factors have also been important, and Jones has shown that there is a tendency for segregation to be most marked in enumeration districts which rate very low on a socioeconomic scale.[49]

He applied an index of segregation to the Belfast enumeration districts by which the proportion of Catholics within each district was compared with the proportion of Catholics in the town as a whole (25.9 per cent in 1951). At 0 per cent and 100 per cent the district has total segregation, and at 25.9 per cent segregation at a district (but not necessarily street) level is absent. Total segregation gives an index of 1, total absence of segregation an index of 0, and levels of segregation midway between 0 per cent and 25.9 per cent and 25.9 per cent and 100 per cent, an index of 0.5. The high level of segregation in Belfast was evidenced by the median at 0.77 and the upper quartile at 0.935.

Where historical segregation is involved, an index of segregation used in urban geography can be applied at a state level to measure the degree to which a particular ethnic group is separated from the rest of the population, using the formula

$$\text{index of segregation} = \frac{\text{ID}}{1 - \sum x_{ai} / \sum x_{ni}}$$

where ID is the index of dissimilarity between the subgroup and the total population (including the subgroup), $\sum x_{ai}$ represents the total number of the subgroup in the state and $\sum x_{ni}$ represents the total population of the state.

Calculation must begin with the index of dissimilarity, derived from the formula

$$\text{index of dissimilarity} = \frac{1}{2} \sum_{i=1}^{k} \left| x_i - y_i \right|$$

where x_i represents the percentage of population of ethnic group x in the ith subdivision of the state (a parliamentary consistuency could be used) and y_i represents the percentage of the ethnic group y in the ith subdivision, the summation being over all the k subdivisions making up the state.[50]

Community conflict segregation and socioeconomic segregation are usually associated with urban situations, in which cases the formula can be applied in its original form, substituting city for state.

5.7 The federal State*

It has frequently been suggested that problems of cultural and regional diversity within States may often be reconciled through the adoption of a federal form of government. The essence of the model federal State, but not necessarily of the real federal State, is a division of powers between the all-union State government and the governments of the component states, with each level of government enjoying autonomy within its allocated sphere of control. This contrasts with the situation in the unitary State whose government may intervene on any matter at any administrative level. The division of power in the model federal system is such that the State government has responsibility for matters affecting the federation as a whole, such as foreign policy and tariff and immigration control, while the state governments manage affairs particular to their states. This division of power implicit in the federal model might be expected to preserve regional diversities and permit the coexistence of different outlooks and cultures, provided of course that these differences are spatially grouped. These conditions underlie the often quoted statement that federalism is 'the most geographically expressive of all political systems'.[51]

In practice, federalism takes on a wide variety of forms, often diverging widely from the federal model. The fact that a State has a federal constitution need not imply that it behaves federally, and contradictions often appear between formal political structures and actual political practices. The constitution of the Soviet Union makes it theoretically the most federal of all States, the constituent Union Republics being awarded the right to secede. This right, however, is compromised by the rights accorded to the Communist Party, which is non-federal and the source of all real political power. Functionally, the Soviet Union is perhaps the most centrally organised State in the world, despite also being the largest, with a regime which has proved distrustful of delegating all but the most trivial powers. Some unitary States are found to behave in a more federal way than many federations; the United Kingdom embraces a separate assembly for the Isle of Man, a temporarily suspended arrangement for home rule in Northern Ireland, and separate Scottish legal and educational systems. Federal constitutions may be adopted by States which appear to be relatively homogeneous and not needing of federal safeguards, such as the Federal German Republic and Australia, while other States with considerable regional and ethnic diversity, such as China and Zambia, are unitary.[52]

The model condition of a clear-cut division of power between State and states envisages a dualism which is no longer compatible with the tasks and

* In this section, to avoid confusion, 'State' refers to the federation and 'states' to its components, the capital letter designating the sovereign unit.

complexities of government. In an age of economic planning and pervasive social legislation, State intervention in almost every sphere of government is inevitable, and ideally federal systems should shift from dualism towards a cooperative integrated federalism in which the state works in partnership with the State, recognising the latter's supremacy while protecting the principle of regional autonomy.[53] Once adopted, a federal constitution is likely to become entrenched; thus Hawaii and Alaska have inherited a set of federal privileges beyond their real needs and representing the maximum programme of cooperation acceptable to the divergent interests of the original states of the Union.[54]

Though Livingston drew attention to the variety of forms that federalism can take and suggested a scaling of forms between the federal and unitary extremes, it remained to Tarlton to explore the different relationships existing between State and state and between state and state, since no two states in a federal system are likely to share identical relationships with either the federation or other member states.[55] This led him to develop the concept of symmetry and asymmetry in federal systems. In the ideal symmetrical model, the units are similar in geographical, economic, cultural and political terms, so that each state is a microcosm of the whole, facing similar problems and similar relationships with the central government. The ideal asymmetrical model is composed of unique states, each with different problems and competitive interests, and each standing in a different light with other states and the federation as a whole.

There has been a tendency for the theory of federalism to blur the facts, but provided that the aspects of diversity are spatially grouped and not distributed on a class or intralocal fashion, federalism may in certain cases provide a medium for cooperation in the face of diversity. However, if the particular situation tends strongly towards the symmetrical pole, then a federal constitution is an unecessary complication and a unitary system of government will suffice, while if the situation is strongly asymmetrical then the provision of a range of federal autonomies will assist irridentism and only centralised coercion can hold the State together. Between these extremes, federalism may provide a solution in circumstances where regionalism is strong but there is a common interest in cooperation such that the centripetal forces exceed the centrifugal.

Case studies

That federalism is not a panacea to which all problems of regional diversity are amenable has been emphasised in recent years by tensions within federal systems which have in some cases led to their collapse. The extreme of asymmetry was approached in the Central African Federation, which was formed in 1953 to link the self-governing colony of Southern Rhodesia with the British protectorates of Northern Rhodesia and Nyasaland. The British and Rhodesians saw economic complementarity in the coal of

Southern Rhodesia, the copper of Northern Rhodesia and the surplus labour of Nyasaland, while the British doubted the economic viability of a separate Nyasaland and did not wish to incur the expense of administering the protectorate as a separate entity. The government of Southern Rhodesia was settler-dominated, though the colonial office had followed a policy of native paramountcy in the protectorates, and within the federation the colonial office retained a responsibility for the protectorates while Southern Rhodesia had settler government under a franchise system which virtually debarred Africans from influence. Parity between the constituent units is fundamental to the operation of a federal system, but in this case Southern Rhodesia controlled three-quarters of the electorate, and the protectorates were regarded as dependencies, while white interests controlled twenty-six of the thirty-five federal assembly seats; not surprisingly, the African majority had no confidence in the federation.[56] After this lack of confidence was echoed by the British-appointed Monckton Commission and native leaders came to power in the protectorates, Nyasaland seceded in 1962, to be followed a year later by Northern Rhodesia.

Yugoslavia provides a rather different example; formed in 1918 as a kingdom, the State brought together a number of large and small Slavic groups which had developed separately under Austrian and Ottoman control within a highly compartmentalised geographical environment, along with substantial non-Slavic Magyar, Romanian, Albanian and Italian minorities. Of the three leading ethnic groups in the population, the Greek Orthodox Serbs spoke a similar language to the Roman Catholic Croats, who shared their religion but not their dialect with the Slovenes. The Serbs formed half the population; their territory was centrally placed within the state and included the capital at Belgrade. As part of the Hapsburg empire, Croatia and Slovenia experienced greater economic development than Serbia, which had stagnated before winning independence from the Ottoman empire.

The only unifying factor between the groups making up Yugoslavia was a tradition of opposition to empire and a vague belief among some Slavs that long ago the South Slavs had been a united people. Even if this had been the case, it was no consolation for the non-Slavic Magyar and Albanian peoples who sought futures in enlarged Hungarian and Albanian States. It soon became apparent that the Croats and, to a lesser extent, the Slovenes considered that the State was being used as a vehicle for Serbian advancement, while the Serbs themselves were considered to be culturally and economically backward. Following a long series of difficulties, a federal constitution was introduced in 1939 in an attempt to satisfy Croat demands for autonomy.

During the 1939–45 war, Yugoslavia was split between the Axis powers, while Croatia became a Fascist puppet state. After the war the country was partly unified in revulsion at the massacre of Serbian minorities by Croatian separatists, and under the personal charisma of Tito. The system of government adopted in 1945 was federal only in name, but an intensification of regionalist sentiment prompted the introduction in 1953 of considerable concessions to regional autonomy, and six republics were redrawn to approximate more closely to the cultural divisions of the country while the ethnically fragmented Voivodina and Kosovo areas became autonomous areas. The persistence of separatist sentiments led to further devolutions of power under the constitution of 1963 and amendments of 1971.[57] It began to seem to the government that the more concessions were made to the regionalisms, the more the demands for further autonomy were forthcoming, and by 1972 it appears that the government had become disenchanted with the federal solution and reverted to a policy of centralised coercion as the best method of maintaining the federation intact. The Croat party leadership was purged of 'bourgeois nationalists' and the Serbian communists were accused of 'ultra-left libertarianism'. The Yugoslavian example supports the contention that federalism works only within a limited spectrum of regional differences.

Federalism is based on consent, and when this is withheld only a recourse to force by the central government can keep the federation intact—but no longer truly federal. In 1967, the distrust of the Nigerian military government by the largely Ibo population of the former Eastern Region of federal Nigeria was confirmed when the regime replaced the five federated units with twelve new states. The Ibo territory was to be divided between four new states, and the Ibo leaders saw this as signifying the end of regional autonomy. They appealed for a more rather than less federal system, a confederation of sovereign Nigerian States. The rejection of the appeal led to the abortive attempt at secession and the creation of the State of Biafra, which collapsed under the force of arms of the Nigerian government in January 1970.

Economic opportunity alone does not provide an adequate basis for federal association, as demonstrated by the demise of the Central African Federation in 1962–3 and the West Indies Federation in 1962. Political factors must also be favourable, and popular feeling such as to provide the federation with a positive *raison d'être*. The West Indies Federation lacked a state idea of greater potency than the individual personalities of Jamaica and Trinidad; however, the gradual strengthening and augmentation of remaining inter-State links may yet produce a permanent Caribbean federation. CARIFTA has brought internal free trade and may provide a framework for economic integration, while the Caribbean peoples are developing their own locational perspective based on opposition to neocolonialism and common problems of urbanisation, urban unemployment and rural labour shortage. A new federation which develops gradually from the realisation of common outlooks will have a sounder basis and better prospects of survival than the old.[58]

5.8 The insurgent state

Minority separatism is not the only source of tension within states; political and ideological factors can also threaten the status quo and initiate geographical change. Any change of government or even of a minister brings new perceptions to bear on the landscape, and consequent landscape change follows. Depending on the degree of contrast with preceding perspectives, the change may merely institute a new stage within a broader continuity or it may initiate a complete reappraisal of the landscape, as when communist regimes came to power in China and Cuba. Alternatively an existing regime may choose to adopt radically different policies, as when Stalin, faced with peasant non-cooperation in the delivery of produce quotas to the state, abandoned his policy of conciliation of the peasantry and launched a massive collectivisation drive which completely transformed the Russian rural landscape.

Those who work for political change are usually seeking to replace one government with another while retaining the territorial framework of the state. Where ideology is a major issue, attempts may be made to gain control of a portion or the whole of a state, and either to use it as a focus for ideological change or to alter its international orientations. When the Bolsheviks, after heated arguments, decided to seize control of the Russian state in 1917, they did so in the hope that a socialist revolution in Russia would catalyse similar revolutions in industrially developed states of West-

---

Figure 5.3.   Revolution and the insurgent state.

(a) Why do revolutions occur?—after Davies (ref. 59). Davies suggests that revolutions are likely to occur when an intolerable gap develops between popular expectations of need satisfaction and actual need satisfaction produced by the political system. Developments preceding the Russian revolution provide an example.

(b) Stages in insurgent expansion—after McColl. A stage of mobile war leads to the establishment of a guerilla area, ideally in a location where popular unrest has occurred, with access to political and military objectives, favourable terrain and cover for guerilla operations, economic self-sufficiency, and on a provincial boundary leading to a division of government forces.

(c) Expansion from guerilla base areas has taken place, producing liberated areas, and attacks are mounted on towns and villages, and on vital communications, which may be controlled by the government by day and the rebels by night.

See ref. 60 for (b) and (c).

(d) NLF expansion in Vietnam. In 1961 the Saigon government controlled most of Vietnam. By 1968 great NLF advances had been made, an NLF system of territorial administration had been introduced, and expansion from base and liberated areas was taking place with attacks on transport lines and provincial capitals. Men and materials were being moved through Laos and Cambodia and assembled in the 'Fish Hook' and 'Parrot's Beak' salients of Cambodia for infiltration into Vietnam. The maps are from an NLF source and somewhat overstate the NLF advantage. Not all the places arrowed were under constant attack, or all communications permanently paralysed.

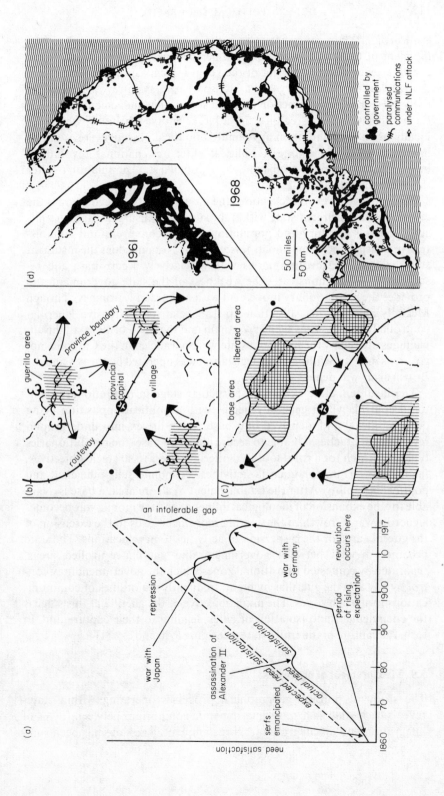

(a)

an intolerable gap

need satisfaction

war with Japan

repression

war with Germany

revolution occurs here

period of rising expectation

assassination of Alexander II

expected need satisfaction

actual need satisfaction

serfs emancipated

1860 70 80 90 1900 10 1917

(b)

guerilla area

province boundary

provincial capital

routeway

village

(c)

base area

liberated area

(d)

1961

1968

50 miles
50 km

controlled by government

paralysed communications

under NLF attack

ern Europe. When communists gained control in Cuba, a complete realignment of Cuban relationships and perspectives followed. McColl has drawn attention to the neglect of the geographical aspects of revolution, though control of territory has a vital part to play in revolutionary activity.[60] He makes a distinction between secessionist movements aimed at the withdrawal of one region from a larger entity; rebellions, which are locally orientated and often have limited political objectives; revolutions involving struggles among a political elite; and national revolutions involving an attempt by a substantial portion of a state population to alter the entire state structure.

He believes that the basic tactic of the modern national revolution is the creation of an insurgent state within the state. The insurgent state or antistate controls territory and population, has its core areas and administrative divisions, its army and its *raison d'être*. Not only does the insurgent state provide the revolutionaries with a relatively secure base and resources, it also demonstrates the weakness of the state government and provides the revolutionary movement with an aura of legitimacy. Though McColl confined his attention to the relatively extensive guerilla-controlled areas in states such as Vietnam and the Cuba of 1958, all the advantages offered by the insurgent state were paralleled in the Catholic 'no-go' areas in Derry within which legislation was operated by the IRA and the British army was denied access.

The insurgent state exists at a particular stage in revolutionary territorial control, which generally begins with a political opposition being declared illegal and, deprived of a base, being driven into underground revolutionary tactics. Unable to secure an urban base, the revolutionaries typically search for a rural foothold offering access to strategic objectives, favourable terrain for guerilla activities, economic self-sufficiency and political instability. After the establishment of a core area, a base is available for the expansion of ideological influence and the mobile war becomes a guerilla war. Growth of the guerilla movement leads to the extension of the guerilla area or the dispersion of activities to new locations. The state becomes divided between government and guerilla-controlled areas, separated by contested transitional zones which the government may control by day and the guerillas by night; frequently major lines of communications form such zones. The main objective of the guerilla at this stage is the encirclement and isolation of cities, leading to their capture and, in turn, the capture of the entire state (see figure 5.3b and c).

5.9 Measurement of processes

The study of political-geographical processes operating within states reveals each state as a stage in a dynamic equilibrium between forces of integration and disintegration and realignment. The state has been summarised as an embodiment of relationships between people, territory and government, and the closer the attitudes towards territorial and political organisation of the various elements in the population are to one another and to those of the government, the more internally stable the state is likely to be.

Measurement of the relative intensities of forces and tensions existing within a state framework presents a series of so far insoluble problems owing to the nature and diversity of the variables concerned. Some measure of the tendency towards or resistance to the integration of political-geographical regions can be derived from the application of interactance hypotheses or transaction flow analysis, used in the measurement of trading patterns and boundary friction.

Working from Deutsch's assertion that the fundamental factors drawing together and separating human groups are variations in the level and efficiency of communication, it can be argued that the changing levels of communication or information flow between communities reflect the strength of their relationship and the tendencies towards greater integration or separation.

Before Tanzania, Uganda and Kenya became independent in the early 1960s, it seemed probable that they would combine to form an East African federation. However, after independence each government was driven towards tasks of internal unification, and during this phase of introspection the prospects for federation receded. Soja applied transaction flow analysis to this situation and measured the change in orientation of the communities involved. He measured telephone flow traffic between twenty-four East African exchanges, for 1961, before independence, and for 1965, after independence, and comparisons were made.[61] To measure the degree of salience in communication, the relative acceptance index was used, based on the actual number of calls or transactions between two regions, minus the number predicted by an indifference model, divided by the expected value

$$RA_{ij} = \frac{A_{ij} - E_{ij}}{E_{ij}}$$

The number of calls expected from the indifference model will be based on the prediction that the percentage of A's calls to B will be equal to the number of calls received at B divided by the total number of calls within the system, minus the number received at A.

The relative acceptance index provided a measure of salience, the degree to which actual communication between two regions exceeds the amount predicted by the indifference model, though Soja considered that for two regions to be considered salient, the flow of calls in both directions should be at least 25 per cent greater than predicted. The survey revealed that

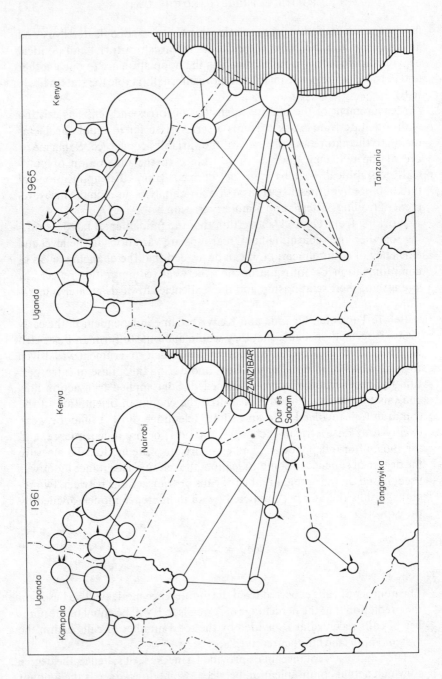

Figure 5.4. Salient transaction flows in East Africa, 1961 and 1965. Solid lines: $RA > 0.25$ and $D > 1$ in both directions. Dashed lines: $RA > 0$ in both directions but $RA < 0.25$ at least one way. Arrows: $RA > 0$ in one direction only. The size of circles is proportional to the percentage of total trunk calls made between twenty-four exchange regions in East Africa. See ref. 61.

after independence there was a fairly general decline in inter-state communication and an intensification of certain intra-state links, paralleling the decline of interest in federation and preoccupation with nation-building in the three states concerned (see figure 5.4). Though Soja's investigation was criticised by Prescott on the grounds that a clearer picture of the changing orientations could have been obtained from a study of speeches made by the political leaders, the techniques used offer interesting possibilities for future political-geographical investigation.

Some years earlier, MacKay[62] used the interactance relationship to study patterns of communication in Canada; French-Canadian cities in Quebec were paired with other Canadian cities, and Canadian cities with cities in the USA, and measurement was made of levels of telephone communication and intermarriage between the city pairs. The results showed that cultural and linguistic differences made the English-speaking and French-Canadian cities effectively five times further apart than the actual distances separating them, while cultural and political factors made the Quebec cities fifty times further from the US cities in terms of social communication than the actual distances would suggest.

If political geography is one of the more backward branches of geographical science, it is not because of a shortage of empirical studies but because of a deficiency of techniques. Hartshorne provided a conceptual framework for the analysis of political-geographical processes within states by drawing attention to the existence of centripetal and centrifugal forces, and it remains for political geographers to augment the concept with a range of techniques for the more accurate measurement of these processes.

The most advanced and comprehensive quantitative analysis of processes of national development, integration and interaction was undertaken by Deutsch.[63] Unfortunately space does not permit a proper appraisal of his techniques, calculations, models and far-sighted attempts at graphical presentation, and the student who is interested in the application of quantitative methods to problems of political-geographical investigation at the state level is strongly urged to study Deutsch in the original, as referenced. The basic terminology used by Deutsch in his analyses is useful in itself, can form the basis for a variety of equations, and is outlined here. The 'mobilised population' M is the portion of the area's total population P which is mobilised for mass communication (such communication is crucial to Deutsch's theories, as outlined in section 5.3 above) and roughly corresponds to the non-rural and non-parochial element in P, the remainder of the population being termed the 'underlying population' U. The speakers of the predominant language of the area concerned are termed the 'assimilated population' A, the remainder of the population being the 'differentiated population' D. The most active carriers of nationality are those mobilised for intensive communication and assimilated to the predominant language or culture, who constitute group N. The persons who are mobilised but differentiated are the most likely to experience national conflict and were designated as the nationally hetero-dox, H. The ratio $H:P$ is the crudest indicator of the probable incidence and strength of national conflict.

When conflict develops within M between A and H, two additional groups may become significant: firstly the underlying assimilated popula-tion, assimilated to the predominant language and culture but not mobil-ised for social communication and with no immediate occasion to participate in national conflict. If and when members of this group do become mobilised, they enter on the side of N, of which they then become a part. Members belong to the quiescent population reserves of the domin-ant language or culture, and this is designated Q. The ratio $Q:P$ provides the crudest expression of the long-run strength of the dominant language or culture of the area. The other group consists of the underlying differ-entiated elements in the population, R, a potential reserve for a national irridenta who may join H providing that mobilisation proceeds faster than assimilation. An extremely rapid mobilisation of R at a rate far faster than the mobilisation of Q could produce a situation in which one dominant language and culture is replaced by another.

Census material and other statistical records are available for a number of countries which allow specific numerical values to be attached to the groups identified by Deutsch for different countries at different points in time. The projection forwards or backwards of different trends in the pro-cesses of mobilisation and assimilation requires the calculation of rates of change; these are

p the natural rate of increase of P
b the natural rate of increase of M
a the natural rate of increase of A
d the natural rate of increase of D
m the rate of entry into M of people born outside M,
      calculated as the average net increase of those
      who enter M over those who leave M
c the rate of assimilation at which people born
      outside A are entering it at a later date,
      calculated as for m

Deutsch used these categories to construct several models as a basis for more advanced mathematical enquiry, and applied them to a number of specific cases relating to actual processes of assimilation and mobilisation, as with the case of Finland where, in the nineteenth century, the transfer of the country from Sweden to Russia, coupled with the rapid mobilisation of the Finnish R group, caused the replacement of Swedish by Finnish A and N groups.

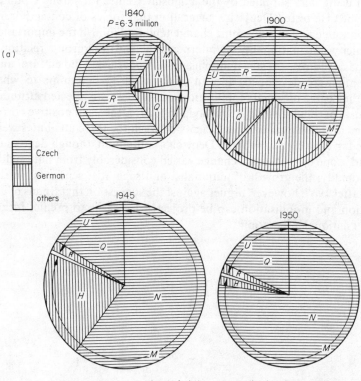

(a)

1840
P = 6·3 million

1900

Czech

German

others

1945

1950

Areas of circles are proportional to P

Figure 5.5. A diagrammatical representation of some concepts and techniques developed by Deutsch.

The changing ethnic balance of power in Bohemia, Moravia and Silesia. A key to the letters used is provided in the text. Note that in 1840 the dominant cultural group and the largest element of the mobilised population were German. In 1900 the Germans remained politically dominant under the Hapsburg Empire but the Czechs now outnumbered them within the mobilised population. After Czechoslovak independence the Czechs became politically dominant and rapidly mobilised elements from their substantial underlying population, while the Germans lacked necessary reserves of underlying population. In 1946–7 the vast majority of the German minority in Czechoslovakia was forcibly repatriated. Based on techniques and statistics provided in ref. 15. See also figure 5.1, page 87.

An interesting development of Deutsch's ideas was undertaken by Bertsch using data supplied by the Yugoslav Centre for Public Opinion Research.[64] He tested Deutsch's suggestion that forces of contemporary socioeconomic and demographic change tend to diminish the importance of ethnicity and nationality in interpersonal and intergroup relations. Three basic indices—of social mobilisation, modernism, and cultural universalism—were developed, and an effort made to determine to what extent the degree of social mobilisation and modernism affected attitudes to cultural particularism in Yugoslavia in 1967. Degrees of positive correlation measured by gamma coefficients between the three attributes were obtained in each case to support Deutsch's contention, though degrees of rate and scope of attitudinal change varied considerably from nationality to nationality; the growth of nationalist and separatist sentiment in the period after 1967, however, argues against the suggestion that trends of assimilation and mobilisation can be projected forwards to predict future levels of national integration.

PART 6

Frontiers and boundaries

Located at the interfaces between adjacent state territories, international boundaries have a special significance in determining the limits of sovereign authority and defining the spatial form of the contained political regions. Frontiers and boundaries have usually been studied in terms of their geographical relationships to the human and physical landscapes through which they pass, and though political geography is rich in morphological, empirical and generic boundary studies, the economic and psychological functioning of boundaries has not received the attention it merits. Boundaries have been loosely described as being linear; in fact they occur where the vertical interfaces between state sovereignties intersect the surface of the earth. Frontiers, in contrast, are zonal and therefore contain various geographical features and, frequently, populations. As vertical interfaces, boundaries have no horizontal extent, though the factor of border location can characterise surrounding landscapes, while a past frontier location may be marked in a landscape long after the frontier concerned has advanced, receded or contracted. The seaward extent of the coastal state is also marked by boundaries, and often by frontier-like extensions of diminished state control beyond the outer limit of sovereign authority; this contrasts with the situation on land, where frontiers associated with boundaries normally represent areas which are being integrated into the functioning state system and which are contained within the state boundaries.

6.1 Frontiers

The existence of land frontiers is indicative of a particular stage in the expansion of effective state area, and frontiers are usually studied in terms of their relationship to the effectively organised portion of the state and to the areas lying ahead of the frontier. At the outset, the distinction can be made between, firstly, the circumstances in which 'political frontiers' exist, the state lacks *de jure* boundaries and the *de facto* limits of the state advance with the advance of its frontiers; and secondly, the situation in which 'settlement frontiers' mark stages in the expansion of the state ecumene within pre-existing *de jure* boundaries. The expansion of the Russian state into Kazakhstan and Soviet Central Asia was associated with political frontiers, while the colonisation of the interior of Australia involved the advancement of settlement frontiers within territory already claimed.

A further distinction can be made between primary and secondary settlement frontiers. The primary form mark the vanguard of advancing colonisation and state control, and disappear when the legal limits of the state are reached. As the primary settlement frontier advances, so apparently unattractive areas will be bypassed, leaving enclaves of uncolonised territory behind, and secondary settlement frontiers mark the stages of subsequent colonisation in these neglected areas. Prescott suggests that primary settlement frontiers are associated with higher population densities, lawlessness and more diverse economic opportunities, while the relatively unattractive nature of secondary settlement frontiers and the lateness of their colonisation give them an association with lower population densities and greater state involvement in their development.[1] A third type of settlement frontier is the hollow form described by James in Latin America, where a consolidation of settlement did not always occur in the wake of frontier advance. Rather, the crude and speculative exploitation of frontier resources led to the exhaustion of soils and minerals, causing the retreat of settlement from colonised areas to new frontiers or longer-established areas of development.[2]

As the sovereign state has replaced earlier forms of political region, so it has become essential that sovereignty should have a known and exact extent. Consequently precise boundaries have been defined between neighbouring states where previously zonal frontiers existed, and the only surviving political frontiers are today found along the southern margins of Saudi Arabia. However, frontier characteristics may persist within former frontier zones now divided by an international boundary, or betwen tribal territories contained within states.

The division of frontiers into political and settlement categories is only one of a number of classifications which can be applied, as table 6.1 shows. Frontiers of inclusion are associated with the assimilation of indigenous populations in areas over which the frontier passes, while segregation is characteristic of frontiers of exclusion. Examples of the former type include to some degree the Roman, Arab and Spanish American frontiers, while resistance to assimilation was characteristic of the North American, Australian and Boer frontiers.[3] Such resistance can come from either the indigenous population or the colonists; in the Soviet Union, the Siberian natives showed a greater readiness to mix with Great Russian colon-

Table 6.1

Classification criteria	Type A	Type B
1 In relation to the sovereign territory of the state	political	settlement (a) primary (b) secondary (c) hollow
2 In relation to the indigenous population of the frontier zone	inclusion	exclusion
3 In relation to the pace of frontier advance	dynamic	static
4 In relation to the degree of trans-frontier contact	contact	separation

ists than did the Moslems of Soviet Central Asia, whose religion opposed mixing with infidels.

Dynamic frontiers are in motion and involve the continuous colonisation of new territory; they may become static when advance is checked by environmental barriers, effective resistance by indigenous peoples, or a lack of colonists. Until suitable passes could be found, the Appalachian Mountains and Dividing Range checked the early colonisation of the interiors of the United States and Australia, and the militancy of the Apache Indians retarded the Spanish and American colonisation of the American south-west, while the colonisation of Siberia would have been more rapid had not serfdom tied many potential colonists to the estates of their landlords. Frontier advance involves both 'pull' and 'push' factors, the attraction of new opportunities and empty areas and the escape from poverty, lack of opportunity, and prosecution or persecution in the area of departure. For each frontier and each individual colonist, the combinations of these incentives will vary.

Levels of trans-frontier contact and accuracy of perceptions are also variable, and in extreme cases there may be no knowledge of the areas beyond the frontier; for example, in the early eighteenth century the British settlers in South Africa were unaware of the formation of an aggressive Zulu state in the area to the north. The final stabilisation of the frontier may be in areas which facilitate or inhibit trans-frontier interactions, though ultimately the levels of these interactions will reflect degrees of political and cultural complementarity rather than terrain factors. In the earlier part of the twentieth century there was considerable debate upon the relative merits of frontiers of contact which, their advocates claimed, would facilitate peaceful intercourse between states, and frontiers of separation, involving zones of difficult terrain and scarce population which were said to minimise the risk of war by separating potential enemies.

Hartshorne suggested that such zones of separation had a static aspect, as areas of difficulty and low population, and a kinetic or hindrance aspect, deriving from the difficulties encountered in traversing them.[4] He then made a rather unsatisfactory attempt to code frontiers of separation whereby, for example, the Sahara Desert would be coded II B I: II as an area nearly but not entirely unpopulated, B as an area difficult but not impossible to traverse, and I as an area of the first magnitude.

Comparative studies of frontier history were lacking until Mikesell attempted in 1960 to compare the similarities and differences of a number of frontier experiences.[5] The American west, for example, involved a dynamic frontier of exclusion; like the Russian advance into Siberia, it had a 'safety-valve' function in respect of the population of the effective state area and was advanced by road and railway construction, though contrasts resulted from the differing imperial monarchistic and republican nature of the states concerned and the differences between Russian serfdom and American homesteading. The Australian frontier was also a frontier of exclusion which became dynamic after the discovery of passes through the Dividing Ranges, but, in contrast to the American experience of homesteading and open range ranching, the Australian colonists were largely rich sheep-herders and their wage-earning ex-convict employees. Also, there was no single Australian frontier, rather a pattern of radial expansion inwards from a number of separate coastal footholds.

The legal and psychological differences between frontiers and boundaries have been elucidated by Kristof.[6] The frontier is seen as a 'manifestation of the spontaneous tendency for growth of the ecumene'.[7] As the forerunner of the advancing state it is associated with movement ahead of the state's ability to integrate territory, and its population is essentially outer-orientated, looking beyond the frontier to areas of opportunity and danger. It is an area in which populations may mix, external relations are not subject to state monopoly, and frontier outlooks and life styles develop. As such the frontier expresses centrifugal forces, while the state boundary reflects centripetal tendencies. Lacking the zonal extent of the frontier, the boundary has no cultural identity and is inner-orientated, being created and maintained by a central government anxious to define the limits of its sovereignty and to monopolise the allegiances of the enclosed population. Frontiers are therefore associated with a phase of state growth preceding the stabilisation of patterns of sovereign control, while the introduction of boundaries reflects an acceptance of the territorial status quo and an emphasis on assimilation and organisation rather than expansion. An intermediate stage may be represented by the appearance of temporary political regions within the frontier zone, such as the marcher lordships of the Welsh and Scottish marches of early medieval England, the autonomy of which diminished as the border areas became integrated into the effective state area of England. In 1893, in a rather romanticised account of American colonisation, Turner visualised the frontier as an area of rapid Americanisation associated with a movement away from European influence and the creation of a society of resourceful individuals in a zone of cooperation, mixing and challenge, with each new phase of colonisation resulting in a renewal of society as new opportunities and challenges were faced.[8]

Territory left in the wake of an advancing frontier becomes subject to processes of effective integration into the state. Witthuhn studied the pattern of the diffusion of postal agencies which were established in Uganda by centralised colonial dictate, and sought evidence of political action and spreading political control and of spatial bias in their location, testing the hypothesis that political impress occurred along the forward edge of a diffusion wave.[9] In the latter case, use was made of trend surface analysis in which the z coordinate for each postal agency represented its date of opening, the data being used to produce a best-fit time interval contour map. The number of postal agencies in Uganda increased from five locations in 1904 to 194 in 1965, and though the agencies existed as symbols of British control, their primary function was to serve an intrusive European population which was tightly linked to the govenor in Kampala. Witthuhn showed that the nearer a location was to Kampala, the higher were its chances of obtaining a postal agency, but that there was no support for the diffusion of agencies along the forward edge of a diffusion wave. Rather, the expansion of the network sought to maximise the range of territorial coverage, proceeding firstly by long movements necessary to effect maximum coverage and then by shorter steps. In the case of Uganda, British colonisation took place rapidly within preexisting superimposed boundaries, and in cases where a clear-cut frontier of expansion was evident, and operative over a longer period, then analysis of the type used by Witthuhn, based on the diffusion of functional symbols of state control, such as postal agencies or police stations, could be used to demonstrate the penetration of effective state control into areas over which a frontier has passed.

6.2 Border and relict frontier landscapes

Proximity to a state boundary can be expected to affect human activities and landscapes in a variety of ways. The most obvious, but usually among the least important, manifestations of border location are likely to be the physical structures of the boundary, customs posts, boundary markers and, frequently, defensive installations. The degree to which these structures are evident in the landscape will usually depend largely upon the nature of international relations between the neighbouring states; for example, movement between Benelux and EEC members Belgium and the Netherlands is largely through almost permanently open single-pole barriers, while the border zone between East and West Germany has been deeply carved into the landscape. On the East German side are a depopulated zone, minefields, barbed-wire entanglements and numerous large

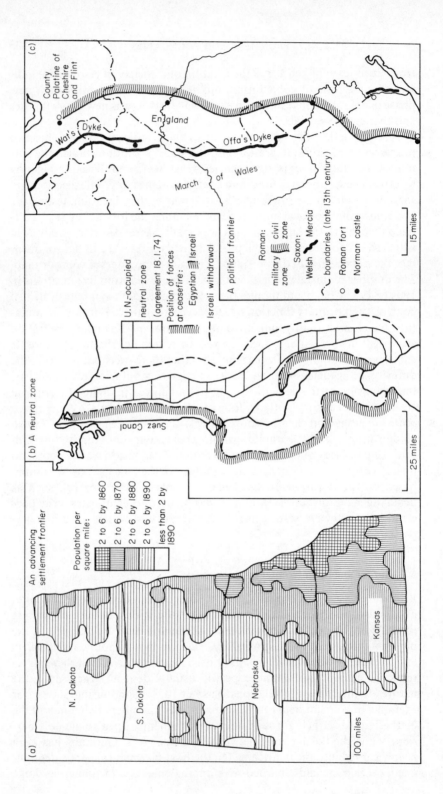

(a) An advancing settlement frontier

Population per square mile:
- 2 to 6 by 1860
- 2 to 6 by 1870
- 2 to 6 by 1880
- 2 to 6 by 1890
- less than 2 by 1890

N. Dakota

S. Dakota

Nebraska

Kansas

100 miles

(b) A neutral zone

Suez Canal

U.N.-occupied neutral zone (agreement 18.1.74)

Position of forces at ceasefire:
- Egyptian
- Israeli

Israeli withdrawal

25 miles

(c) A political frontier

County Palatine of Cheshire and Flint

Wat's Dyke

England

Offa's Dyke

March of Wales

Roman:
- military zone
- civil zone

Saxon:
- Welsh Mercia
- boundaries (late 13th century)

Roman fort

Norman castle

15 miles

military bases, while populations living within the more general area of the boundary are carefully vetted for reliability. On the West side are a series of settlements which have experienced economic decline as a result of their peripheral and potentially unstable locations, such as the former railway node of Helmstedt.

The economic, sociological and psychological characteristics of the border zone are much more significant, though less obvious than the physical structures of the boundary. Though their barrier effect varies from case to case, boundaries define separate economic, political and social *milieus*. As the most peripheral portions of their states, border zones have the lowest levels of economic, transport and social connectivity with the remainder of the state. Their industries are likely to be relatively remote from major national markets, and the distributional spheres and service areas of border towns are restricted and perhaps unable to extend beyond the boundary because of economic or political controls, though the border zone may contain industries which specially exploit a border location. The economic barrier effect of international boundaries is discussed more fully in section 6.5 below. The social and psychological habits of border-zone populations differ from those of the remaining state population in a number of ways, the degree of difference depending on the barrier effect of the boundary and the degree of trans-boundary political compatibility. Border populations are usually the first to feel the shock of inter-state conflict, and usually as such they are particularly politically aware. It is generally accepted that the most intense anti-British sentiments in the Irish Republic are to be found in the zone bordering Northern Ireland. Communications systems are usually developed along nationalistic lines, and consequently the orientations and social contacts of border-zone populations are normally directed towards the interior of the state. In studying the shopping behaviour of residents in the zone of the Maine–Maine–New Brunswick international boundary, Reynolds found that a shift in the scale of perception occurred at the boundary, and inhabitants had a closer knowledge of conditions on their own side of the boundary than beyond it. 75 per cent of New Brunswick residents asked where the trans-boundary route led to, simply replied 'to the boundary' or 'to the States'.[11] Transaction flow analysis provides a valuable tool for the examination of the nature of boundaries as barriers to trans-boundary communication, and its application by MacKay and Soja is mentioned in part 5.

Figure 6.1. Examples of settlement and political frontiers and a neutral zone. (a) An advancing settlement frontier (based on ref. 10). (b) A neutral zone. (c) A political frontier. Wat's Dyke was built *circa* 750 and Offa's Dyke *circa* 784–96 by the Mercians to mark their frontier with the Welsh. Offa's Dyke, by following the western scarp of hill slopes, gave a defensive advantage to the Mercians. Note the persistence of the zone as a political frontier from the Roman to the medieval periods.

Almost every portion of the earth has probably at some time been passed by a frontier, but in some cases the former frontier character remains clearly marked in the landscape. Many centres which began as frontier garrison posts have subsequently acquired economic activities to replace declining political functions; examples include many of the main service centres of the Great Plains, such as Fort Worth and Fort Dodge, and former garrisons of the Russian advance in the Ukrainian steppes, Kazakhstan and Soviet Central Asia, such as Rostov on the Don, Krasnovodsk and Alma Ata. Routeways originally laid out as military roads by General Wade in the pacification of Celtic Scotland form a basic element in the present communication system of the Scottish Highlands.

The Welsh landscape is particularly rich in frontier relics. Extending from Brymbo in the north to Sedbury in the south is Offa's Dyke, an impressive late eighth-century earthwork constructed to mark the agreed frontier between Anglo-Saxon Mercia and the Welsh mountain kingdoms to the west. The Dyke was overrun by subsequent colonisation from England, with the Norman invaders being particularly interested in securing a land route through Wales as a preliminary to a conquest of Ireland mounted from Welsh ports; the importance of frontier relics in Welsh border towns has been described by Wood.[12] The pre-industrial Welsh border town was an English military creation designed to consolidate areas absorbed in the expansion of the English political *milieu*. Stages in the expansion of English influence in Wales were marked by the establishment, by marcher lords or by the king, of planted fortress towns in advance of the lines of earlier fortresses. These towns were castle-dominated, and accomodated intrusive military and commercial populations. As one zone became subdued and castle-dominated, so new advance lines of garrisons were established, the process culminating in the conquest of Gwynedd in the Edwardian period. More than a hundred towns were established or substantially influenced by their frontier garrison function; examples include Ludlow, Hereford, Flint and Montgomery, and frontier relics remain their most characteristic features, though this differentiation is evident only in their locations and cores, not in their suburbs.

6.3 Classification of boundaries

Though political geographers seem to have had a preoccupation with boundary studies, the morphological, genetic and generic aspects of boundaries have virtually monopolised attention at the expense of more significant functional studies. The nature of boundaries as interfaces between adjacent state sovereignties, intersecting the surface of the earth as radial plains from its centre, has already been discussed in section 3.1. A number of schemes for the classification of boundaries have been suggested, and usually boundaries have been classified in respect of their locational relationship to physical or cultural landscape elements.

Discussion on the relative merits of rivers and mountains as boundary-containing zones has been a time-honoured source of political-geographical debate. Rivers both divide and unite flood plain and valley cultures; while providing variable barriers to communication between adjacent banks, rivers are frequently highways for intense commercial activity, and their basins tend to include communities which are homogeneous, at least in an economic sense. River boundaries tend to encourage cooperation between the political communities which they separate, since special arrangements must be negotiated with regard to bridging, damming, and the ownership of territory affected by a change in river course. It has become a convention in international law that river boundaries follow the river thalweg, a line joining the deepest points on the river bed; such boundaries provide both states with access to the navigable channel, and are therefore more satisfactory than median-line boundaries which may shift with changes in water level or deprive one state of navigation where the river bed is asymetrical and the thalweg winding. Boundaries following one river bank are rare and undesirable, since one state may be completely deprived of access to the river. River basins as areas attractive to settlement have tended to be associated with the historical cores rather than the peripheries of states, and consequently riverine international boundaries are more common in the new world, where boundaries were sometimes drawn along distant watercourses which provided convenient reference lines in little-known country.[13]

Table 6.2.   Boundary classifications

Classification criteria	Type I	Type II	Type III	Type IV
1 Relationship to physiographical features	mountain	river	maritime	other
2 Historical relationship to cultural landscape	antecedent: pioneer relict	subsequent	superimposed: colonial truce line other	
3 Relationship to barriers to trans-boundary interaction	contact	separation		
4 Duration	.... various time categories			
5 Supposed level of pressure on boundary	living	dead	(not acceptable)	
6 Supposed relationship to landscape	natural	artificial	(not acceptable)	
7 General: S. W. Bloggs's classification	physical	anthropo-geographical	geometrical	complex

Mountain ranges, as areas unattractive to dense settlement, frequently mark the limits of politically integrated ecumenes and provide defensive frontiers of separation between neighbouring political communities. The possible drawbacks with frequently favoured watershed boundaries are that mountainous areas frequently contain homogeneous mountain-dwelling cultures which will be divided and possibly severed from their seasonal migration routes by the enforcement of such boundaries. The nomadic peoples of Soviet Central Asia have been obliged to abandon their traditional migratory habits by the hardening of the Sino-Soviet boundaries, while the Kurds are an example of a mountain culture divided against their wishes by the mountain boundaries between the Soviet Union and Turkey and between Turkey and Iran. Further, most mountain ranges consist of a series of parallel *cordilleras* rather than having a single clearly defined range; the general watershed may be difficult to define, and may not correspond to the line of highest peaks. The difficulties which resulted in the classic case of the disputed boundary between Chile and Argentina are discussed in part 7.

Despite his unfortunate use of a confusing geomorphological terminology, Hartshorne suggested a useful classification of boundaries which relates them to the development of cultural landscapes.[14] 'Antecedent' boundaries are those which have preceded the full development of associated cultural landscapes, and in the course of this development the presence of the boundary is taken into account. Totally antecedent or 'pioneer' boundaries exist in 'virginal' form until the arrival and settlement of colonists. 'Subsequent' boundaries postdate the development of cultural landscapes, and they can be described in relation to their degree of conformity with established cultural patterns; where this conformity is notably lacking, the boundary is said to be 'superimposed'. Antecedent boundaries, such as that in the Great Plains between Canada and the United States, were characteristic of early stages of European colonisation in circumstances where territorial disputes were avoided by the anticipation and definition of patterns of colonisation and control. Subsequent boundaries typically seperate the European nation states where, at various stages, political patterns have been made to conform to national distributions, while superimposed boundaries are common in colonial situations after the negotiation by imperial powers of spheres of control at European conference tables, often in ignorance of actual cultural and physiographical distributions.

When a reconstruction of European boundaries seemed imminent following the defeat of the Central European empires, there was very active political-geographical debate concerning the relative merits of boundaries in zones of contact or separation. Sir Thomas Holdich adopted a military perspective on the problem, and argued for boundaries of separation which would minimise contacts between neighbouring states and facilitate defence, while Lyde supported boundaries in zones of contact which would necessitate inter-state cooperation and lead, he hoped, to better mutual understanding.[15] In reality, the barrier function of boundaries will be determined far more by adjacent state attitudes and policies than by the nature of the border terrain.

As well as being studied in terms of their conformity to physiographical and cultural phenomena, boundaries may also be mapped, analysed and possibly categorised in terms of their duration. A quantitative extension of a cartographical exercise by Gilfillan[16] was suggested by Learmonth and Hamnett, whereby sections of the total boundary lengths of European states were ascribed to seven appropriate time categories, according to their duration, and the percentage of total boundary length in each category was calculated.[17] The categories used were over 475; 300–475; 200–300; 50–200; and under 25 years' duration. The percentage of total boundary length in the over-475-year category was then multiplied by 10, that in the next category by 9, down to multiplication by five for the percentage in the under-25-year duration category. The resultant quotients were then summed for each state to provide a composite index of duration of land boundaries, which could be used for ranking. The following calculation is for Italy.

Duration category	Percentage of boundary length			
475+	34.6	×	10 =	346
300–475	30.7	×	9 =	276.3
200–300	–	×	8 =	–
50–200	19.2	×	7 =	134.4
25–50	15.4	×	6 =	92.4
under 25	–	×	5 =	–

Composite index   849.1

Ranking   6

Portugal, Spain and Switzerland, each with maximum indices of 1000, headed the list; at the foot were Greece and Albania, each with indices of 600, and East Germany, with an index of 561.

The classification of boundaries as 'living' or 'dead' and 'natural' or 'artificial' is unacceptable. Dead boundaries were supposed to exist when neighbouring states reached equilibrium in their relationship and ceased to press for extensions of their territories beyond the boundary. Prescott has pointed out that boundaries may be stable but rigorously enforced, while policies towards expansion may. change with changes in regime and circumstance.[18] Both Hartshorne and East have shown that since all political boundaries result from human decisions, actions and choices, all must be man-made and consequently artificial.[19]

The categorisation of boundaries is of value in the organisation of political-geographical material, but it does not constitute an end in itself; it should be based on, and in turn enhance, detailed empirical study. One must agree with House that 'An excessive emphasis seems traditionally to have been placed on the classification of boundaries largely as an end in itself, rather than as an intermediate hypothesis for the understanding and comparison of the character and problems of the frontier contact-zones between distinctive sovereignties'.[20]

6.4 The choice and construction of boundaries

The adoption of precisely known and clearly demarcated boundaries was related to the acceptance of sovereignty as an important basis of statehood. Typically, a number of stages are involved in the development of international boundaries, and these have been identified by Jones as 'allocation', 'delimitation', 'demarcation' and 'administration'.[21] Allocation involves general political decisions on the division of territory; delimitation, the final selection of a specific boundary within a frequently broad allocation zone; demarcation, the marking of the boundary location by posts, buoys or other markers; and administration, the continuing arrangements for the maintenance and operation of the boundary. In particular cases one or more of these stages may be absent, and there is considerable variation in the actual sequence of events.

Kristof states that in the modern world involving the 'coexistence of many creeds and states it is important to have the spheres of the several centripetal, integrating forces legally delimited',[22] and the acceptance by a state of a particular set of boundaries is a force for stabilisation and marks the ascendancy of internal integration over external expansion. States have acquired their boundaries in a variety of ways; in some cases they mark the territorial limits of a phase of political expansion and conquest, as in the cases of the boundaries of the Soviet Union in central Asia or the USA in the south-west. In other cases, they have been imposed by external powers, either through acts of conquest or through negotiation; Hungary and Czechoslovakia were awarded their boundaries by the allied powers after the 1914–18 war, while the final delimitation of the boundary between Chile and Argentina was achieved by invited British arbitration. Boundaries frequently represent the final stage in the contraction of a frontier zone between separate politically integrated communities, and are defined by bipartite negotiation. In the developing world it has been common for states to inherit the boundaries of former European colonies, originally determined by processes of negotiation and power politics in Europe. Though conquest is outlawed by international law, the post-1967 boundaries of Israel show that it remains a means of obtaining de facto if not de jure control of territory, and the boundaries of many states, particularly in Europe, reflect earlier military solutions to the problem of boundary definition.

The defeat of the Central European coalition in the 1914–18 war provided a unique opportunity for the practical application of contemporary theories of nationality and boundary-making, though perhaps unfortunately the principle of national self-determination was compromised in areas where the victors required compensation, and retribution was taken against the defeated. Therefore, while boundaries between Slav and Slav tended to be guided by the nationality principle, those between Slav and vanquished or between victor and vanquished tended to reflect the intrusion of power politics.

Not only was the principle of the rights of nations to self-determination applied selectively (and never within the colonial empires of the victors), but also the redrawing of boundaries according to this principle involved inconsistency in the use of techniques. National leaders in exile were taken to be representative of the wishes of entire nations, and though the larger Slav nations were well-organised and vocally represented, the national aspirations of several smaller groups such as the Slovaks and Sudeten Germans were often confused and poorly developed. As well as listening to the councils of national leaders, the allied politicians despatched commissions of inquiry into an (insufficient) number of areas where the knowledge of the aspirations and ethnic composition of populations was inadequate. In the subsequent construction of boundaries, language was generally assumed to provide an adequate expression of nationality, and in a few areas plebiscites were held, frequently with British support, since the British had less faith in the objectivity of nationality than had the Americans. All parties seemed prepared to sacrifice more altruistic considerations for the pursuit of vested interests: for example, the Germans argued for plebiscites to be held to determine the future of Alsace and Lorraine but were opposed to a plebiscite in East Prussia; the Poles favoured linguistic tests on their western frontier but opposed their being held on their southern and eastern frontiers.[23]

The practical problems facing the boundary-makers were severe. Ethnic maps were frequently incomplete, while the interested parties supplied maps which were distorted and designed to emphasise different aspects of the cultural landscape; Italian, Jugoslav and Albanian sources provided different versions of the national distributions in the Jugoslav Kosmet, where rural populations were largely Albanian though Turks and Serbs predominated in the towns.[24] In other areas the principle of nationality contravened economic realities; in Upper Silesia the Prussian industrialisation of the coalfield area involved a policy of Germanisation, and the new industrial towns contained islands of German population standing in a largely Polish countryside. A plebiscite held in 1921 resulted in more than half the population, including many Poles, voting to remain in Germany. A boundary was drawn through the coalfield, dividing it into German, Polish and Czechoslovak sections, though the interdigitation of population was such that many Germans were left in Poland and *vice versa*. The threefold division of the single and formerly integrated economic region necessitated a convention in 1922 to regulate and unify its administration, though disputes continued throughout the interwar period, culminating in the Polish seizure of the Czech district of Teschen and the German invasion of Poland.

Though objectivity in the application of the principle of national self-determination was frequently lacking and sometimes difficult to determine in the construction of boundaries in central and east-central Europe, in Africa and some other parts of the colonial world ethnic principles were completely neglected. 'The political map of Africa today is the product of diplomatic chess amongst the colonial powers, a game played on European council tables since the 1880s by men who never saw Africa.'[25] The nineteenth-century colonisation of the continent initially involved inland penetration from coastal footholds established at assembly points for the export of tropical products. When contact was established in the interior between representatives of separate colonial movements, there usually followed an agreement to define respective spheres of influence, either through the adoption of geometrical boundaries following particular lines of latitude of longitude, or boundaries connecting prominent but often little-known landmarks.

The launching of a series of German claims in Africa prompted the convention of the Conference of Berlin in 1874, and in 1875 guidelines were adopted for the completion of the partition of Africa involving rules for consultation between the imperial powers concerned and for the effective occupation of territories claimed. There then ensued the final scramble for territory, with pressure for claims coming well in advance of progress in geographical knowledge, and boundaries were superimposed on areas of which the claimants were largely ignorant. In establishing political territories, each colonial power attempted, firstly, to maximise its sphere of control and to connect its possessions into large compact units which might also act as barriers to the continuous expansion of rival colonial territories; secondly, to control river basins which provided highways for trade to established coastal footholds and for further inland penetration; and thirdly, to avoid conflict over colonial territories which might be escalated into a European confrontation. In general the first and second principles would be pursued until boundaries were superimposed in the little-known voids between expanding spheres of influence, in accordance with the third rule. As a result, patterns of political control were established which compromised indigenous cultural realities; tribesmen were divided from fellow tribesmen or from their traditional grazing lands, and implacable tribal enemies were united in the same colony.

The 49th-parallel boundary between Canada and the United States is considered antecedent in terms of its relationship to subsequent colonisation (its superimposed nature in terms of the indigenous populations over

which it passed being generally neglected). Like other geometrical boundaries, it is unrelated to underlying patterns of terrain, and though the
boundary was politically acceptable to both parties, Boggs pointed out
that the International Joint Commission was concerned with problems
involving no less than fourteen rivers and lakes crossing this boundary.[26]

Problems concerning maritime boundaries are in a rather different category, and though there has been some standardisation of procedures for
boundary construction, a number of important matters await resolution.
The conventional baseline from which the breadth of the territorial sea is
measured is the mean low water mark, though a judgment in favour of
Norway and against Britain by the International Court in 1951 suggests
that states with exceptionally indented shorelines may draw baselines by
connecting promontories; since this judgment a dozen states, not all of
which have highly indented coasts, have simplified the construction of
maritime boundaries and extended their spheres of control by adopting
straight baselines. Where bays are concerned, the question becomes more
complicated; certain bays are considered as part of the internal waters of
their state, and baselines drawn across their mouths. There has been disagreement on the maximum length of lines which can be drawn to close off
bays, though according to the 1958 Convention of the Territorial Sea it is
24 miles, and a feature is considered to be a bay if it will contain a semi-
circle of diameter equal to its mouth. However, a number of states base
their claims to bays as internal waters on historical grounds, and several of
these, such as Hudson Bay, claimed by Canada, Peter the Great Bay,
claimed by the Soviet Union, and Santa Monica Bay, claimed by the USA,
do not satisfy conventional criteria for defining internal waters.

Territorial waters may be drawn around insular possessions provided
that these are natural and always stand above sea level, though politically
independent archipelagos present a particular problem. Both Indonesia
and the Philippines employ straight baselines which connect the entire
insular systems. The Indonesian claim of 1957 has the effect of including
the Java, Celebes and Banda Seas as part of Indonesia, and places important world shipping lines within Indonesian territorial waters. The claim
has been actively opposed by the Dutch, though the international legal
situation seems to be unclear.

Where two states are opposite or adjacent to each other, the territorial
sea of each extends to a median line which is equidistant from each shore-
line. In the former case, the effect may be completely to partition straits
used by international shipping; the Straits of Malacca, between Indonesia
and Malaysia, are in places less than 24 miles wide, and twelve-mile limits
affecting the straits have been claimed by both states since 1971. These
claims have not been recognised by the USA which, like other states, would
be required to obtain permission before sending its warships through the
straits, and in 1973 an American warship was sent through the straits in a
gesture of defiance. At the time of writing, the construction of the Kra

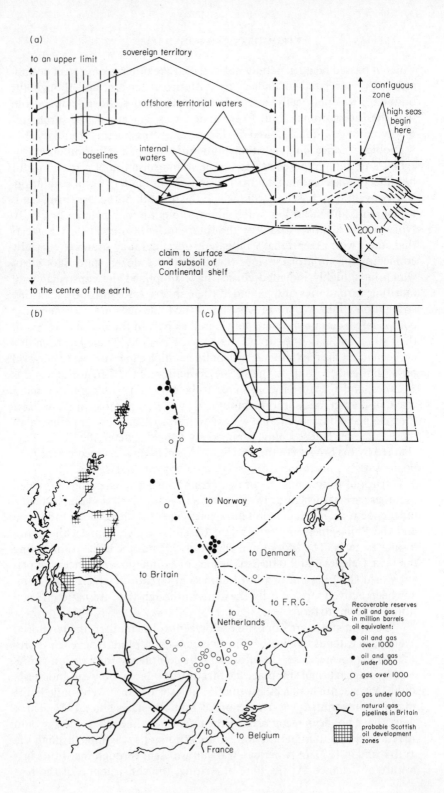

to an upper limit

sovereign territory

offshore territorial waters

contiguous zone

high seas begin here

baselines

internal waters

200 m

claim to surface and subsoil of Continental shelf

to the centre of the earth

(b)

(c)

to Norway

to Denmark

to Britain

to F.R.G.

to Netherlands

to Belgium

to France

Recoverable reserves of oil and gas in million barrels oil equivalent:

● oil and gas over 1000

• oil and gas under 1000

○ gas over 1000

∘ gas under 1000

natural gas pipelines in Britain

probable Scottish oil development zones

canal project across Thailand is being evaluated in the USA as a means of bypassing the Malacca Straits.

Enclosed within the baselines of the coastal state are internal waters, which are legally treated as part of the land surface of the state. Beyond the baselines are territorial waters, the extent of which is subject to considerable disagreement, and international law has not yet been able to resolve the problem (see part 7). Full state sovereignty extends to the outer limit of territorial waters. However, within territorial waters international shipping enjoys the right of innocent passage, subject to the restrictions conditioned by the security interests and fishery control policies of the coastal state, though the rights of warships to innocent passage in peacetime are disputed among legal authorities.

The seaward limit of the territorial sea, whatever the breadth of that sea, marks the termination of the sovereign territory of the coastal state. Special rights may be claimed beyond the territorial waters in what has come to be known as the contiguous zone. International legislation concerning contiguous zones is far from complete, though there are well-established precedents for customs controls beyond territorial waters, and the USA has operated them over a four-league zone since 1790, extending inspection to cover ships within one day's sailing time of the seaboard during the Prohibition era. There is also precedent for the operation of sanitary controls in a contiguous zone, though the prevention of oil pollution is governed separately by the International Convention for the Prevention of Pollution of the Sea by Oil, signed by thirty-eight parties and in force since 1958, rather than by the Convention on the Territorial Sea. The most controversial use of contiguous zones concerns fishery control. There now appear to be thirty-eight states which claim fishery zones beyond their territorial waters, and here the territorial sea convention appears to have been modified by subsequent practice, though there would be substantial legal support for the view that, in respect of customs, fishery protection and security, the contiguous zone can extend no further than 12 miles seawards from the baselines of the coastal state. Therefore such contiguous zones would only be available to states which claim less than 12 miles of

---

Figure 6.2. The offshore zones of the state.

(a) Model of offshore political zones. A contiguous zone beyond the territorial waters of the state may or may not be present, while some writers have referred to a 'zone of diffusion' beyond the contiguous zone and associated with the operation of a specialised function, such as weapon testing or pollution control. Note that when sovereignty is claimed over a continental shelf, sovereignty does not apply to overlying waters beyond the territorial waters.

(b) The division of the bed of the North Sea into national sectors. Only definitely proven oil and gas reserves are shown (see ref. 27).

(c) This inset shows an enlargement of a portion of the British sector, showing the allocation of concessions. Twenty companies took up concessions in the area shown, and those of one company are shown by the diagonal.

territorial waters. In 1970 Canada claimed control of a 100-mile wide zone off the Arctic seaboard for the purpose of pollution prevention, a claim which is challenged by the USA.

Claims to rights over adjacent continental shelves date from 1944, when Argentina claimed rights over offshore mineral reserves, and this was followed in 1945 by a more forceful US claim to rights over the seabed and subsoil of its continental shelf. Further such claims resulted in the Continental Shelf Convention of 1958. Several important ambiguities remained; continental shelves vary considerably in their width and depth, and the Convention, in stating that control is given to the adjacent coastal state 'to a depth of 200 metres or, *beyond that limit*, to where the depth of the superadjacent waters admits of the exploitation of the natural resources. . .' fails to provide a definitive outer limit for permissible claims, which could be interpreted as being relative to technological ability, and the US government has granted exploration permits affecting areas at depths up to 5000 feet. Rights to the control of continental shelves apply only to the sedentary organisms of the seabed and the geological resources below, the overlying waters remaining part of the high seas.

The division of the North Sea basin between adjacent and opposite coastal states for the allocation of oil concessions resulted in a number of cases being considered by the International Court in 1969–70. It was decided that the delimitation of separate spheres of control should be by mutual agreement and guided by the principle of awarding to each party zones equivalent to the natural prolongation of their land territory seawards. Difficulties arose because West Germany was not a signatory to the Continental Shelf Convention and therefore not bound by the established principles of division.

Beyond these areas subject to various controls and claims to ownership are the high seas which, with regard to the increasing number of maritime claims and the lack of international legal agreement, can only be described as being areas of the sea in which no claims or rights of ownership are current. The high seas are traditionally open to the vessels of all nations, free of any interference, though at various times states have exerted *de facto* but not *de jure* controls, the most recent case involving the closure to international shipping of an area of the high seas around Mururoa Atoll during French atomic tests.

6.5 Boundaries as barriers

The actual function of boundaries, surely their most important characteristic, is but lightly stressed in a political-geographical literature which is boundary-rich; yet

The concept of a dynamic process appears to be crucial to the study of barriers in a social context. If barriers are studied only in relation to static distributions, then the whole character of the barrier may be easily misinterpreted or distorted.[28]

In defining the extents of particular political systems, boundaries act as barriers to social and economic processes which would otherwise transgress them without interference. In the sociological and perceptual senses, boundaries contain regions of political and social integration, and restrict the flow of communication and the formation of social and psychological associations with areas and populations lying beyond the boundary. In an economic sense, boundaries enclose national economic systems, and through their function as tariff and quota barriers they protect national economies by artificially restricting the 'normal' patterns of production and exchange.

In 1919 Brigham pointed out that boundaries drawn in respect of the principle of national self-determination would be economically disruptive, and in producing numerous small national political regions they would resist economies of scale in production and would be therefore less 'natural' than boundaries which ignored physiographical divides.[29] Boggs returned to this theme in 1940, stressing the interruptive aspect of boundaries and suggesting that this could be roughly measured from the ratio between the total length of boundaries and the total areas contained within them.[30] On a continental basis, this ratio gave North America an index of 1.3 : 1000 and Europe (excluding the Soviet Union) an index of 7.3 : 1000. More realistically, the interruptive effect of boundaries derives from the international and economic policies adopted by governments and applied at their borders; Boggs compounded his error by suggesting that pressure on boundaries increases according to population density, and he multiplied his indices by a value for population density, producing the even more dubious indices of 1400 for Europe and 27 for North America.

In the measurement of barrier effects, the researcher faces the problem of existence; existing levels of cross-boundary interaction can be measured, but it may be impossible to measure the level of interaction which would take place were the boundary not present.[31] Both MacKay, in his study of telephone communication between Canada and the USA[32] (see part 4), and Lösch, in his study of the financial sphere of El Paso,[33] interpreted the barrier effect of boundaries as adding an extra distance factor to cross-boundary transactions. The problem of existence may be partially alleviated by the construction of a null model such as those used by MacKay and Soja and described above, whereby actual levels of interaction are contrasted with the levels predicted by the indifference model.[34] This technique is effective in demonstrating the barrier effect of boundaries to communication, as expressed by expected and actual levels of telephone communication, and has also been applied to international trading patterns, as discussed in part 7. It should be remembered, however, that the industries producing goods in world trade have developed in the 'unnatural' economic environments created by barriers, and that therefore the indifference models used do not take into account the patterns of production which might exist if boundaries were never present; the models simply provide a guide to some non-economic factors influencing exchange.

In the development of perceptual environments and patterns of social communication, barriers emphasise the difference between geographical distance and functional distance. Communications networks provided by the state are usually very much influenced by the objective of national integration, while movement across boundaries is only possible at certain regulated crossing points. Therefore the extra distance friction caused by movement to and from a crossing point, coupled with the inconvenience and delays encountered at such places, may reduce to almost negligible levels communication between two settlements only a short linear distance apart but separated by an international boundary. In North Dakota, east of Grand Forks, 175 kilometres of the USA–Canadian border are approached by fifteen northbound railways which either extend to the boundary or to within 10 kilometers of it, and only two of these railways actually cross the boundary. Reynolds and McNulty suggest that the least mobile individuals are likely to be those living near a political boundary yet distant from a crossing point, since their action spaces are highly curtailed by the presence of a boundary.[35] Similarly, such border locations are not normally attractive to industrialists, since trading can take place only in one direction, though some exceptions to this rule are discussed below.

The barrier effect of boundaries may reinforce cultural preferences in consumption and so affect national patterns of production. Lösch was interested in the effect of national character upon production, which he considered to be significantly influenced by the acquired skills of the workforce and the established preferences of national consumers. 'The diversity of production of a people is determined by how far they can resist a general levelling.'[36] Each group of producers has the choice of specialisation in the production of a familiar range of goods for the domestic market or an unfamiliar and more standardised range of goods for a larger international market.

Boundaries are most significant in the economic sense through their association with tariff and quota restrictions, the basic effect of which is to create an artificial economic environment for domestic producers by adding to the cost or restricting the quantity of imports which would otherwise be preferred by domestic consumers. Tariffs, quotas and trade embargoes convert an otherwise open world economic system into a series of partially closed national economic systems. Trade restrictions may be used by developing states to protect newly established industries and to accelerate economic growth, or by developed states to buttress outmoded industries. Alternatively they may be politically motivated (for example, the US embargo on trade with Cuba); preferential, and designed to encourage trade within certain economic groupings at the expense of more general trade, as in the case of the EEC; or tariffs may be used as a crude means of raising state revenue, as in the case of US charges against imported tropical products which cannot be produced in North America.

Governments also add to the artificiality of economic environments through tax concessions and other economic incentives; for example, industrialists have been attracted to Puerto Rico since tax concesssions were made available by the US government, with longer-term incentives being offered in the less developed parts of the island.

Models have been devised to highlight the effects of boundaries as economic barriers; Lösch symbolised the effect of customs duties as additional transport costs operating over zero distance, as exemplified in figure 6.3a. Any theory of industrial location which simply attempts to explain patterns of production in relation to production and distribution costs, without allowance being made for the creation of a series of artificial economic environments through government economic policies, will prove inadequate. The economic favourability of certain industrial locations is almost totally dependent upon peculiarities of tariff and quota regulations; the Virgin Islands watch industry provides an excellent example.[37] The islands are lacking in conventional attractions to industry, raw materials, skilled labour and large domestic markets. However, legislation passed in 1954 gave duty-free access to the US customs area to all articles produced in the American insular possessions, provided that less than 50 per cent of their appraised value on arrival represented foreign materials, and in the same year duties on foreign watches were doubled. In 1959 the first company to import unassembled parts or subassemblies of watches to be assembled in the Virgin Islands was located, and by 1966 sixteen such firms were operating, supplying one-ninth of the US market and employing 500 workers. These firms were solely attracted because the nature of import controls provided a lucrative basis for establishment, though in 1966 legislation was introduced to stem this expansion, which was taking place at the expense of domestic watch producers; the importation of watches from American insular possessions was limited to one-ninth of US watch consumption for the previous year.

Models can be used to demonstrate the impact of the introduction of an international boundary into an economic landscape and, conversely, the removal of such a barrier. In figure 6.3c, the natural hinterland of a plant producing commodity Q at location B is shown, along with the level of tariffs necessary to induce the introduction of a similar plant in state A. In figure 6.3d, it is shown that tariffs can in some cases be regarded as additional transport costs operating over zero distance, and the relationship between transport costs and the number of available crossing points on an international boundary is also shown.

The movement or the removal of an international boundary has the effect of placing locations affected in new economic environments. German areas in Schleswig–Holstein which were transferred to Denmark after 1918 suffered economically as a result. Under German control they had been associated with the export of agricultural products to German industrial areas in a market protected for domestic grain and cattle production. As part of Denmark the areas found it difficult to adapt to Danish free-trade farming based on milk and pig exports. Though the Danish government offered easy credit loans, rates of farm bankruptcy were four times as high in the acquired territories as in the rest of Denmark.[38] In 1947 the Netherlands joined the customs union of Luxembourg and Belgium; adjustment to the new economic environment brought contraction in the Belgian brewing industry and difficulty in the development of a competitive agriculture, but expansion in Belgian coal-mining and steel production. France lost Alsace and Lorraine to Germany in 1871, and regained them in 1918; the effects of repeated economic readjustment were severely felt, particularly in Alsace, while industrialists were frequently reluctant to invest in areas whose political future seemed unstable. The transfer of German territory to Belgium in 1918 provided the town of Aachen with a border location, as a result of which the town experienced considerable economic decline.

In certain exceptional cases, economic activity is attracted to international boundaries. Lösch quoted the examples of pre-war Swiss firms which established their enterprises on the German side of the boundary in order to have customs-free access to the German market while their head-

----

Figure 6.3.   Boundaries as economic barriers.

(a) An identical good is produced at location X in state A at a cost of 50 cost units, and at location Y in state B at a cost of 60 cost units. Increasing transportation costs are incurred with increases in distance from the points of manufacture. At the boundary CD, state B levies a tariff on the good produced at X of 20 cost units, so making it no longer competitive with the good produced in state B at Y.

(b) If an international boundary and interaction barrier is introduced into the system of service areas shown around centres X and Y, the central place function of X will be diminished, with resultant economic decline; Y will capture the trade of X in the area separated from X by boundary CD (shaded) and will expand accordingly.

(c) An enterprise in state B can produce good Q at a price of 20 cost units. At the best location in state A the same good can only be produced at a price greater than 20 cost units; a tariff at least equal to the difference in production costs between enterprises in states A and B must be introduced at the boundary before competitive production can be begun in state A. The pecked line symbolises the natural trading area of the enterprise in state B.

(d) The reduction of market areas by a tariff. If duties equivalent to transport costs of a height DJ are collected by Eastland, the market of A in Eastland would be marked by line CDE if goods could be delivered across the boundary at any point, and by FDG if the only customs house were at B. If HK were not a political boundary with tariffs, but a river with the only bridge at B, the Eastland market area would be bounded by HJK.

(e) The financial sphere of El Paso, 1914. Lösch has delimited the area (shaded) within which banks kept accounts with El Paso banks; note the effect of the international boundary in restricting the area in Mexico.

(b), (c), (d) and (e) are based on models given in ref. 33.

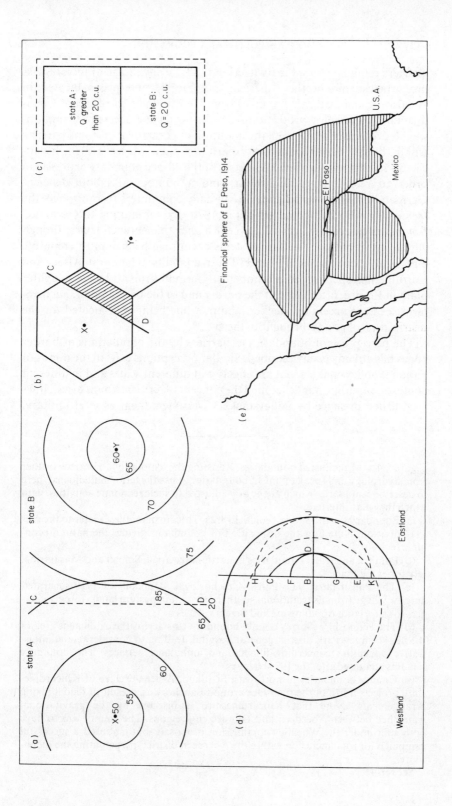

(a) state A   state B

(b)

(c)
state A:
Q greater
than 20 c.u.

state B:
Q = 20 c.u.

(d) Westland   Eastland

(e) Financial sphere of El Paso, 1914

U.S.A.

El Paso

Mexico

quarters remained based in Switzerland to take advantage of lower Swiss profit taxes, and of the American automobile enterprises located in Windsor, Canada, only a few miles from Detroit, in order to escape Canadian tariffs and enjoy protection from the tariffs and access to Commonwealth preferences.[39] Despite the abolition of permanent customs barriers within the EEC, major economic disparities remain. Mercedes Benz has located a factory within a few kilometres of the Alsace boundary expressly in order to recruit Alsatian labour, and a number of labour-deficient German border towns rely heavily on daily commuters from France, the *frontaliers*, who numbered 16 700 in 1970. By commuting to Germany, *frontaliers* can earn wages 50 per cent higher than French levels, though variations in national welfare systems encourage bachelors to commute and family men to work in France. The availability of labour in Alsace and Lorraine has encouraged a number of German firms to locate daughter plant in France, often close to the border and to the parent plant. Such enterprises have access to cheaper labour, while being well-located for the distribution of goods throughout the EEC.[40]

The perception of boundaries as barriers by the populations of border zones has already been described. Similar perceptions exist in the minds of national policy-makers, but are effective at different scales and in different contexts. Boulding has developed the concept of 'critical boundaries', lines established in space by policy-makers who view them as vital military,

---

Figure 6.4. Maladjusted boundaries. Resisting the temptation to borrow further from hydrology and speak of 'misfit boundaries', I use the term 'maladjusted' here to describe boundaries which are poorly adjusted to socioeconomic activities, with which they may interfere.

(a) Boundaries in the Silesian coalfield area. Titles in parentheses refer to the pre-1914 division. Note how the disposition of boundaries divides the natural economic region.

(b) Political and tribal boundaries in north-east Africa. Somali and Masai tribal territories are shaded.

(c) The Polish tatra. The Polish–Czechoslovak boundary of 1919 separated Jurgow village from its traditional southern mountain pasture lands, forcing villagers to share lands of Bukowina and Brzegi villages.

(d) The Hampshire–Surrey county boundary cuts across the catchment area of the new Frimley Park district general hospital, leading to considerable administrative difficulties concerning finance and ambulance services. The boundary remains unaltered after the 1974 changes.

(e) County boundaries in north-east Scotland. A pene-exclave of Kincardineshire projects north of the river Dee around Banchory as a result of feudal taxing arrangements. Note that Kincardineshire is bisected by the gravitational watershed between Aberdeen and Dundee city regions. The county was to have been split under the Wheatley commission proposals, but mounted a successful campaign for total inclusion within the Aberdeen district, perpetuating the dichotomy.

See ref. 41.

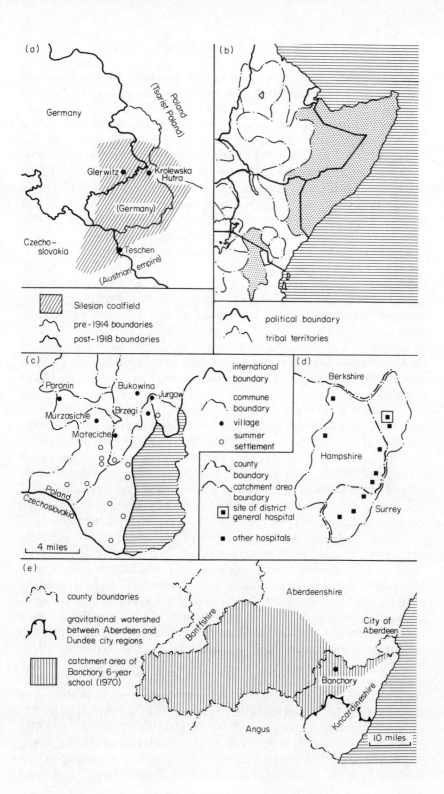

(a)

Germany

Poland (Tsarist Poland)

Glerwitz ● ● Krolewska Hutra

(Germany)

Czecho-
slovakia

● Teschen

(Austrian empire)

▨ Silesian coalfield

〜 pre-1914 boundaries

〜 post-1918 boundaries

(b)

〜 political boundary

〜 tribal territories

(c)

Poronin ●

● Bukowina

● Jurgow

Murzasichle ●

Brzegi

Mateciche ●

○

Poland

Czechoslovakia

4 miles

—— international
boundary

—— commune
boundary

● village

○ summer
settlement

(d)

Berkshire

Hampshire

Surrey

〜 county
boundary

—·— catchment area
boundary

▣ site of district
general hospital

■ other hospitals

(e)

〜 county boundaries

▬ gravitational watershed
between Aberdeen and
Dundee city regions

▥ catchment area of
Banchory 6-year
school (1970)

Aberdeenshire

Banffshire

City of
Aberdeen

● Banchory

Kincardineshire

Angus

10 miles

political or ideological divides across which interaction is to be resisted.[42] Some useful examples of such mental critical boundaries were provided by Bradshaw,[43] and include the critical boundaries implicit in President Johnson's statement of 1965 that 'We must say in south-east Asia—as we did in Europe—in the words of the Bible, "Hitherto shalt thou come but no further", ' while a Ministry of Defence advertisement asked readers, 'Isn't it better to have our frontier on the Elbe than on Brighton beach?'. Perceptions of critical boundaries, like all other perceptions, are liable to change; thus Louis XIV of France, when hearing that his grandson had inherited the throne of Spain, remarked, *'Il n'y a plus de Pyrénées'*—the Pyrenees had ceased to constitute a critical political boundary.

As well as having economic barrier functions applied at them, boundaries may be selected, fought for or enforced as defensive barriers. At the tribal frontier level there is the example of Kikuyu territory which was skirted by belts of forest in which the marauding Masai, who were invincible on the plains, could be ambushed and defeated by Kikuyu defenders. At several stages in recent history, France has striven to obtain an eastern frontier along the Rhine, avowedly for defensive reasons. The Israeli seizure of the Golan Heights in 1967 provides an excellent recent example of a state fighting for defensive boundaries; until then Israeli *kibbutzim* had been exposed to frequent shelling from the overlooking Golan summits. Defensive considerations frequently explain the noncontinuity of communication lines across boundaries, and the construction of the Channel tunnel between Britain and France was deferred on several occasions by British fears that it might be used in a Continental invasion of Britain. Where aggression from across a boundary is considered possible, the state concerned will normally seek to ensure that it has the transport capabilities to assemple troops and war materials at the frontier but that facilities for cross-boundary movement are minimised.

A macro-scale solution to the problem of strengthening barriers to undesirable interaction involves the creation of buffer states. Certain weak states, strategically located between powerful rivals, have at various times functioned as buffer states, though not all were specifically created by great powers to serve this purpose. The buffer states of Iran and Afghanistan were maintained by the British in the nineteenth century as a *cordon sanitaire* between British and Russian imperialism. Though the east-central European nation states which were created after 1918 largely originated from the application of the principle of national self-determination, the creation of a *cordon sanitaire* between defeated Germany and Bolshevik Russia was not overlooked by Allied policy-makers, and strategical considerations influenced the detail of the boundaries of the new states.

On a less grandiose scale than the buffer state, demilitarised zones may be imposed to enhance the defensive barrier function of an existing divide. The settlement terms of the Treaty of Versailles of 1919 demanded the occupation of the western Rhineland and the creation of a demilitarised zone covering the eastern Rhineland, thus providing France with greater security along its eastern frontier until the illegal reoccupation of the area in 1936. During the 1930s the French undertook the costly construction of the Maginot Line in an attempt (in the event, unsuccessful) to strengthen defensive capabilities in the region between Dunkirk and Weissembourg. The disengagement of Egyptian and Israeli armies under United Nations supervision, which is proceeding at the time of writing, will likewise create a *cordon sanitaire* between the opposed forces.

Journalist Simon Hoggart provided a fascinating microgeographical study of the difficulties involved in the defensive sealing of the border between Northern and Southern Ireland in the Newry area, where a maze of country lanes cross the boundary and were used daily by the Republican-orientated northern population, which used churches and shops in the south and would be faced by fifty-mile detours in the event of road closure.[44] The only practical means of closure involves the blasting of deep trenches across the roads, obstacles set in the roads being found to be easily dislodged by the concerted efforts of the local communities, though blasting is only possible where the roads are a safe distance from farmsteads and where they are not surrounded by flat fields which could provide detours.

During the post-war period, functionalist writers in political science have criticised the illogical nature of boundaries which are enforced as barriers to political integration; their viewpoint is encapsulated in the following statement by Claude.

The state system imposes an arbitrary and rigid system of vertical division upon global society, disrupting the global unity of the whole, and carving the world into segments whose separateness is jealously guarded by sovereignties which are neither able to solve the fundamental problems nor willing to permit them to be solved by other authorities.[45]

However, rather than there being the optimistically predicted submergence of international barriers by increasing inter-state interaction, most boundaries remain rigidly enforced, though some of the more important international boundaries now surround blocs of states engaged in the reduction of intra-bloc barriers.

PART 7

Political geography and the international system

The state can be studied in terms of the changing pressures within it, as a stage in a dynamic equilibrium between people, territory and government. Each state is also an actor in an international system, and since each state by virtue of its sovereignty is an independent actor, unable to recognise any power as superior to its own sovereignty, the international system is an anarchical one lacking a supreme authority which can impose order upon it.

Interactions between states take many forms and find varied geographical expressions. In the following sections an attempt is made to explain the dynamic and geographical significance of inter-state relations as expressed in state power, international organisations, trade, empire and conflict. In the past, political geographers were often content to describe the spatial causes and manifestations of inter-state relations without exploring the dynamic of the system which was affected by spatial phenomena or which produced geographical change. This task was perhaps considered to be the preserve of the political scientist. Such an approach is, and was, out of step with methodologies and approaches in other branches of the subject; it is difficult to imagine a geomorphologist restricting himself simply to the measurement or topographical description of tors or eskers without attempting to explain their mode of formation. Neither would a population geographer be content to describe a population distribution without any attempt to understand the processes by which it had developed. Some writers have seen political geography as a link between political science and geography, while others have emphasised the geographical connection. In either case, a fuller appreciation of political process can only enhance the understanding of spatial patterns developed under political-geographical influences.

7.1 Geography and international relations

States are the behaviour units in an international system consisting of states, their colonies and protectorates, and international organisations. The relationship between these units is of interest both to the political geographer and to the student of international relations. 'The differentiation of the space accessible to man appears to be the *raison d'être* of both geography and international relations.'[1] Variations in the nature of society and its economic activities form the bases of social and economic geography, and were there not likewise variations in political objectives, there would be no politics and no political geography. The difference between geography and international relations is one of perspective, and while both are concerned with the behaviour of units in the international system, the behaviour and its fairly immediate causes are the central subject-matter of international relations; the political geographer is primarily concerned with the *geographical* causes and effects of this behaviour.

Fewer problems of definition face the student of international relations, whose subject is virtually defined by its title, though the political geographer has difficulty in legitimising his interest in the field without reference to the central geographical aim of interpreting spatial variation and change.[2] Both subjects are experiencing controversy between traditionalists and the advocates of newer quantitative approaches, and acrimonious exchanges occur frequently in the literature of each ('Having read the criticisms of the traditionalists, I am convinced that they understand neither the simpler assertions nor the more sophisticated techniques employed by the advocates of newer methods'[3]). Recent advances in methodology in international relations have a considerable bearing on political geography, though they have been little explored despite the fact that economic geography, for example, gained so much from the application of techniques developed by economists.

Considerable overlaps of interest occur between the disciplines. Political scientists are interested in spatial variations in that they influence international behaviour, while political geographers are concerned with international behaviour because it may reflect or affect spatial patterns.

7.2 State power

Many political scientists cast state power as the motive force in the international system; according to Morgenthau, 'International politics, like all politics, is a struggle for power'.[4] Great controversy surrounds the definition of 'power', though there is some agreement that the power of one state should be seen in relation to the power of others, and that state power is reflected in an ability to obtain favourable results in both internal affairs and external relations. In the latter case, the power of the state as perceived by external decision-makers may be more influential than the actual power of the state.

Power is of interest to geographers both because of its effect on state behaviour and because the power of states is partly based on their geographical characteristics. In fact one of the standard, though seldom adopted, approaches to political geography is based on power analysis. When a state exerts its power it is attempting to change the international system in some way favourable to itself, and at the same time these efforts are likely to produce geographical change within the state, ranging from a small-scale redeployment of resources to a mobilisation for war. However, the deeper the investigation of state power, the more elusive the quarry becomes. It is not only relative to the power of other states, but also to situations; thus the power of the USA was sufficient to play a large part in the defeat of the Nazi war machine, but not sufficient to overcome the Vietnamese peasant guerilla.

Power analysis may begin by a division of power into its component groups. A variety of categories have been suggested, and the following is used for its simplicity.

1. *Morphological power*. In this category may be included the power which derives from the size, shape, location and topographical features of the state.
2. *Demographical power*. This aspect of power is affected not simply by the numerical strength of the population but also by its skills, health, structure, and more elusive characteristics such as morale and national character.
3. *Economic power*. Here we may include the commercial resources of the state, the efficiency with which they are utilised, the rate of technological diffusion, trading relationships, and the vulnerability of the state to severance from suppliers of imports or from export markets.
4. *Organisational power*. This will involve the quality of government and subordinate levels of administration, the stability of government, and the regard in which the government is held at home and abroad.
5. *Military power*. In this category will be included the number, type and quality of weapons and military personnel, their deployment, and the quality of current tactics and strategy.
6. *Power from external relationships*. This will involve all aspects of the international relations of the state, its membership of international organisations and alliances, the power and reliability of allies, and also its international prestige.

It might appear that, by calculating together the various positive aspects of state power, a figure might be produced which was a measure both of the power of a state and of its ranking in the international power spectrum. Several such attempts have been made, but with little success.

Firstly, variables which can be quantified are crucially affected by those which cannot; for example, it is a simple matter to add up the population or numbers of fighter aircraft which a state possesses, but so far impossible to gain an accurate measure of the morale, aptitudes or national character of the population or the deployment and effectiveness of the fighters in changing and unforeseen situations. Secondly, simple comparisons of different elements of state power are inadequate; one knows that the USA and the USSR produce roughly the same amounts of steel, but other factors to be considered in a valid comparison would include the vastly greater reserves of coal and iron ore possessed by the USSR and the threat of depletion of domestic resources to the USA, the fact that the Russians utilise very low grade ores which would be considered uneconomical in the USA, and the marginal social utility of much of the American steel production while Soviet steel is utilised in areas where it is of maximum assistance to the state's economy. Thirdly, the elements of power continually interact with one another and cannot be evaluated in isolation; for example, an efficient military machine may be compromised by incompetent government intervention, or a resource may be held in quantities far in excess of the demand for it, as with hydroelectric potential in Norway. Fourthly, the calculation of an index of state power would be impossible even if the individual elements of state power could each be measured, since a value for efficient government could not be equated with one for, say, coal production. Finally, Frankel has pointed out that the influence exerted in international affairs need not correspond to state power; in the late 1920s the USA could be ranked as the most powerful state, followed by Germany, the UK, France, the USSR, Italy and Japan, while France's influence in international affairs was far greater than that of the USA, which would on this count have been placed near the foot of this list.[5]

In one of the more elaborate attempts at power analysis, German considered twenty-six relevant variables, including plus factors for morale and minus factors for food deficit; the key to the calculations alone amounted to over a thousand words.[6] Even so, many important variables were omitted and much depended on subjective estimates, the rankings produced representing little more than an informed guess. A different approach was adopted by Fucks, who decided that the evidence suggested that

$$power = P^3 \sqrt{B}$$

where P represents production and B represents population.[7]

State power cannot be gauged by studying the relationship between just two variables, and it seems unlikely that a complete measure will ever be obtained. Rough estimates of state power can be derived from selected statistics, from studies of the success of state policies in international affairs and from subjective impressions, and after all, international politics is affected by perceptions of power more than by real state power. A few indicators of the power of selected states are included in table 7.1, though it must be emphasised that the power of a state is relative not only to that of others but also to situations; though Britain is a much greater power than Iceland, British policy suffered a defeat in the first 'cod war'.

Table 7.1.   Some indicators of state power

Ranking	State	Area (million sq. miles)	Population (millions)	Steel production (million metric tons)	Army (100 000s men)	ICBM and Polaris-type missiles
superpower	USA	3.53	203	131	14.3	1710 (1971 est.)
	USSR	8.65	246	133	20.0 (approx.)	1900 (1971 est.)
near-superpower	China	3.70	750 (approx.)	?	25.5 (approx.)	20? (1974 est.)
great powers	Japan	0.14	104	82	1.7	—
	UK	0.08	54	24	1.6	64
powers	Sweden	0.41	8.1	5	0.01	—
	Turkey	0.30	35	1.3	5.1	—
mini-powers	Andorra	0.0002	0.02	—	—	—
	Maldive Republic	0.0001	0.1	—	—	—

It is geographically pertinent to enquire into the relationship between the area of a state and its power, and the population of a state and its power. Because of the impossibility of calculating a realistic index of state power, this is not possible. It is, however, possible to select the single indicator which appears to be most expressive of state power, GNP, and to work out Spearman rank correlation coefficients of GNP (substituting for power) against area and population, using the formula

$$S = \frac{1 - 6\sum d^2}{n^3 - n}$$

where d is the difference in ranking for each state and n is the total number of cases. This was undertaken for 132 sovereign states for which data on area, population and GNP (1969, or nearest previous estimate) were available. If our assumptions are correct, then there is a remarkably close correlation between population size and state power, and a much weaker one between state area and state power. For GNP against area, the coefficient is 0.346; for GNP against population, the coefficient is 0.955; and for area against population, the coefficient is 0.879.[8]

At any time, international systems tend to have been dominated by their most powerful members, and periods of relative international stability have been correlated with the operation of a balance of power between these members, such as operated and was maintained between 1648 and 1914. During this period the distribution of power was multipolar and the system involved at least five and less than ten great power actors. The basic rules by which the system operated included a rough parity of power between the great powers; observance of European norms of sovereignty and diplomacy; that each power should attempt to increase its power, influence and territory; that alliances could be formed; and finally that states should be prepared to combine to prevent the system being dominated by any single power or alliance. Crucial to the operation of this system was the balancing power, prepared to restore equilibrium by lending its strength to a weaker power or alliance. This role was generally played by Britain, since the British, with international commercial interests, had strong reasons for desiring political stability. Kaplan has described five other ways in which power may be distributed within the international system, with the conditions which have prevailed since the 1939–45 war somewhat corresponding to the 'loose bipolar' model which is characterised by two leading states with blocs centred upon each and the presence of nuclear weapons and international organisations.[9]

The remainder of his models are more theoretical, and comprise the 'tight bipolar' system, in which there are no neutrals, all actors being integrated into one or other of two opposed power blocs; the 'universal actor' system, in which a global organisation is sufficiently powerful to outlaw war, and the remaining actors retain their identities and jockey for power within its framework; and the 'unit veto' system, in which every state has the capability to destroy every other. These models are geographical in that they describe different spatial distributions of power and different capabilities of transmitting power across space.

Kaplan has described different periods in history as being typified by the prevalence of a particular power system, each system being a complex of variables which include norms of international behaviour, and the effect on these standards of developments outside the system, and actors—the states, organisations and statesmen involved, their capabilities and the levels of information available to them.[10] A particular system will only prevail so long as a certain set of necessary conditions exists, and the replacement of one type of system by another will engender changes in the nature of international behaviour. This behaviour in the loose bipolar system is governed by different rules from that in the balance-of-power system; alliances become prolonged and of an ideological nature rather than concerned with short-term expediency, shifts in alliance are rare, and interbloc warfare is restrained by the nuclear threat.

In the near future, a tripolar power system is likely to emerge as China joins the ranks of the superpowers, while further ahead, a multipolar system involving the USA, USSR, China, Japan and Western Europe may appear. Each new power system will generate new rules of international behaviour, different from those of any previous power system.

Though not the very core of political geography, the study of state power provides ample scope for relevant research. There seem to be two main directions which such studies can take: firstly, the investigation of the geographical components of state power, where, for example, one might attempt to explore the implications for the USA of the depletion of domestic petroleum reserves and the consequences of dependence upon foreign sources of supply. The second direction of study concerns the effects upon landscape of the existence of a particular power system and of attempts to mobilise state power for particular political ends. It is difficult to imagine a state policy that is not in some way intended to enhance the power position of that state, but in many cases the political motive is paramount, as with the inter-war development of the German synthetics industry, which sub-stituted imports vulnerable to wartime blockade and was located in east-ern regions considered secure from Western aircraft.

7.3 International organisations

The fundamental actors in the international system are sovereign states, and the main motive force directing their behaviour is the pursuit of the 'national interest' of each as it is perceived by the decision-makers compos-ing the various state governments. Pursuit of this perception of the national interest leads states variously towards conflict, competition and cooperation. Cooperation may become institutionalised in an inter-national organisation of states, but such organisations are created and operated as vehicles for the furtherance of the interests of their member states, and no government will countenance a wholesale compromise of the perceived national interest for the good of the organisation, though the organisation itself may develop a dynamic and vested interests of its own.

International organisations can be classified according to the nature of the formal ties which hold them together, and also in relation to their func-tion. When the ties between the linked units are so strong that sovereignty passes from the units to a central government, one is dealing not with an in-ternational organisation but with a federation. In a confederation the member states retain their sovereignty, and therefore centrally made decisions are not binding upon the member states; direct contact between the population and the central agencies is absent in confederations, whose structures are designed for intergovernmental contact.

A league may lack the central organs of government and the permanent intent apparent in a confederation, and is an intermediate stage between a confederation and an alliance, which is a temporary political association, restricted in its sphere of operation. Dikshit quotes NATO as an example of an alliance, the British Commonwealth and the United Nations as examples of leagues, and the EEC as an example of a confederation.[11]

The latter example is an interesting one, questioning some basic ideas about the nature of international society, since membership of the EEC requires certain sacrifices of sovereignty necessary for the acceptance of common economic policies, the common negotiation of commercial agreements and eventual monetary union, while lip-service is paid to the goal of further political unification which began in 1970 with biennial consultations of Foreign Ministers. Since the EEC exercises sovereignty in certain limited fields, it appears to represent an intermediate stage between a confederation and a federation, though within the community there is considerable disagreement concerning rights of veto and acceptable degrees of political unification.

When classed according to function, international organisations fall under the following main headings.

1. *Global.* In formal terms, the United Nations is an association of states pledged to maintain and further the causes of international peace and security. The organisation has no sovereignty and no authorisation to intervene in the domestic affairs of states. In effect it provides a platform for political debate and propaganda, and a medium for informal contact between diplomats; it supports fourteen agencies which are mainly concerned with assisting economic development, human rights, world health, trade and the advancement of science.

The organisation has a membership of 124 states, not all of which are sovereign, since the USSR is also represented by Byelorussia and the Ukraine. The principal organs of the organisation are as follows.

(a) The General Assembly, in which each member state is represented and has one vote. The assembly meets annually or by special convocation, and contains six major committees and a number of lesser committees.
(b) The Security Council, which is in permanent session and has fifteen members, of which the USA, USSR, Britain, France and China are permanent members and may operate a right of veto. The Security Council is directly responsible for the maintenance of world peace, and may instigate armed intervention.
(c) The Economic and Social Council, responsible for implementing the economic and social functions of the organisation.
(d) The Trusteeship Council.
(e) The International Court of Justice.
(f) The Secretariat, consisting of the Secretary-General, the organisation's chief officer, and his staff.

On rare occasions the United Nations has resorted to armed intervention, attempting to prevent civil war in Cyprus and the Congo, but only once has the organisation initiated intervention in a great-power confrontation, during the Korean war. It is virtually debarred from this role by the power of veto in the Security Council. Resolutions made in the General Assembly are frequently flaunted and are not enforceable upon the greater powers, and therefore the organisation has failed in its more grandiose aims. It is probably most effective through the less spectacular activities of its various agencies, and as a medium for informal contacts between diplomats. There is little to suggest that governments are prepared to devolve substantial powers to an international organisation which they cannot control, and it is unlikely that the United Nations provides a stepping-stone to world government. This has led some political scientists to regard the strengthening of regional links as a more promising prologue to world unity. Russett writes, 'there is a long and honourable tradition . . . which regards regionalism as the proper basis for world order, an alternative both to fragmentation and to universalistic solutions'.[12] Though the formation of regional groupings may reduce the number of inter-state conflicts, there is no evidence to suggest a reduction in the intensity of conflict.

2. *Economic*. The post-war period has witnessed a proliferation of economic organisations whose formation has been largely influenced by the need for a pooling of markets by member states in order to create conditions favourable to large-scale production and specialisation in industry. There is considerable variation in the scope of economic organisations; the EEC, with its sovereign attributes, is the most comprehensive, while others such as CARIFTA provide members with a free trade area but have no separate legislature. The scope of EFTA, three members of which have merged with the EEC, was even more limited, and the removal of tariff barriers affected only selected goods, while tariffs on agricultural products remained.

3. *Defensive*. Defensive alliances have probably existed as long as there have been states to threaten one another, though modern defensive organisations reflect the crisis of the territorial state in a world dominated by two aggressive superpowers. The bipolarisation of the post-war world found expression in the accretion around the superpowers of defensive blocs, linked to them by ties of treaty, ideology or fear. On the one hand there are those formed to facilitate the US policy of containment, such as NATO, SEATO and CENTO, and on the other, the Russian response to this policy, expressed in the Warsaw Pact, combining the armed forces of the Russian satellites under Soviet hegemony.

4. *Political*. A number of organisations exist to further a particular political idea; in this category could be included the Arab League and the Organisation of African Unity, designed to develop greater common purpose between the member states and peoples.

Several other international organisations exist which do not fit easily into any of the above categories. Some are concerned with cooperation of a limited and specialised nature, such as the Danube Commission, involved with navigation on the river Danube, or the Colombo Plan, an organisation which attempts to promote technical assistance between the developed countries and a number of Asian states, while the British Commonwealth is an unusually amorphous organisation, surviving precariously in the face of few bases for common agreement and British membership of the EEC.

International organisations can be classified according to their function and the closeness of their political linkages. It is also possible to distinguish between the hegemonial relationship, in which a great power or superpower serves as a nucleus around which lesser powers cluster, either for protection against another major power or through fear of their protector, and on the other hand the relationship of more equal powers uniting on a cooperative basis.[13] Examples of the hegemonial form of relationship include the Organisation of American States, NATO, SEATO and CENTO, for which the USA forms the nucleus, and the Warsaw Pact and CMEA, formed under Russian hegemony. Organisations reflecting a more equal relationship include the EEC, the Arab League and CARIFTA.

Table 7.2. A framework for the classification of international organisations. Strength of political links increases to the right; asterisks denote hegemonial relationships.

Function	Alliance	League	Confederation
defence	NATO* SEATO* CENTO* Anzus Pact	Warsaw Pact*	
economic	Andean Group	CMEA* CARIFTA	EEC
political	Council of Europe	United Nations Arab League	EEC

Not all international organisations are organisations of states, and other forms include international religions (of which the Roman Catholic, with over 400 million members, is the most widespread; the Vatican has diplomatic relations with 67 states), international industrial corporations such as Unilever or Philips, the two competing international federations of trade unions, and international scientific, sporting and cultural societies.

7.4 The geographical significance of international organisations

The political geography of international organisations has been neglected, though highly significant studies could be made concerning the geographical factors underlying regions of political integration, the geographical and related inducements to membership of a particular organisation, the effects of membership on the geography of the states concerned and on the organisation as a whole, and the effect of the formation or broadening of the organisation on non-member states.

Case study

The United Kingdom gained membership of the EEC in January 1973; the inducements for EEC membership were numerous and complex, but probably of greatest importance was a recognition that Britain is primarily an industrial state operating in a highly competitive world environment and with a domestic market insufficiently large to provide the economies of scale necessary for competitive production in fields such as aviation and possibly automobiles and defence. Membership of the EEC was seen to provide Britain with a domestic market comparable in size, and almost comparable in standards of living, with that of the USA. During the last decade, British industry was considered highly competitive with its European counterparts, but improvements in efficiency within the EEC were reducing the British lead, adding urgency to the British application for membership.

Industrial expansion in Europe during the 1960s was much more dynamic than in Britain; in the period 1960–5, the British annual growth rate averaged 2.8 per cent, while during the same period, though that of Luxembourg averaged only 1.6 per cent, the growth rates of the remaining EEC members ranged between an average of 4.7 per cent for France and one of 6.5 per cent for Italy. Even though Britain stood outside the community and was faced with EEC import tariffs, there was a tendency for British trade with the EEC to increase while the Commonwealth connection weakened, as the statistics of table 7.3 show.

Table 7.3. UK imports and exports in £ million

	Imports (c.i.f.)			Exports (f.o.b.)		
	1958	1964	1967	1958	1964	1967
Commonwealth	1307	1800	1686	1254	1313	1261
EEC	533	941	1265	461	963	1041
EFTA	434	747	942	331	640	780

Consequently, the British government considered that a brighter future waited on EEC membership, despite the hardships the public would face through incurring high EEC food prices after decades during which cheap food had been a cornerstone of British policy.

It is too early to assess the geographical implications for Britain of EEC membership, though one may anticipate an intensification of the drift of industry to the south-east, with the southern container ports being particularly affected. The degree of the adverse effect upon the northern and western development areas will depend on the level of support which can be made available under EEC regional development strategies. In recent years the tendency towards industrial concentration in the south-east has been retarded through the government's power to refuse industrial development certificates, but as Jay points out,

Any firm refused an IDC in a congested area in Britain would be able to say: if we cannot have this where we want it, we shall build our new factory in Antwerp or Rotterdam. . . . As a result, the whole Development Area policy which rests much more on IDC control than on financial grants and loans, would be disrupted; and a new and powerful pressure would set in for industrial development to concentrate in the south-east of England, or Belgium and Holland.[14]

The prospects for British agriculture seem varied, though the Common Agricultural Policy was designed to protect inefficient European peasant farming rather than to suit British circumstances. If high grain and fodder prices persist in the EEC, they will cause a shift of emphasis in British farming away from meat and milk, and could cause the somewhat marginal production of grain on land which has supported efficient livestock production. In general one may expect the new conditions to benefit the already prosperous arable farming of southern and eastern England, while making the formerly subsidised, uneconomical but socially desirable hill farming of highland Britain even more marginal.[15]

The consequences of British membership on the EEC community as a whole will be diverse and complex, though perhaps the main effects will include firstly, the expansion of the market by a further 54 million consumers, to which may be added the 4.7 million Danish and 3 million Irish consumers; secondly, the industrial benefits resulting from the introduction of relatively advanced British technology; and thirdly, the political effects of replacing the bipolar power structure based on France and Germany with a more balanced three-way distribution of leadership.

British membership of the EEC will also rebound upon states outside the community, and Britain's Commonwealth trading partners will be particularly affected. In anticipation of Britain's joining the EEC, the Australian and New Zealand governments and producers began to explore new export outlets. This reinforced a tendency which already existed, with the share of Australian exports destined for Britain dropping from 54 per cent in 1938–9 to 17.4 per cent in 1965–6. Australian wool and minerals found a ready market in Japan, wheat in China, and meat in the USA. The New Zealand economy is in a rather more vulnerable position, though in 1965 Britain took 48 per cent of New Zealand exports as compared to 65 per cent in 1950. For Canada, the prospect is one of increasing the association with the USA while exploring Asian export outlets, despite the traditional Canadian policy of offsetting dependence on the USA with British links. The economies of some African states seem particularly vulnerable, and associate membership of the EEC provides inadequate protection.[16] There can be little doubt that British membership of the EEC will catalyse or intensify geopolitical changes of great significance.

Case study

Voluntary membership of an international organisation involves national sacrifices made in the expectation that they will be exceeded by ensuing advantages. The new association may in some cases produce serious disadvantages, as proven by the Romanian experience in the CMEA (Comecon).

The organisation was formed in 1949, but until 1956 its activities were largely limited to the registration of bilateral agreements between members. After 1956, however, attempts were made to harmonise supply and demand within the Soviet bloc and to develop patterns of regional specialisation. Before the 1939–45 war, Romania had suffered a virtually colonial existence as a supplier of primary products to more developed states, and the post-war communist regime was anxious to bury this relationship by industrialising the country.

Discord within CMEA became apparent in the mid-1950s as the Romanians reacted against bloc pressures that they should serve as suppliers of primary products—petroleum, cement, timber and agricultural produce—to the more industrialised members. The Romanian leaders articulated the dissent of the less-developed CMEA members in arguing that the simpler standard industrial products such as tractors and trucks should be made by them as a stimulus to industrialisation and diversification away from primary production. The counter-attack was led by Czech economists, accusing the Romanians of harbouring autarchic tendencies, and arguing that regional specialisation was the best way to remove inequalities in development and that the Marxist principle that production of producer goods should exceed other sectors of production was applicable only to the bloc as a whole and need not apply to individual members.

In 1966 Romania established foreign trade links outside the provisions of CMEA, setting up direct links with foreign buyers and joint production schemes with western companies; by this time Romanian trade within CMEA had dropped by 20 per cent to 60 per cent of her total.[17]

7.5 International trade

If international trade simply involved the exchange of commodities between regions of relative surplus and deficit, and were not subject to political restrictions or incentives, tariffs or quotas, or unequal trading relationships, then the political geographer would have little to add to the analyses of the economic geographer. In fact the pattern of world trade is conditioned by political factors of affinity and animosity to a very considerable degree. As Alker and Puchala state,

Economic logic . . . accounts in large part for the directions and intensities of international trade. But such factors as geographic proximity; ethnic, cultural or linguistic similarity; traditional affinities; and formal political linkage and commitment also help to determine trade flows.[18]

Therefore one may expect higher-than-normal levels of trade to be encountered between states which are politically sympathetic, with the reverse in the case of hostile states. Extreme political hostility may find expression in terms of trade embargo or economic warfare; in 1966, the United Nations Security Council called on United Nations members to break off economic relations with Rhodesia, while Britain was authorised to enforce an oil embargo, causing Rhodesian exporters to explore trade outlets through South Africa and Moçambique where the embargo was not upheld. Hostility between Mali and Senegal following the collapse of their union led to the closure of the Mali rail link to the Senegalese port of Dakar, and Mali was obliged to redirect its overseas trade through Upper Volta and Ivory Coast.

The extent to which political factors may condition trade has been demonstrated by the trading patterns of the USSR. Foreign trade is organised as a state monopoly, and is governed by import and export licences issued in accordance with an annual state plan. During the 1960s trade with other communist bloc countries accounted for 75 per cent of Russian imports, a level explained only by political rather than economic complementarity. Political rather than economic considerations influenced Russian trade with non-bloc members; for instance, during the entente with Egypt large quantities of Egyptian cotton were imported, despite the abundant Russian domestic cotton production. In order to woo and influence post-revolutionary Cuba, itself affected by a crippling USA trade embargo, Russia imported Cuban exports excluded from western markets, at such a level that Russian trade with Cuba was greater than her trade with the rest of the western hemisphere combined. As a reflection of the developing dispute with China, Sino-Soviet trade dropped by two-thirds between 1959 and 1962.[19]

A further political dimension to Russian trade is added by the unequal nature of exchanges formerly carried out between Russia and its satellites. Cliff claims that in 1958, for example, tractors were being sold to the satellites at prices 51 per cent higher than those charged to non-members of the bloc, while the price for Russian cotton goods was three times that charged outside the bloc. At the same time, the seventeen commodities for which prices are available were being bought by Russia from the satellites at prices 20 per cent lower than those charged to other buyers.[20]

State interference with the economic logic of trade is also effective through imposed tariffs and quotas (discussed fully in part 6). The imposition of tariff and quota restrictions against foreign imports has been a favourite form of state protection for otherwise uncompetitive domestic industries, and on the broad scale it has been the developing world that has suffered. The textile industry, as a large employer of semi-skilled labour, has been adopted as the first stage in industrialisation by a number of underdeveloped states. A number of advanced manufacturing states, notably the USA and Britain, have resorted to import restrictions in order to protect domestic textile industries, while a more rational approach to the problem might involve a retraining of textile workers in activities more appropriate to advanced technological economies. In 1960 the USA introduced quota restrictions on cotton textile imports which have been estimated to have cost the underdeveloped producers $850 million per annum in sales lost.[21]

Political factors also affect the choice and utilisation of trading routes. Hostility between Israel and the Arab states has interrupted the development of natural trading routes in the middle east; the Arab–Israeli war of 1967 was partly precipitated by the Egyptian ban on Israeli vessels' using Egyptian territorial waters or the Suez canal, followed by an Egyptian blockade of the Strait of Tiran cutting access to the Israeli port of Eilat. Thereafter Egyptian and Israeli forces confronted each other across the Suez Canal, which remained closed since the Israeli advance, blocked by sunken shipping. While world shipping was obliged to circumnavigate Africa via the Cape of Good Hope route, there is evidence to suggest that some of the oil from the Persian Gulf states was shipped to Eilat and piped across Israeli territory to the Mediterranean port of Ashkelon for transshipment to Europe.[22] The Panama Canal was also a source of political contention, and the Panamanian government has been involved in an attempt to regain Panamanian sovereignty over the canal and its zone, compromised by the unequal Panama Canal Treaty of 1903 which accorded special rights to the USA. Tensions involving the world's two major international canals were reduced early in 1974, with the implementation of the ceasefire agreement of the 1973 Egyptian–Israeli war, involving the clearance and reopening of the Suez Canal to international and Israeli shipping in return for Israeli military withdrawals, and the USA's surrender of its claim to sovereignty over the Panama Canal.

The international trade in oil provides another example of the political factor in world trade. In 1948 Venezuela, then the leading oil-exporting state, partially nationalised its oil concerns, dividing profits between the extracting companies and the government. As a result, posted prices for oil were introduced, based on the selling price for oil in the USA, and were accepted by most of the oil-producing states. In 1957 the US government, partly motivated by strategical considerations arising from the possible dependence upon foreign oil producers, imposed quotas on oil imports. The effect of this was a fall in the price of oil, estimated to have cost the oil-exporting states $1.5 billion per annum.[23]

In 1960 five leading oil-exporting states formed the Organisation of Petroleum Exporting Countries, with the aim of increasing the world price for oil, and OPEC membership now includes the producers of half the world's oil. OPEC pressure on the oil companies increased throughout the last decade, and demands for higher prices and better shares in petroleum profits were joined by demands for greater participation in the running of the industry. Under Libyan leadership the oil-producing states are discovering the political leverage which possession of oil and control of its exploitation and distribution can give, at a time when there is a growing thirst for oil in Europe while US domestic oil reserves are faced with depletion. A decade ago the destinies of most oil-exporting states were in the hands of American oil companies, but in the foreseeable future the destiny of the USA may be controlled by the governments of the oil-exporting states to a considerable degree.

If one is to isolate the political factor in world trading patterns, an answer must be found to the insoluble question of existence—of what trading patterns would exist if there were no political influences. Though this is impossible, transaction flow analysis related to the form described in part 5 may provide some valuable clues. In 1960 Savage and Deutsch studied deviations from a null model as indications of non-random trading partnerships.[24] The null model derived the expected trade between states; for example, if the USA were the destination of 20 per cent of world trade, it would be expected that each trading state would send 20 per cent of its exports to the USA. Then deviations from the null model were measured in terms of a relative acceptance coefficient

$$RA_{ij} = \frac{T_{ij} - \hat{T}_{ij}}{\hat{T}_{ij}}$$

where RA_{ij} is the relative acceptance coefficient for countries i and j, describing the extent to which the acceptance by j of the exports of i exceeds the expectations of the null model, T_{ij} is the actual trade from country i to country j, and $\hat{T}_{ij}$ is the trade from country i to country j predicted by the null model. A zero RA value would indicate actual levels of trade equal to those predicted by the null model, a value of -1.00 that there was no trade between i and j, and a value of 2.00 that actual trade was double the expected level.

Certain refinements to the model enabled Alker and Puchala to study trading patterns between and within international groupings of states in the North Atlantic area between 1928 and 1963.[25] A range of notable features emerged, including the surprising fact that multiple economic partnership between the six original EEC member states was higher during the pre-EEC Marshall Plan era, 1948–51, than ever before or during the early years of the EEC, with 1948 as the peak of economic 'Europeanism'. Clear indications emerged that directions and intensities of trading were related to political developments. Alker and Puchala decided that the economic separation of Germany from Western Europe in 1928 symbolised a more general social, cultural and political chasm, that 'The patterns of relative economic acceptance remarkably reflect the picture of political disunity in the North Atlantic Area during the interwar period', and that '. . . changes in trading relationships between 1928 and 1951 appear to reflect major European political realignment brought about by the conclusion of World War II and subsequent American foreign policy'.[26]

A final example of the intervention of political phenomena in international economic transactions is the pattern of US ore, metal and scrap imports. As well as demonstrating the relative non-acceptability of communist sources of imports, according to Prestwich, these figures clearly demonstrate the shift in purchasing from politically 'unreliable' developing producers to 'reliable' developed producers.[27]

Table 7.4. US imports of ores, metals and scrap from
major world blocs: percentage averages for 1955–6
(a) and 1966–7 (b)

	total		ores		metals		scrap	
	(a)	(b)	(a)	(b)	(a)	(b)	(a)	(b)
advanced	55.3	71.6	37.0	46.1	62.5	79.5	83.0	78.2
developing	44.5	27.8	63.0	53.1	37.5	19.8	16.9	20.4
communist	0.2	0.6	0.0	0.8	0.0	0.7	0.1	1.4

Economic geographers have tended to explain international trading patterns by reference to distributions of areas of supply and demand and spatial variations in material assembly, production and distribution costs, and
have frequently underestimated the significance of political factors. The
purpose of this section has been to highlight the importance of political intervention in trading patterns and to demonstrate that international trade
can be an important area of political-geographical study.

7.6 Imperialism

Different political regions may form an association through joint membership of an international organisation. The alternative form of association
of political regions is through the operation of an imperial system. The
basic political difference between the two forms is that international
organisations have a membership of sovereign states, while the imperial
system is dominated by its only sovereign member. The distinction, however, is not as clear-cut as it may appear, and a transition exists from the international association of equals, such as the EEC, through hegemonial
associations formed by mutual consent, such as NATO, to hegemonial associations in which the coercion of lesser members is a fundamental characteristic, as with the Warsaw Pact, and to imperial associations.

Since imperialism has been such an important political and geographical phenomenon, it is surprising that theories about imperialism are
so sparse; the topic may have been bypassed by academics because of its
emotive nature, though this point of view is invalidated by the very reality
of imperialism.[28] The most influential analysis was that undertaken by
Lenin, many of whose conclusions have been accepted by non-Marxists.
Writing in 1916, Lenin sought to interpret the world war as a clash of imperial interests and to explain the persistence of the capitalist system, the obi-
tuary of which had already been written by Marx. Drawing upon the
earlier writers J. A. Hobson and R. Hilferding, Lenin deduced that the
free-competition phase of capitalism had passed into one of finance capital, with power transferred from industrialists to the large banking and finance interests. Colonies provided an excellent outlet for finance-capital
investment, constituting not only captive markets but also sources of
cheap raw materials. He predicted that the struggle for control of colonies
would lead to increasing great-power rivalry which would destroy the stability of the capitalist bloc. Meanwhile, the vast profits derived from impe-

rialism permitted the payment of higher wages to workers in the imperial homelands, so reducing their revolutionary fervour, while the exploitation of native labour in the colonies created a new revolutionary class, and the class struggle became internationalised.[29] Lenin provides an explanation for the dynamic of late nineteenth and early twentieth-century imperialism, though his analysis does not explain the various earlier forms of imperialism, nor the imperialism resulting from the acquisition of imperial military and naval bases for the furtherance of the geopolitical policies of the metropolitan country.

Several geographically relevant attempts have been made to classify forms of imperialism. S. H. Frankel has made a distinction between the primary colonisation, which involves the occupation of lands and domination of the indigenous population, and secondary colonisation, involving the occupation of virtually uninhabited territory.[30] Cohen's suggestions amount roughly to using 'imperialism' to describe the former process and 'colonialism' to describe the latter.[31] However, in common usage 'imperialism' and 'colonialism' are interchangeable terms, and it would be more apt to use the term 'colonisation' to describe the extension of state control into areas devoid of indigenous peoples.

In spatial terms, a fundamental distinction can be made between the expansion of the state into contiguous territory and control of non-adjacent territory, usually in the form of an overseas empire. Perhaps then the terms 'peripheral' and 'remote' imperialism and colonisation would be appropriate, with the British Empire in India an example of remote imperialism, the expansion of Tsarist Russia into Central Asia an example of peripheral imperialism, British control of the Falkland Islands an example of remote colonisation, and Australian penetration and absorption of the outback an example of peripheral colonisation.

Where the territory concerned is peripheral, its assimilation by the expanding state is likely to be more permanent, and (disregarding intervention by other states) the tendency has been for adjacent territory to become integrated into the state and for remote possessions to succeed in severing themselves from the mother country. Peripheral expansion is normally accompanied by attempts to assimilate the acquired territory into the state ecumene, and Kristof has described the frontier as an area of outer orientations and centripetal tendencies whose political loyalties the state must attempt to monopolise.[32]

The problem of noncontiguity and political integration was investigated by Merritt, using examples of fragmented states and exclaves, though his enquiries are relevant to the question of the assimilation of noncontiguous colonial and imperial possessions. He considered that the centrifugal effect within politics of noncontiguity is stronger than that of distance alone; 'It is somewhat more likely that two noncontiguous portions of a polity will drift apart than that a pair of communities with territorial continuity will do so, even though the actual distances involved may be the same'.[33]

Problems concerning the noncontiguity of imperial possessions with the imperial power were investigated by Tiwari, who developed the concept of administrative distance.[34] Distance was partly a function of time, and therefore became reduced during the imperial period from a matter of months to a matter of hours as a result of technological improvements in transport and communications. Though the European powers usually installed makeshift administrations in their possessions, decision-making authority remained in the mother country. Distance was not expressed solely as a function of time; there was also a social distance separating the European decision-makers from their colonial decision-implementers, and a more extreme social distance between the colonial administrators and the African masses. The distance between the reaction to decisions and the decision-makers was affected by bureaucratic processes, reaction being heavily filtered so that only favourable components were allowed to proceed officially to Europe.

The result of the operation of administrative distance was partially to insulate the European decision-makers from the areas upon which their decisions were effective. Taking the example of land ownership, the Europeans often assumed that, as in Europe, all vacant land was the property of the government; decisions regarding such land were made effective by the decision-implementing authorities in Africa, who were replaceable in their jobs and unlikely to oppose decisions, and as a result many African tribes were deprived of access to forest and grazing lands.

Political-geographical analysis of imperialism involves the study of the spatial impact of an imperial system on the empire as a whole and on the various subsystems within it. Though more altruistic motives may be indirectly involved, the basic function of an imperialist policy is the creation of a system in which the imperial state has its power enhanced through the practice of an unequal relationship with its colonies. Imperial powers therefore draw upon their colonies in order to increase the power they can bring to bear in relationships with one another and with other great powers. In order to maximise its advantages, the imperial power must bind its colonies to itself through various forms of dependency while avoiding undue dependence upon them. This dependency is achieved through mercantilism, involving the monopoly of the external trade of the colonies, the fostering of their trading dependence upon the imperial power, and the discouragement of their production of goods produced by the imperial power.[35] The effect of a policy of mercantilism is to cast the colonies in the role of producers of primary products and purchasers of the manufactured goods of the imperial power. This is unfortunate for the colonies, since the general tendency has been for the price of primary products to rise at a much slower rate than the prices of manufactured goods.

Though the basic economic and political motives have been the same, variations in the detail of colonialism have left their mark on the landscape. De Blij has drawn attention to the differing perceptions of colonies held by imperial powers. British imperialism aimed to reduce the impact of empire upon indigenous societies through a policy of indirect rule which limited the pace of change and in many cases preserved native power structures as agencies of the empire. Though the British were pledged to eventual withdrawal, the surge for independence frequently overtook their plans, while difficulties in the allocation of power resulted in areas where white settlers formed a considerable portion of the colonial population. The Belgian attitude was one of paternalism aimed at the control of territory for colonial purposes rather than the organisation of territory according to its particular characteristics. French imperialist policy was based on the concept of assimilation which relied upon the creation of an educated indigenous elite immersed in French culture and values. Until the events of May 1974, the Portuguese had remained oblivious to the 'wind of change' in Africa, and clung tenaciously, if precariously, to 'an imperial colonial policy which is reminiscent of another century'.[36]

One can also identify differences in imperial attitudes concerning the political relationship of the imperial possessions to the metropolitan country, and to the desirability of the formation or retention of enlarged or large independent units. The British never considered their colonies as an integral part of the British state, though until the adoption of the de Gaulle constitution of 1958, French overseas territories were assumed to be an indivisible part of France. In 1951 the Portuguese changed the status of their overseas possessions from that of 'colonies' to 'overseas territories', and in 1961 all Africans in these territories were given full Portuguese citizenship. The French, according to Wallerstein, were usually opposed to larger groupings because their leading advocates were also the most vociferous supporters of independence, and the French were much less prepared than the British to accept the legitimacy of the goal of independence.[37] As independence in Africa became an imminent reality, the British imperial policy of 'divide and rule' became redirected into a policy favourable to enlarged independent units, since it was considered that the larger entities showed a better potential for stability and economic development. Belgian policy in the Congo, following the belated acceptance of the inevitability of independence, was to maintain the geographical integrity of the Congo in order to retain a strong economic unit in which they desired continued involvement. However, as development in the Congo after independence threatened Belgian interests, the Belgian attitude became one of connivance with separatist elements.

7.7 The aftermath of imperialism

Two factors have dominated international relations since the 1939–45 war: the emergence of a bipolar power system, and the retreat of West European imperialism in the face of colonial nationalist movements. A useful systems-based framework for the analysis of imperial disintegration has been provided by Merritt.[38] Each imperial system is seen to be composed of a dominant subsystem, the imperial power, and dependent subsystems, the colonies. Under mercantilism, the objective of the imperial power is to monopolise the external ties of its colonies. Policy decisions pass from the imperial power while trade, communications and attention flow between the imperial power and its colonies; at the same time the loyalties and identifications of the colonies are fostered and monopolised. The dominant power seeks to ensure that contacts between its colonies, and between them and other colonies or other dominant subsystems, are minimised.

The imperial system becomes unstable when the colonies succeed in forging commercial and psychological connections with powers outside the system. If this occurs, the disintegration of the system may be outright and result in the formation of new international groupings or in the appearance of a series of unaligned units. Alternatively, some links between the imperial power and its colonies may be retained. The attitudes to loss of empire have varied; the British prepared some of their African possessions for independence by fostering the development of parliamentary systems of government, though in the former Belgian Congo the changeover was traumatic. The emergent state inherited an administrative system of areas which was at variance with ethnic patterns, while the imperial power intrigued with secessionists in the copper-rich Katanga province; the outcome was civil war and armed intervention by the United Nations.

Unless endowed with exceptional mineral wealth, the former colony is likely to begin its sovereign existence in a condition of extreme economic backwardness and vulnerability. With an economy which has been developed in relation to the requirements of the imperial power, the new state will be dependent on the production of a limited range of primary products. The markets for these products lie in the developed countries, and with a few notable exceptions supply has exceeded demand. Politically the state may seek to identify with other former colonies, but in reality it is obliged to compete with these other underdeveloped primary producers for markets in the developed world. In the resultant economic struggle there is a competitive lowering of prices which minimises profit margins, and when profit margins are very low the primary producers may attempt to increase production, so flooding the world market and causing prices to drop even further.

Two-thirds of Ghana's exports are cocoa. Between 1953 and 1961, cocoa exports increased by 71 per cent, but the revenue rose by only 23 per cent. In the same period European goods shipped to West Africa went up 25 per cent in cost. So a piece of machinery that cost Ghana the equivalent of 10 tons of cocoa in 1953 cost 25 tons of cocoa in 1961.[39]

At the same time, the industrialisation of the new state, necessary to reduce its economic dependence upon the export of a limited range of primary products, is frequently retarded through tariff barriers and quota restrictions erected to protect domestic industries within the developed states.

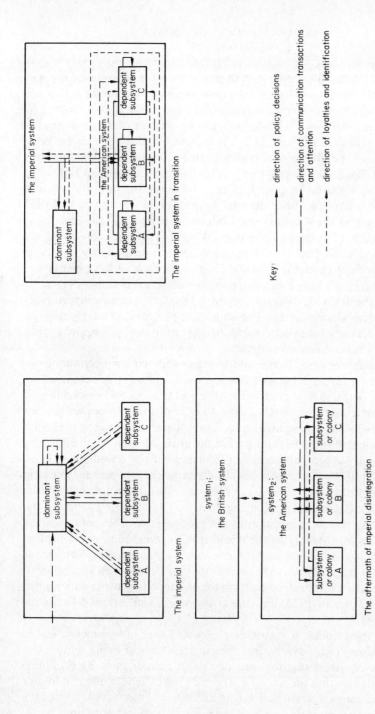

Key:

— direction of policy decisions

— — — direction of communication transactions and attention

– – – – direction of loyalties and identification

The imperial system

system₁: the British system

system₂: the American system

The imperial system in transition

The aftermath of imperial disintegration

Figure 7.1.   The disintegration of an imperial system, as described by Merritt (reproduced from ref. 38)

Unless a politically provocative programme of nationalisation is undertaken, plantation and mine ownership in the post-independence era will remain with companies based in the metropolitan world and the benefits derived from plantations may amount to no more than the wages paid to the plantation workers. Sri Lanka provides an extreme example, where exploitation of plantation workers by the foreign-based companies has been tolerated since the labour in the tea plantations is largely supplied by members of the Tamil minority, whose welfare has been a matter of little concern to the Sinhalese majority. The nationalisation of foreign-based companies is likely to be countered by economic warfare or political intrigue such as the Cubans and Chileans experienced following their nationalisation of US-based companies. Where the resource concerned is a scarce and valuable one, the values of nationalisation are likely to exceed any possible repercussions; in 1967 the nationalisation with compensation of Union Minière which controlled copper production in Congo Kinshasa prevented the drain of 50 per cent of the state's GNP to foreign investors. If the primary producing states are to obtain fair treatment in world markets, it will be necessary for them to band together to control prices and supply through organisations such as OPEC.

In the inter-war period, commodity prices suffered from economic depression in the developed world. The boom in commodity prices caused by the Korean war was tempered by the effects of the pre-1945 stockpiling of strategic materials and metals in the USA, and prices thereafter drifted steadily downwards, being on average about 10 per cent lower in 1962 than in 1952, though during the same period the prices of manufactures rose by more than 20 per cent, and between 1956 and 1973 by about 40 per cent. However, in 1971 an upsurge in commodity prices began, perhaps marking a long-term rather than a short-run phenomenon and coinciding with the signing of the Teheran–Tripoli oil agreement. The concerted action of the oil producers was an inspiration to the producers of other commodities, and other factors underlying the recent rises in commodity prices include the exhaustion or higher cost of non-renewable resources—which for example has probably caused a shift from petroleum-based synthetics to natural fibres—the industrial boom in the developed countries which gathered momentum in 1972, and the rising worldwide demand for foodstuffs.[40]

Within the colonies it was widely expected that independence would bring freedom from poverty, but rises in standards of living require not only more equitable distributions of wealth accompanied by economic growth, but also that the rate of economic growth should outstrip that of population increase. Unfortunately the former colonies have inherited the means to reduce mortality without the means to support or to limit populations which are generally tending to grow more rapidly than economic expansion.

Almost all the states that have gained independence during the post-war retreat of European colonialism have been prey to a series of vicious-circle effects. It might be expected that many problems would have been offset by foreign aid and special trading arrangements, but in most cases this has not been the case. When allowance is made for inflation, the amount of aid given by the richer to the poorer countries has dropped steadily through-out the last decade. In 1948 US foreign aid amounted to 2.79 per cent of the state's GNP, in 1960 to 0.5 per cent, and in 1970 only 0.3 per cent, while be-tween 1965 and 1969 British aid to Commonwealth countries rose from £156 million only to £157 million. More than half of the aid received by underdeveloped countries is immediately paid back to developed countries in the repayment of loans. Further, foreign aid is not distributed on an equitable basis to areas where it will be of the greatest value.

We can see the types of countries that the US has tended to favour—reactionary or military regimes whose principal virtues have been either militant anti-Communism or a location next to the Communist bloc. In 1966-7, 25 per cent of our aid went to South Vietnam.[41]

The figures published showing the amounts of aid given tend to disguise the fact that considerable proportions are in the form of weaponry which is of debatable value to the populations of the recipient countries; though the value of military aid is frequently classified, between 1953 and 1965, of US aid to Taiwan and to South Korea, two of the largest recipients, 65 per cent and 39 per cent respectively was of a military nature.[42] Foreign aid is seldom given without the expectation of specific political or economic favours; in 1967 the USA offered a loan of $25 million provided that the Peruvian government purchased inferior American fighter aircraft, with-drew their demands for shares in the profits of a U.S.-owned petroleum company and allowed American fishing vessels access to Peruvian terri-torial waters.[43]

At the United Nations Conference on Trade and Development held in 1964 the underdeveloped states appealed unanimously, but with little suc-cess, for 'trade not aid', in particular a lowering of tariff and quota barriers operating against their exports. In recent years, former colonies have ex-perienced an erosion of such trading advantages as they had with their col-onial overlords, while British protection of domestic agriculture against Commonwealth producers began two decades ago. Several of the leading former imperial powers have united in the EEC and there has been a strong tendency for trade between developed countries to grow at the expense of trade between the developed and underdeveloped worlds. Between 1960 and 1970 the proportion of British imports coming from the Common-wealth dropped from 38 per cent to 24 per cent. In 1963 the Yaoundé agreement was concluded between the EEC and eighteen African countries, abolishing all EEC tariffs against unprocessed coconuts, coffee, pepper, pineapples and tea. Though the agreement might facilitate trade in the short term, in fact it serves as an inducement to the African countries to remain as primary producers, dependent on fluctuations in world prices, controlled by foreign monopolies and subject to low growth rates. Yet since the underdeveloped countries tend to produce similar commodities and share similar shortages of capital, a solution is not to be found in the intensification of trading within the underdeveloped world, and in fact between 1965 and 1969 exports between Commonwealth countries dropped from 31 per cent of all exports to 23 per cent.

On the broad scale, imperialism and its aftermath may be seen sequentially in terms of the creation, through processes of European exploration, commercialism, colonialism and imperialism, of a single worldwide closed system to replace a series of regional systems which were partly closed, each located within an environment with which interaction and connection was slight. The next stage involved the establishment of several imperial systems, each consisting of a dominant and several dependent subsystems, and the latest stage is the retreat of imperialism as colonies have become sovereign states. The reality of these changes has involved the precipitation of colonial peoples into a world composed of competing sovereign states and the imposition or adoption of a form of political and territorial organisation developed elsewhere and in different sociological and historical circumstances.

The state was a product of European evolution, a response to an environment to which it was well-adapted, but its imposition upon tribal societies and village and nomadic communities has produced many incompatibilities. Political-geographical investigation of imperialism, as well as being concerned with spatial variation in the nature of imperialism, may involve the consideration of the human and geographical responses firstly to the imposition and operation of an imperial system, and secondly to its removal.

The Tuareg of Mali provide an example of a culture which has found its post-imperial existence to be at least as difficult as its imperial one. Bad relations with the Mali government began in 1963 when the government attempted to impose a poll tax on the Tuareg herds, and this triggered off a three-year guerilla war, the Tuareg refusing to pay the tax since they were unable to perceive what they were receiving from the government in return. Further, the hardening of boundaries between the former colonies of south-Saharan Africa closed off many of the established Tuareg grazing grounds. The independent nomadic tradition of the Tuareg prevents many from accepting the menial urban employment available, while according to their cultural values money has no intrinsic worth except as a means of

---

Figure 7.2.   Aid and export prices. (a) Net aid as a percentage of GNP, 1960 and 1970. (b) Total aid at current prices (US $ million), 1960 and 1970. See ref. 44. Statistics were not provided for Russian economic aid, but Korner lists Russian economic aid totalling US $69 million for 1960, rising to US $244 million in 1967. (c) World export prices. Prices for primary products and manufactures are compared to a price of 100 for each in 1962. See ref. 40.

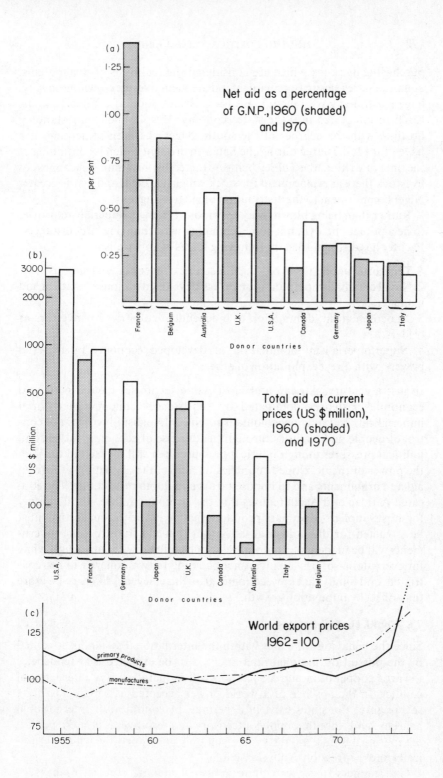

(a) Net aid as a percentage of G.N.P., 1960 (shaded) and 1970

per cent

Donor countries

(b) Total aid at current prices (US $ million), 1960 (shaded) and 1970

US $ million

Donor countries

(c) World export prices 1962 = 100

primary products

manufactures

purchasing livestock which are considered the real basis of wealth. This, and the Tuareg desire to remain an independent livestock-owning society, have frustrated government plans for their adoption of commercial pastoralism integrated into the state economy. Despite their long-standing hostility with the negroes of the south, Niger has been something of a haven for Mali Tuareg during the Saharan drought which is continuing at the time of writing, the Tuareg being attracted by the relative cheapness of livestock there as replacement for stock which has died, and by the greater Niger commitment to the distribution of aid to refugees.[45]

Rather than being blown away by winds of change, imperialism proved to be a potent and dynamic force, changing with changing circumstances. Pachter has distinguished the following forms of imperialism.

1. Territorial imperialism: old-fashioned rule over conquered nations.
2. Naval colonialism: exploitation of less-developed nations by settlers and managers.
3. Neocolonialism: domination of independent countries by investors or traders.
4. Superimperialism: domination of developed economy by imperial powers, with direct exploitation of others.[46]

In just a century, African and most Asian territories have experienced economic existences dominated by subsistence economies, territorial imperialism, and now neocolonialism. Neocolonialism involves the control of people and territory through the exercise of economic rather than political pressure, though political pressures can still be exerted through the power of the developed countries to control the allocation of foreign aid and armaments and to impose tariffs and quota restrictions. The educated African and Asian realises that the economic future is still gloomy for most suppliers of primary products, that investment from abroad must be attracted for the industrialisation but that aid from foreign governments will be inadequate and will seldom be offered without strings, while for every dollar of private investment coming in two dollars will be repatriated, and finally that any economic growth achieved is likely to be more than offset by population growth.

7.8 Conflict between states

Since the behaviour of states within the international system is governed by the pursuit of 'national interest', it is to be expected that tendencies towards cooperation and association will be paralleled by international conflict. In the absence of a world power accepted as superior to state sovereignty, the states exist in a permanent condition of international anarchy, and since the supply of territory and resources is limited, pursuit of separate national interests can result only in competition which periodically finds expression in physical conflict.[47]

Geographers have been quite active in making studies of the geo-

graphical causes of warfare and of post-war recovery, though the geography of warfare itself (as opposed to military geography, which has
consisted largely of supplying basic geographical information of value to
soldiers) has been largely neglected. They have also been reticent where the
geography of armaments industries is concerned. There are restrictions on
data involving state security, but again a certain coyness towards emotive
issues is apparent, which is regrettable since warfare is one of the most important agents of landscape change, and armaments one of the leading industries.

The contemporary geography of Vietnam is the geography of a quarter
of a century of almost uninterrupted warfare, and the ecological problems
alone present a topic of major interest. At the beginning of the 1970s the
destruction of vegetation through the spraying of defoliants and bombing
was reducing the forest of Vietnam at the rate of 1000 acres per day, and
now the commercially valuable forest reserves have been reduced by one-
third and agricultural land by one-tenth. In 1974 American scientists estimated that the ecological effects of spraying 6 million acres of South Vietnam with a million pounds of chemical agents between 1961 and 1971 will
last for at least a century. The recolonisation of the battered landscapes is
by tenacious weeds, and reversion to the forest climax will be an extremely
slow process; the country is pitted by an estimated ten million bomb cra-
ters which disrupt natural and man-made drainage systems and provide
ponds in which mosquitoes can breed. Numerous less important ecological effects have resulted; for example, an explosion in the tiger population
of the mountainous areas has been caused by the general availability of
human corpses.

Roughly 7 per cent of the world GNP is spent on the production of armaments, a sum equal to the combined incomes of all the population of Latin
America, southern Asia and the near east.[48] It has been estimated that arms
expenditure amounts to one-half of gross capital formation throughout
the world,[49] while the military–industrial complex creates one job in nine in
the USA, involves 100 000 companies and creates around one-tenth of
GNP.[50] In 1972 France, the third largest supplier of armaments, sold weapons to the value of £500 million, equivalent to 8 per cent of the total value
of French exports. Using constant 1968 prices, it can be estimated that between 1963 and 1973 US arms sales to the developing world increased in
value by 260 per cent and Soviet arms sales by 500 per cent, the respective
1973 values being 775 million and 1000 million 1968 dollars (see figure
7.3).[51]

The causes of international instability may change, but there is little to
suggest an overall reduction in tension. Kristoff has suggested that boundary disputes as a major cause of conflict have been replaced by struggles at
the frontiers of ideological worlds.[52] One of the main themes in contemporary geopolitics concerns superpower competition for the allegiance of
intervening unaligned states, a probing of pressure points within respective

spheres of influence, with a concentration of effort in certain geostrategic shatter zones such as the middle east and south-east Asia.* Ideological issues apart, however, there is no shortage of narrower territorial disputes involving disputed rights of ownership of, access to, and exploitation of land and marine areas.

The instability of patterns of territorial control has been highlighted by Joos, who estimates that between 1815 and 1965, within Europe alone, no less than twenty-seven sovereign states were born, twenty-three disappeared, while five states 'died' and subsequently reappeared. Over the past 150 years, a European state has appeared or has disappeared on average once every three years, while there have been at least sixty-seven boundary changes since 1815, approximately one every twenty-seven months.[53] Excluding the complicated case-histories of Germany and Italy, of the twelve European states which have existed without interruption since 1815, only three have not undergone frontier changes: Switzerland, Portugal and Spain. In case it should be thought that these states represent a residue of relative stability, it should be noted that Switzerland is currently faced by a strong secessionist movement by the Bélier ('mountain goats') demanding self-government for the Jura region, that the territorial integrity of Spain was preserved only by foreign intervention in the Spanish civil war of 1936–9, that contemporary Spain is pressing a territorial claim on Gibraltar and is threatened by a number of secessionist movements, particularly from the Basques and Catalans, and that democratic processes in Portugal (which has a boundary dispute with Spain) were suspended for a number of years. The position at the time of writing is extremely unstable.

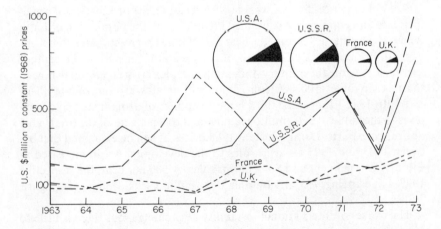

Figure 7.3.   Arms sales to the third world. The inset proportional circles show the proportion of GNP spent on defence by the leading arms vendors in 1969 (shaded). The size of the circles is proportional to 1969 GNP. See ref. 51.

* These are discussed in part 8 below.

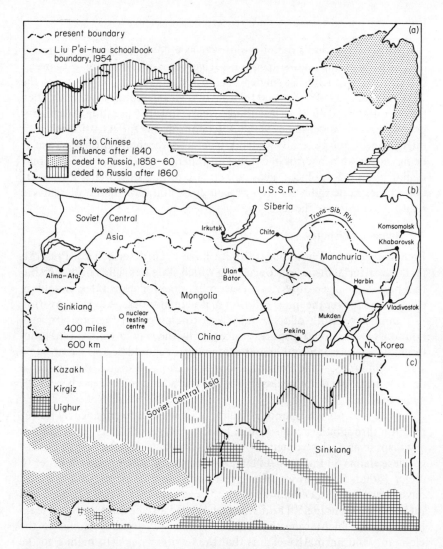

Figure 7.4. The Sino-Soviet border dispute.

(a) The disputed boundary. The area shown by Liu P'ei-hua in 1954 as Chinese territory taken by imperialism roughly corresponds to the pre-1840 frontier of the Chinese empire.

(b) Railways and major towns. Note the vulnerability of the trans-Siberian railway to attack which would sever the Soviet Union from its connection with its far eastern territories.

(c) National minorities which overlap the boundary in Sinkiang and Soviet Central Asia.

Estimates of the strength of opposed forces along the border vary. In 1974 the Soviet infantry strength was between 0.5 million and 1 million men, the Chinese probably over 1 million. The Russians had up to 10 000 tanks and 1200 combat aircraft, the Chinese up to 140 obsolescent medium bombers and around 50 IRBMs, and might be installing a small number of LRBMs.

See ref. 55.

If we accept Wood's definition of war as a conflict of over one hour's duration, involving regular troops on at least one side, shooting with intent to kill, and if we include as single wars the first and second Balkan wars, the 1914–18 and 1939–45 wars and fighting in their immediate aftermath, then between 1900 and 1970 no less than seventeen wars were fought on European soil, five of them since 1950.[54] After considering the statistics above, it might appear that generally we tend to perceive the international system as being more stable in terms of conflict and change than it actually is. Of particular interest to political geographers are disputes involving inter-state boundaries, state rights involving resource exploitation, and state rights in relation to the law of the sea.

7.9 Boundary disputes

Four categories of boundary dispute have been described by Prescott: firstly, territorial disputes, concerning which state has rights of ownership to a particular piece of territory; secondly, positional disputes, involving disagreement over the interpretation of documents describing the position of a boundary. Both of these may lead to changes in the position of a boundary. Functional disputes concern only the way in which state functions such as customs and immigration control should be applied at inter-state boundaries, while Prescott's fourth category, disputes over resource development, need not necessarily affect the boundary and are here dealt with separately.[56]

A state may press a boundary claim in an attempt to enhance its power position through the acquisition of more territory, or it may use a boundary dispute as an instrument of its foreign policy. Prescott suggests that Chinese claims on Indian-held territory may have been pressed in order to direct Indian funds away from prestigious developments which would have enhanced India's reputation in the eyes of other Asian peoples, and into defence spending.[57] The distinction should also be made between legalistic claims which argue that a piece of territory legally belongs to the claimant, and normative claims that the territory *ought* to belong to the claimant for historical, ethnic, geographical or strategical reasons. The Japanese–Soviet territorial dispute over ownership of the southern Kurile Islands is of the legal type: the Russians claim that the entire Kurile archipelago was awarded to Russia at the wartime Yalta conference; the Americans claim that the Russians were only sanctioned for a military occupation; the Japanese regard the islands as part of their national territory.[58]

Examples of the 'ought' type of claim include the Russian claim of 1939 to Finnish territory in the vicinity of Leningrad based on the need to give the town greater security against artillery attack, or the Spanish claim to historical rights of ownership to Gibraltar. Also included would be the pre-war German claim to ownership of the Sudetenland in Czechoslovakia, for which an ethnic justification was advanced. The counter-claims of Ghana and Togo to ownership of the entire Ewe homeland is based on arguments concerning the need to create a united territory for the Ewe people who were divided by superimposed colonial boundaries.[59] When Czech negotiators claimed territory around the largely Polish town of Teschen in 1918, they advanced arguments based on the need for the area's coal in the nearby Ostrava industrial region and on the importance of railways traversing the area in maintaining the connection between Bohemia–Moravia and Slovakia.

Positional disputes are most likely to affect areas where boundaries are antecedent or superimposed and where the negotiation of a boundary between neighbouring states has predated the compilation of accurate maps and records. A notable example concerned Chile and Argentina; the original allocation of a boundary in 1871 was based on the assumption that the watershed corresponded to the line of highest peaks, though it was subsequently discovered that headward erosion by streams draining to the Pacific had shifted the watershed well eastward of the line of highest peaks. British arbitration in 1902 produced a boundary that was mutually acceptable until further exploration brought an area in the Rio Encuentro locality into dispute concerning which of two candidates was the true upper course of the river. The Chilean candidate had greater length, discharge and catchment area, and was the master stream according to the Horton system of stream ordering, though the Argentinian candidate had greater linear continuity with the undisputed lower course and was of the same order as the Chilean candidate according to the Strahler system of ordering. Further British arbitration produced a mutually acceptable boundary in 1966.[60]

Functional disputes of any consequence are uncommon, though in several cases the rights of pastoralists to access to traditional grazings from which they have become separated by new or more strictly observed boundaries have caused problems. Examples include the current dispute concerning the rights of Somali pastoralists to use grazings in Ethiopia, and the difficulties which formerly faced French and Italian peasants separated from their respective traditional transhumance pastures in the Alpes Maritimes until the problem was resolved by a minuscule exchange of territory.[61]

Though boundary disputes may have diminished as sources of major international tension, no less than fifty-two pairs of states appear to be involved in current land-based territorial disputes (I may have overlooked one or two cases in my survey). Some states have territorial disputes with two or more neighbours, and at least sixty-nine states at the time of writing share disputed boundaries with one or more neighbours; therefore almost half the states in the world are in one way or another directly involved with boundary disputes.

Prescott suggests that geographical investigations of boundary disputes should begin with discussions of the initial cause of the dispute and then consider the trigger action which creates a situation in which a claim is made; an analysis should follow of the aims of the parties involved and the arguments invoked, and lead to an assessment of the results of the dispute and its local and wider implications.[62]

Case study (see figure 7.4)

Of all boundary disputes, that between China and the Soviet Union is potentially the most dangerous in global terms. In attempting to apply Prescott's framework for analysis, difficulties emerge in isolating and separating initial causes and trigger actions. The basic cause of the dispute is involved in the contraction over three or more centuries of the frontier zone between two expanding land empires, and the imposition upon the Chinese, during a phase of Russian ascendency, of a series of unequal treaties concerning the Sino-Russian border in the later nineteenth century. Russian advance and Chinese counter-advance in Sinkiang were stabilised under the Treaty of St Petersburg in 1881, and though the treaty embodied the recovery of some Russian-held lands, some territory which the Chinese claimed remained in Russian control. The Russian penetration of the area was facilitated by Chinese weakness and inability to exercise effective control over the subject population. In 1895 Chinese weakness prevented participation in the Anglo-Russian agreement on the Russo-Afghan borders, and Russia negotiated an advance into debatable territory in the Pamirs. During the Chinese revolution of 1911 the Russians encouraged the people of Outer Mongolia to assert themselves against Chinese protection and influence; the Chinese attempt to regain control in 1919 was unsuccessful, and in 1924 a fully independent Mongolian Republic was proclaimed. In Manchuria a frontier, if not a boundary, was negotiated between China and Russia under the Treaty of Nerchinsk in 1689. However, after 1850 large-scale Russian penetration of the Amur basin took place at a time when China was threatened by Britain and France, and the Russians, acting as peace negotiators, obtained 185 000 square miles of territory under the terms of the Treaty of Aigun. Then in 1898 the Chinese were compelled to give Russia a twenty-five-year lease on the Kwantung peninsula, which would have served as a preliminary to the Russian annexation of Manchuria, but this was thwarted by the Japanese occupation and victory over Russia in 1905.

If the initial cause of the Sino-Soviet boundary dispute concerns these unequal treaties, the dispute lay dormant for several decades, and some trigger action must be found to explain the recent eruption of tension. A single trigger action is not to be traced, but a number of events can be found which contributed to the atmosphere of rivalry and suspicion. Even before the Chinese communists came to power in 1949, relations between them and the Soviets were not always cordial; the relationship between Stalin and Mao Tse-tung was soured by practical and ideological disagreement, and the Chinese communist victory was a vindication of principles rejected by Moscow. The Chinese were also aware that Russian material and verbal support for their struggle had been miserly. In 1954 the Russians made important concessions to China, returning Port Arthur and Dairen and dissolving the much-resented joint stock companies set up to exploit the economic resources of Sinkiang and controlled by the Russians who held 41 per cent of their stock. However, about this time the Chinese began a bid for leadership in Asian affairs, and parity with the Soviet Union within the communist camp. The Russians refused to lend their support to Chinese attacks on nationalist-held Quemoy and Matsu in 1958 or to the Chinese advance on India in 1959, at a time when the Chinese were becoming suspicious of Russian intentions towards Manchuria and particularly towards Sinkiang, where the Russians may have been courting the Sinkiang Kazakhs. In the early 1960s the Russians appear to have reduced their purchases from China, defaulted on crucial technological deliveries and withheld some military assistance.

By 1962 the breach had become public knowledge, and about this time there was an exodus of 60 000 Uigurs and Kazakhs from Sinkiang into Russia.[63] No single trigger action was responsible for the dispute, which developed in an atmosphere of growing Chinese mistrust and resentment towards the Russians. Though it was not until 1962 that the Chinese began to make public declarations concerning the return of territory held by Russia, a schoolbook map published in 1952 marked extensive areas beyond the Russian boundary as 'seized by imperialist Russia'.

The Chinese aims in the border dispute are open to various interpretations; it can be argued that the border issue has been raised as a lever in a broader ideological and geopolitical conflict. Considering the amount of territory at stake, this argument alone is inadequate, for the Chinese claim that the unequal Aigun, Peking, Tahcheng and Ili treaties have cost China 1.5 million square kilometres of territory, while they appear to be reserving the right to claim a further 2.6 million square kilometres in Soviet Central Asia and Kazakhstan. Obviously the reacquisition of only a fraction of these rich but lightly peopled areas would be of inestimable value to a state experiencing population pressure on the Chinese scale. The Chinese attitude and policy is based on a deep resentment of the treatment of China by both Soviet and Tsarist regimes, the desire for greater recognition and influence as at least an equal of the Soviet Union within the communist camp, security considerations, and territorial ambitions intensified by a belief in the justice of the claims.

The Russians have played a more passive if inflexible role in the dispute, and the basic aim of Russian policy in the dispute emphasises the retention of territory held. This marks a retreat from the idealism of the Karakhan declaration of 1919 in which

The Government of the RSFSR declares as void all treaties concluded by the former Government of Russia with China . . . and returns to China free of charge, and for ever, all that was ravenously taken from her by the Tsar's Government and the Russian bourgeoisie.

Generally the Russians have aimed to de-emphasise the dispute, while casting the Chinese in the light of an ungrateful and delingquent child and at the same time preparing the Soviet population for the eventuality of war. Occasionally Russian comments have seemed to reflect a racial antagonism which stems from the centuries during which Russia was ravaged by Asiatic nomads; a Russian poet has referred to 'Genghis sub-humans', and a witness of a border incident is reported to have said, 'our hair stood on end, only barbarians could commit such outrages against the dead and wounded'.[64] Ideally the Russians would like to revert to the hegemonial relationship of 1950; this no longer seems a possibility, and the present aim, despite Chinese warnings of imminent Russian attack, is probably to avoid conflict while taking precautions against a Chinese attack, and to countenance nothing beyond a possible token return of territory.

Most analyses would recognise the strength of the Chinese claims, particularly in the light of the Karakhan declaration. The value of the disputed areas to the Soviet Union in the foreseeable future is largely of a strategical nature, and despite the encouragement of volunteer immigration in 1955 and 1969, the far-eastern area at least is a poorly integrated and relatively unproductive section of the Soviet Union. The Russians have attempted an urban-based colonisation of the disputed areas which contrast with the apparently more firmly rooted rural-based patterns of settlement established on the Chinese side of the boundary. Since the disputed areas lie much closer to the Chinese ecumene, it is arguable that more effective colonisation of them on a commune basis would be undertaken if they revert to China.

The implications of the border dispute have been profound. On the broad scale, the dispute has played a considerable part in recasting the global balance of power system, and the alliance which might have developed between the two potentially most powerful states has disappeared in favour of a tripolar system in which an alliance of any two superpowers against a third is possible. On a more localised scale, the border zone has experienced a massive influx of military and civilian personnel with related settlement and communications constructions. Differences in ideology and strategical doctrines are apparent in the landscape; the Russians have massed armour and defence-works along the boundary, while Chinese deployments are organised in relation to the Maoist concept of people's war('Fight on a fluid and extended front, avoid battle in the opening phases of the enemy's assault, yield territory and so draw the invader in deep so that he can be exposed to the waves of people's war').[65] The Chinese have around thirty-two divisions stationed in Manchuria and four in Sinkiang; the Russians have fifteen divisions and ten armoured divisions in eastern Siberia, and twenty-eight divisions in Soviet Central Asia.[66] Although the boundary dispute has caused the strategical development of the borderlands, as an important element in the wider dispute it has prevented cooperation in the exploitation of the area's considerable economic wealth in a situation in which Chinese manpower could have complemented Russian technology to the considerable advantage of both parties.[67]

Case study

A unique form of boundary dispute concerns the Antarctic. The basic division of the continent was undertaken according to the sector principle, based on sectors with their apices at the pole and with sides formed of two radii and an arc. The principle originates in a proposal made at the beginning of this century as a means of formalising Canadian claims to the Arctic, and though rejected at the time by the Canadian senate, the idea was investigated by Russia and first applied by the British in their creation of the Falklands Islands dependencies. The British lead was followed in the 1930s by sector-based claims in the Antarctic by France, Norway, Australia and New Zealand. In 1940 and 1941 respectively Argentina and Chile announced sector claims in the Antarctic, based on proximity and fifteenth-century papal edicts, contrasting with previous claims which had been justified by discovery and occupation. These South American claims impinged upon each other and together encompassed the British claim. In 1959 twelve interested parties signed the Antarctic Treaty, under which existing boundaries were to be frozen for thirty years; after that, territorial disputes in the Antarctic are to be considered afresh. The treaty, ratified in 1961, served as a model for subsequent agreements concerning the exploration of extraterrestrial bodies. Provision was made for the solely peaceful use of Antarctica, the freedom of, and exchange of information in, exploration, the prohibition of nuclear explosions and unlimited rights of inspection.

Owing to the absence of permanent or indigenous populations, arbitration according to conventional means will be difficult. In many areas the actual coastline is obscured by ice sheets, and where the ice has a saline content it may be claimed to constitute part of the high seas, so the delimitation of boundaries in the Antarctic will present the boundary-maker with some unusual problems.[68]

7.10 Disputes over resource development

Since states are sovereign, their populations and governments are free to develop their resources as they see fit, though political and legal difficulties are likely to arise when this exploitation affects other states. Most disputes over resource development concern water bodies, though atmospheric pollution or the tapping of an oil pool which extends under the territory of a neighbouring state could also cause disagreement.

Where a river constitutes a boundary water, containing the boundary between neighbouring states, difficulties are to be expected if agreements are not concluded concerning rights of navigation, damming, bridging, irrigation and general policy to be applied in the event of the river changing its course. Most of the major rivers accessible to commercial vessels have long been designated as International Rivers, accessible to the shipping of all states, while the use of boundary waters and estuaries and bays shared by neighbouring states usually finds provision in the relevant boundary agreements. An important exception involved the Shatt el Arab, where the boundary between Iran and Turkey, and subsequently Iran and Iraq, followed the low-water line on the Iranian bank, thus depriving Iran of access to the river until a treaty of friendship negotiated Iranian rights of anchorage.[69]

The wandering of the Rio Grande, which contains the USA–Mexico boundary, has caused considerable inconvenience. In 1934 an International Boundary Commission was appointed, with powers to undertake a programme of river straightening in the El Paso–Fort Quitman area which would increase the river gradient and so reduce silting and meandering. A series of parcels of land were cut off by the artificial course, and these were exchanged so that each state should advance to the river but not beyond, each receiving and losing about 3500 acres.[70]

The exploitation of tributaries to boundary waters may also cause problems. Canal construction in 1900, by which the Chicago municipal authority tapped Lake Michigan, caused the level of the lake to drop six inches by 1926, sufficient to threaten navigation and moorings constructed on the Canadian shore of the lake. This prompted negotiations through which a limit was set on the amount of water which could be withdrawn.[71]

Rivers which cross rather than contain inter-state boundaries may be termed 'successive rivers', and provide considerable potential for disputes concerning the drawing off, ponding back or pollution of waters. In 1964 the Israelis produced a plan for the diversion of part of the waters of the Jordan for the irrigation of the southern coastal plain and Negev which would have greatly reduced the volume of water leaving Israel. The idea was met with an Arab counter-plan of reducing the volume of water available to Israel by diverting Jordan head waters into the Litani and Yarmuk rivers.[72] One of the rare instances of cooperation between India and Pakistan produced the Indus Water Treaty of 1960, under the terms of which use of the three eastern rivers of the Indus system was allocated to India, and of the three western to Pakistan, and provision was made for a permanent Indus Commission to facilitate the joint development of the basin.

Pollution of successive rivers or boundary waters by upstream or adjacent states presents particularly thorny problems.

The major obstacles in controlling global pollution have been traditional use and sovereignty rights, the cost of control, and the differing perception of pollution by various cultural groups. Since industrialisation contributes heavily to pollution, the problem of assigning responsibility becomes more difficult.[73]

Various international commissions have been set up to protect international waterways from pollution, and the greatest successes seem to have been achieved where only the interests of two states have been directly involved. The USA and Canada, for example, have agreed to enforce standards of purity for the waters of the Red River flowing into Canada. An international commission set up in 1950 by five countries of the Rhine basin has limited its activities largely to testing the levels of pollution in the waters concerned, despite the considerable damage experienced by downstream states; for example, extreme pollution of the river Ruhr has caused extensive damage to market gardens in the Netherlands.

Fawcett has argued that global approaches to questions of international conservation have proved inadequate, and that the global perspective should be superseded by forceful regional approaches by groups of states and related to specific problems of resource management involving the states and organisations directly involved.[74] As long as governments prefer to pursue the short-term objectives which appear to be dictated by considerations of national interest, a solution to the worldwide threat of pollution will not be forthcoming.

7.11 Disputes involving maritime rights

Alexander writes, 'Ever since man first learned to make use of the sea, he has wrestled with problems of allocating authority within that environment'.[75] Since the oceans are international highways, disputes over maritime rights usually involve not just two parties but conflicts between the rights of individual states as opposed to the rights shared by all states. Most disputes concern rights to territorial waters, contiguous fishery and inspection zones, exploitation of the ocean floor, continental shelves, or the high seas. The law of the sea, like all international law, is seldom enforced and frequently flaunted, while the situation is worsened by its incomplete and ambiguous nature. This has led to a situation in which the world's oceans may be described as the last frontier, where sovereignty is disputed and an acceptable code of territorial rights is lacking.

The full sovereignty of the coastal states extends seawards to the outer limit of their territorial waters, yet no single formula exists for defining this outer limit, and the post-war period has witnessed a dramatic expansion of territorial waters. The ability of the state to enforce a claim to territorial waters of any scale is largely dependent on the ability to coerce foreign shipping into observing the claimed limits. In 1951 Boggs wrote, 'Never have national claims in adjacent seas been so numerous, so varied, or so inconsistent'.[76] Still, as late as 1963, Pounds was able to write that 'A 3-mile limit has become common practice', though he listed thirty-five states which claimed more extensive territorial waters.[77] Now, states claiming three-mile limits are in a minority; in 1968, Alexander was able to list only twenty-eight states with three-mile limits.

My own estimates are that in 1961, of the fifty-five coastal states which claimed fixed territorial waters limits, twenty-eight claimed more than the three-mile norm and sixteen claimed exclusive fishing limits beyond their territorial waters. By 1974, a number of states which had no fixed territorial waters limits formulated precise claims, the number of coastal states was swollen by coastal colonies' gaining independence, and many claims to territorial waters were extended. Thus in 1974, of the 104 coastal states stating fixed limits, eighty-two claimed more than the three-mile norm, and thirty-eight claimed exclusive fishery zones beyond their territorial waters.

The 1958 Geneva Conference on the Law of the Sea was unable to produce agreement on the breadth of the territorial sea or on state rights to exclusive fishery zones beyond the territorial waters, and the second conference convened in 1960 to consider these outstanding issues also became deadlocked. At the latter conference a proposal for a six-mile territorial sea with a six-mile exclusive fishery zone beyond failed to obtain sufficient support, and subsequently states have extended their control over offshore fisheries in quite an anarchic fashion, so now thirty-seven states enforce exclusive fishery zones beyond their territorial waters.

Case study

Icelandic waters at the junction of the warm Irminger and cold East Greenland currents, where temperature differences cause a constant upwelling of water bringing nutritious seafloor material into the sunlit plankton zone, have long attracted both fish and fishermen. In the nineteenth century Icelandic fishing limits were widely ignored by British fishermen, but the development of an Icelandic fishing industry throughout the first half of this century brought unprecedented wealth to Iceland and the threat of conflict over fishing rights. An awareness of the need for conservation developed after 1944 with the departure of the herring shoals, but though minor conservational measures were taken in 1948, overfishing became severe, and in 1952 the Icelanders introduced a four-mile limit seawards of baselines connecting headlands (see figure 7.6).

British interests retaliated with a ban on Icelandic exports, and tension continued until 1956 when pressure from the Organisation for European Economic Cooperation induced a British resumption of Icelandic fish landings. Icelandic catches continued to decline, and in 1958 a twelve-mile

---

Figure 7.5.   The expansion of territorial waters. (a) Territorial waters claimed, by width and macro-regions, 1974 and 1961. (b) Inset showing the macro-regions used; note the inclusion of Israel, South Africa and Japan with the western group. (c) Territorial water and exclusive fishing zones. Note the use of logarithmic scales. Symbols conform to the key above. (d) Mean claims of territorial waters by macro-regions. Shading below mean lines corresponds to the key above. Note the use of a logarithmic scale.

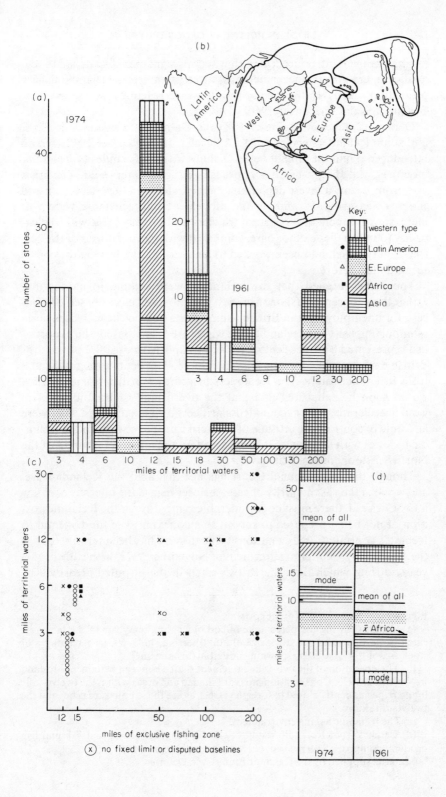

(a)

1974

number of states

miles of territorial waters

3 4 6 10 12 15 18 30 50 100 130 200

(b)

Latin America

West

E. Europe

Asia

Africa

Key:
o western type
● Latin America
△ E. Europe
■ Africa
▲ Asia

1961

3 4 6 9 10 12 30 200

(c)

miles of territorial waters

miles of exclusive fishing zone

Ⓧ no fixed limit or disputed baselines

(d)

mean of all

mode

mean of all

mode

x̄ Africa

mode

1974   1961

miles of territorial waters

fishing limit was introduced. British warships were then dispatched to Icelandic waters in a (rather ridiculous) attempt to arrest Icelandic fishery protection vessels. In the face of hostile world reactions, an almost total British capitulation came in 1960.

Depleted catches in 1967 and 1968 caused a minor recession in Iceland, and some Icelanders emigrated to Australia. In September 1972 Iceland introduced a ban on foreign vessels fishing within fifty miles of headland baselines, and British naval support vessels again intervened. The crisis was prompted by a severe depletion of fishing stocks in the Norwegian and Barents Sea grounds, and by the movement into Icelandic waters of increasing numbers of large stern trawlers and factory ships with the capacity to sweep the seafloor bare, combined with recent failures of the herring fishery which had been worked to near-extinction, leaving the cod as Iceland's last resort.

The British argued that the Icelanders were seeking to monopolise rather than conserve offshore fisheries, and mounted a case based on concern for unemployment in British fishing ports and on the increased costs of importing fish. The Icelandic case was more firmly based: the export of fish represented 81.9 per cent of Icelandic exports against 0.2 per cent of British exports, while foreign ships caught 48.4 per cent of the total catch from Icelandic waters. The Icelanders feared that British home fisheries would soon be exhausted and that the overfishing of Icelandic waters would accelerate as the EEC and Russian fleets turn northwards. They were also able to contrast the attitude of Western European states to the Icelandic fisheries with the way that they carved up the mineral resources of the North Sea floor among themselves.

Though the International Court has not favoured the Icelandic case, and while in the vast majority of cases a closer regard for international law is to be desired, there must be considerable sympathy for the Icelandic position of not being prepared to submit to a court an issue fundamental to Iceland's continuation as a nation.[78] The dispute has been terminated for the moment by an interim agreement of November 1973, with a life of two years, during which time the British catch in the disputed areas will be

---

Figure 7.6.   Some aspects of the cod war.
(a) Graph showing the percentage of cod older than ten years in the Icelandic catch (solid line), and the stock size of adult herring, 1947–69, in percentages of stock size of 1947, based on spawning potential (broken line).
(b) The operation of the two-year agreement signed between Britain and Iceland in November 1973. Conservation areas are shaded and areas within the twelve-mile limit are permanently closed to foreign vessels, as are the stippled areas beyond the twelve-mile limit.
(c) The Icelandic fishing environment.
(d) Catches from Icelandic waters, 1945–70; the inset shows that fish and fish products composed 81.9 per cent of Icelandic exports (in 1969).
Material supplied by the Icelandic Embassy in London.

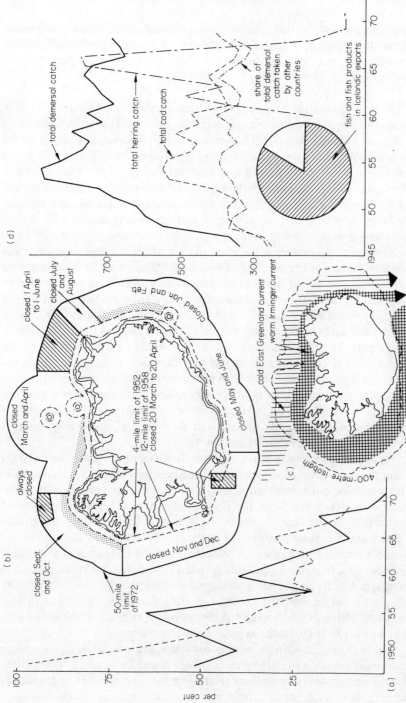

(a)

(b)

closed 1 April to 1 June

closed July and August

closed Jan and Feb.

closed March and April

always closed

closed Sept. and Oct.

4-mile limit of 1952
12-mile limit of 1958
closed 20 March to 20 April

50-mile limit of 1972

closed May and June

closed Nov. and Dec.

(c)

cold East Greenland current

warm Irminger current

400-metre isobath

(d)

total demersal catch

total herring catch

total cod catch

share of total demersal catch taken by other countries

fish and fish products in Icelandic exports

per cent

700

500

300

1945 50 55 60 65 70

100

75

50

25

1950 55 60 65 70

limited to about 130 000 tons, while not more than sixty-eight trawlers of
more than 180 feet in length and not more than seventy-one of less than
that length will be allowed to fish the areas, and freezer and factory trawlers are entirely excluded.

Claims to rights over an adjacent continental shelf can be traced to 1945,
when the US government, anxious to monopolise Gulf Coast submarine oil
reserves, claimed sovereignty over the seabed and subsoil of the continental shelf. Though submarine geomorphologists may find it difficult to
provide an exact definition of a continental shelf, the 1958 Convention of
the Continental Shelf allows the adjacent state exclusive rights to the exploitation of the seabed, but not over the overlying waters up to a depth of
200 metres outside territorial waters, and apparently deeper still, dependent only upon technological ability.

Successful, at least from the point of view of the main participants, was
the carving up of the North Sea basin into a series of national sections
(drawn on the basis of median lines extending seawards between bordering
nations) for the sharing out of the submarine oil and gas fields. In 1964 the
British government divided its share into concessions of about 100 square
miles each, and twenty companies were granted licences for exclusive dril-
ling rights. The divisions removed the possibility of conflict between the
states and the companies involved, and the main controversy which has
arisen concerns the cheapness with which the British government disposed
of concessions in an industry which may produce profits of over £4000 million per annum by 1980; advocates of nationalisation can quote an estimate that Britain stands to lose well over half of a possible eventual
revenue of more than £50 000 million.[79].

As improvements are made in the techniques of discovery and extrac-
tion, the ownership of submarine oil reserves beyond territorial waters is
likely to cause considerable disagreement. Already the entrepreneurial collection of pyrolusite from the floor of the Atlantic poses problems of
ownership. In the face of growing pressures on the high seas, the British
representative recently suggested to the United Nations a division of the
world's oceans into blocks for allocation among the states of the world.
The construction of an equitable division would be a fascinating exercise
for the political geographer. A division based on median lines or proximity
would be unfair, and the landlocked state would be entirely deprived,
while a raffling of predetermined blocks might provide many states with
blocks too distant to justify exploitation.

The high seas, in terms of international law, are open to all states, and no
state may regulate the activities of others above or beneath them. However, international conventions relating to the high seas have periodically
been flouted, while the zone itself is contracting as claims for the extension
of territorial waters and other exclusive rights are pressed. The high seas
have been described as a last frontier where states compete for resources

and attempt to extend their frontiers.[80] In 1963 the US Navy took action on the high seas to prevent Russian ships delivering missiles to Cuba, while at present Canada is laying claim to the right to control ships within 100 miles of her Arctic shores in order to protect the area from pollution by giant oil tankers.

Case study

During summer 1973 the French government instigated the latest of a series of nuclear tests to be held above Mururoa Atoll in the Pacific, and banned foreign shipping from a zone extending sixty miles beyond the island's twelve-mile territorial waters. This interference with the freedom of the high seas contravened international law, though a more serious medical and political problem concerns the possible effects of fall-out from the tests. France was not a signatory of the 1963 pact to ban atmospheric testing of nuclear devices, and the latest tests were part of a series considered essential to the French policy of acquiring an independent Polaris-type hydrogen missile capability by 1976. Earlier French tests were carried out in the then French colony of Algeria, and though French testing could have continued there for five years after Algerian independence in 1962, the move to the Pacific was prompted by consideration for the political sensitivities of the Algerians, while rumours circulated that French testing had caused radioactive contamination in Spain. The French were able to point to the use of Pacific test sites, in Australia, Christmas Island and Bikini, by British and Americans, powers which completed test programmes before 1963. In the case of Bikini, at least, unexpected harm was done through contamination; when the Bikini islanders were permitted to return after an enforced exile of over twenty years, it was discovered that all fish and crabs were inedible through strontium-90 contamination, coconut palms were stunted, the nuts were foul-tasting, and the islands were infested with blind rats.

Strong reactions to the resumption of testing came from Australia and New Zealand; Australian scientists claimed that every person in Australia had received radiation from past tests to a point where there was definite harm, and that a resumption of testing would directly cause a further 100–200 deaths and disabilities from cancer and genetic change. The New Zealand government dispatched a warship into the forbidden zone as a gesture of extreme disapproval.

This and many other cases serve to show that the concept of 'freedom of the seas' rests more upon myth than upon reality. Population growth and technological advance have given nations the need and the ability to extend their economic and militaristic activities into hitherto inaccessible or insignificant maritime areas, and this development has not been paralleled by advances in consensus, legislation or international control capabilities. International law relating to the oceans and seas is incomplete, ambiguous, and rendered obsolete by recent developments in technology. A United Nations Conference on the Law of the Sea was, at the time of writing, scheduled to take place in Chile in summer 1974, and it appeared possible that sufficient agreement might be reached to produce a more modern and complete code of international behaviour; the question of how such a code could be enforced upon a system of self-interested sovereign states would, however, remain*.

In this brief review of the political-geographical aspects of inter-state reactions, it has been found that the political processes which derive in part from environmental characteristics and differences, and which in turn either directly or indirectly affect landscape change, are produced by decisions which frequently offend conventional notions of logic and morality.

With regard to mankind as a whole these decisions may be illogical, but in respect to a series of state-bound communities they have a logic of their own. The faults lie more in the nature of the international political system which has evolved than with the decision-makers. In a system composed of independent actors (sovereign states), it is only to be expected that self-interest (national interest) will be the main determinant of behaviour. Individual governments are unlikely to work purposefully for causes of international order and justice, since they are unable to control the activities of other independent actors in an anarchistic system in which competition and conflict are the natural manifestations of sovereignty and national interest.

* The 1974 Law of the Sea conference, held in Caracas, foundered on 19 August, after ten weeks of discussions. Though none of the many items on the agenda reached the stage of negotiations, there was widespread support for the principle of a 12-mile territorial sea and a 200-mile economic zone. A new conference was scheduled for March 1975.

PART 8

Political regions and scale

Regions are defined by geographers in terms of their possession of one or more unifying factors. The regions studied in political geography exist through the presence of some form of internal political unity, which may derive from the unification of the region under a single sovereign government or a single local authority, from the existence within it of a particular political outlook or aspiration, from the functional unity of the region as an area of formal international cooperation, or from the existence of informal underlying supranational characteristics. The state is the traditional and, to a lesser extent, continuing focus of political-geographical attention, and constitutes the most distinctive and developed political-geographical form. Though there are strong political, economic and social forces working in the directions of both intra and supranational regionalisation, the state will retain its paramount political status so long as state sovereignty remains the basis of statehood. While the power of ultimate decision-making remains with the sovereign governments, decisions affecting supra or intranational developments must be made by these governments or in respect of them.

The great majority of political-geographical enquiries have been made with reference to the state, either in terms of the ways in which morphological or ethnographical subregions such as border zones, core areas or minority territories relate to the state as a whole, or in terms of how pairs or groups of states interact within a spatial context. A valuable minority of studies have dealt with political-geographical phenomena operating at intra and supranational levels and without special reference to the state, and these fields of study present continuing opportunities for research. The remaining sections are concerned with scales other than that of the state, at the macro-scale with geopolitics and international regions, and at the micro-scale with electoral geography, administrative areas and administrative area reform.

8.1 Geopolitical approaches

Global strategic views have been presented in a diversity of forms and with a variety of objectives; they are linked by their perspective of the world as a dynamically interrelated whole, a single system where change in one part produces, and may be caused by, change in other parts. Past work in international politics has been basically ethnocentric, focusing on the nation state, and some students consider that the study of international relations will be retarded as long as this approach remains unchallenged, there being a need for geocentric approaches which take the world as a centre of perspective and evaluation. The rapidly mounting problems of the earth are considered to be no longer amenable to ethnocentric attack, and basic political questions could be rethought in the perspective of a large, complex and globalised society.[1] In political geography, available global approaches include geopolitics, along with possible developments of the systems approach, and the delimitation by various means of international regions of the world.

The term 'geopolitics' is a translation of the German *Geopolitik*, coined by Kjellen to mean 'the science of the state as a realm in space', and first used in 1899. Since then geopolitics has been subjected to vastly different interpretations; it has produced probably the most widely read and discussed geographical paper of all times,[2] and it has been misused to the severe detriment of political geography as a whole and the virtual extinction of itself. Recent understandings of the term are exceedingly varied. Some writers would associate the term with the perversion of geographical science by some geographers in Nazi Germany: 'Kristof's revival of the term geopolitics is probably premature and may remain so so long as most people associate the term with the inhuman policies of Hitler's Third Reich'.[3] However, Pounds did recognise the usefulness of the term and of Kristof's approach to geopolitics as a geographically orientated study of politics intermediate between political science and political geography.[4] Other poorly informed writers have interpreted geopolitics as a synonym for political geography, while Hartshorne considered that 'As an applied field concerned with specific problems, geopolitics would appear to be divided into as many different schools as there are independent states'.[5] Geopolitics has its inviting and its repellent aspects, and only its uglier forms correspond to Martin's definition that

Geopolitics is essentially a body of thought developed in a given territory which seeks the maximisation of its own ends. The geopolitician sees all other groups through the spectacles of national interest, often becoming selfish to the point of greed, lust, and violence. The core of this discipline is power; the quest for power provides the guide to method.[6]

Obviously many conflicting interpretations are available, but here geopolitics is considered to include studies of dynamic political processes operating at levels broader that that of the individual state and within a global perspective. Within this framework there is scope for objective enquiry as well as emotive speculation, and geopolitics is not the only branch of political geography that is open to abuse; for example, electoral geography techniques could be misused in the gerrymandering of constituency boundaries.

In 1904 Halford Mackinder presented a geopolitical view of the world to the Royal Geographical Society which, seven decades later, continues to stimulate geographical debate.[7] In a thesis which leans heavily on geographical determinism and the relative merits of the sea and land forms of power transmission, Mackinder claimed to have recognised a 'geographical pivot of history' which he immortalised as the Heartland in a later work of 1919.[8] Very briefly, Mackinder interpreted 'European advance' as being 'stimulated by the necessity of reacting against pressure from the heart of Asia',[9] a response to the periodic invasion of Europe 'by a cloud of ruthless and idealess horsemen sweeping over the unimpeded plain—a blow, as it were, from the great Asiatic hammer striking freely through the vacant space'.[10] Both past and future were translated within the broad framework of a confrontation between the settled societies of the Eurasian continental margins and the mobile and culturally backward inhabitants of the continental interior, and the juxtaposition of sea and land power.

Eurasia was divided between a 'pivot area' and an 'inner crescent', and Mackinder detected a persistent geographical relationship between the two. The pivot area was considered to be that part of the land mass which was inaccessible to ships, having a pattern of drainage which was either internal or towards the frozen polar sea. The open steppelands of the pivot area, reaching westwards towards the Hungarian Plain, provided an open corridor of movement for the mobile horse and camel-riding tribesmen of the Asian steppes, who were able to exert fairly continuous pressure on the developing civilisations of Western and Central Europe. However, Mackinder considered that 'Mobility upon the ocean is the natural rival of horse and camel mobility in the heart of the continent',[11] and that in the post-Columbian age Europeans had reversed

the relations of Europe and Asia, for whereas in the Middle Ages Europe was caged between an impassable desert to the south, an unknown ocean to west, and icy or forested wastes to north and north-east, and in the east and south-east was constantly threatened by the superior mobility of the horsemen and camelmen, she now emerged upon this world, multiplying more than thirty-fold the sea surface and coastal lands to which she had access, and wrapping her influence round the Euro-Asiatic land-power which had hitherto threatened her very existence.[12]

Then in the nineteenth century, in the wake of the Cossack armies, the Russian peasants returned to the steppelands to recover their lands from the nomads after over half a millenium of exile in the forest.

But Mackinder did not consider that the historical confrontation between the pivot area and marginal crescent need end here; he believed that transcontinental railways are now transmuting the conditions of land-power. . . . Railways work the greatest wonders in the steppe, because they directly replace horse and camel mobility . . . the century will not be old before all Asia is covered with railways.[13]

He then asked

Is not the pivot region of the world's politics that vast area of Euro-Asia which is inaccessible to ships, but in antiquity lay open to the horse-riding nomads, and is today about to be covered with a network of railways?[14]

Russia was cast as the heir to the Mongol Empire, exerting pressure on peripheral states, and with a land-power potential which would soon be enhanced through the predicted phase of railway construction. In common with several later geopoliticians, Mackinder was offering political advice rather than writing for a limited academic readership. He considered that under the prevailing balance of power Russia was not equivalent to the peripheral states, but he warned of an alliance between Germany and Russia which would 'permit the use of vast continental resources for fleet building, and the empire of the world would be in sight'.[15] Further, a conquest of the Russian Empire by China 'might constitute the yellow peril to the world's freedom just because they would add an oceanic frontage to the resources of the great continent, an advantage as yet denied to the Russian tenant of the pivot area'.[16]

In 1919 he reiterated his ideas, with modifications, in a small book;[17] the pivot area became the Heartland, and its boundaries were extended to include the Baltic and Black Seas which, as experiences in the 1914–18 war had shown, could be closed to sea power. He thought that during the war the Germans had attempted to secure Eastern Europe as a preliminary to the capture of the Heartland and had shown that the Heartland could be invaded through the East European steppes; he urged the peacemakers to produce a lasting settlement of affairs between Germany and Russia, with the introduction of a *cordon sanitaire* of nation states to separate the Germans and the Heartland, securing the independence of each and providing a balance of power.

When our statesmen are in conversation with the defeated enemy, some airy cherub should whisper to them from time to time this saying:

Who rules East Europe commands the Heartland:
Who rules the Heartland commands the World Island:
Who rules the World Island commands the World.[18]

A third statement of Mackinder's ideas was offered in 1943, narrowly directed towards the events of the war and suggesting the defeat of Germany by an alliance between the Heartland and the North Atlantic community.[19] His obvious neglect of technological change by this time makes the article his least impressive and most dated contribution.

On several occasions the Heartland thesis has been refuted and systematically dismantled, only to rise Phoenix-like for further punishment and to stimulate geopoliticians to present their own revisions. It is vulnerable from a variety of directions; Mackinder overestimated the ability of sea power to penetrate and control rivers (exposed by the plight of the Amethyst on the Yangtse river during the Chinese communist revolution[20]), and he consistently neglected both the might of the USA as a world power and the effectiveness of air power. The strategical railways which Mackinder invoked to endow his theory with overtones of urgency never materialised, while since 1928 the power of the Heartland has come to lie not in its immunity from attack but in its industrial strength. The Heartland is vulnerable to attack by a variety of land and sea-based missiles, and is regularly photographed in detail by US spy satellites using both conventional and infra-red methods; not only has its security vanished, but also its privacy. The economic basis of Russian power has been discussed by East[21] and by Hooson,[22] and by 1943 was realised by Mackinder. 'The Heartland is the greatest natural fortress on earth. For the first time in history it is manned by a garrison sufficient both in number and quality.'[23] Hooson suggests that a new Soviet Heartland is to be found in the richly endowed and developing Volga-Baykal zone, an area which proved immune to German attack and with the marks of a real continental stronghold.

Though according to Malin, 'It would be difficult to find an essay of comparable length and reputation that is more indefensible in terminology and ideas than Mackinder's . . .',[24] the Heartland still has its advocates, who can point to the failure of the Napoleonic and twentieth-century German attempts to conquer the area and can argue that the post-war American policy of containment, which has surrounded the communist states with a ring of treaty-bound groupings (NATO, CENTO and SEATO), represents a validation of Mackinder and an acceptance of the threat from the Heartland.

The Heartland thesis dealt with ideas so broad that it is difficult to topple the concept by the refutation of its detail, though even if a Heartland does exist, the pillars upon which Mackinder's Heartland rested have mostly been undermined by the developments of this century. 'Mackinder was a bold and inspired wielder of the broad brush, and had a rare ability to start intellectual hares, stimulating others to attack or elaborate.'[25] In some ways the pivot-area concept was very much a product of its time, and its geographical determinism, oversimplification, unsupported generalisations and value-judgments about non-European cultures will be distasteful to many modern readers, though some underlying ideas are striking in their modernity. The lasting value of Mackinder's work lies in its emphasis on the functional unity of the world. His aim 'to exhibit human history as part of the life of the world organism', and his statement that 'From the present time forth, in the post Columbian age, we shall again have to deal with a closed political system, and none the less that it will be one of world-wide scope',[26] have a continuing relevance and encapsulate the spirit of acceptable geopolitics.

Since the 1930s geopolitics has been under a dark shadow of academic reaction against the activities of geopoliticians in Nazi Germany, but interest in the subject has been kept alive in the work of several writers who have attempted to reinterpret the Heartland or describe new geopolitical regions. Spykman recognised that Mackinder had seen the potential world domination by the Heartland as dependent upon its organisation in conjunction with a great power of the marginal crescent, but it was to the latter region, redefined as the Rimland, that he gave priority.[27] He demonstrated that historical alignments, rather than expressing a basic opposition between land and sea power, had frequently involved an alliance between the Heartland and a Rimland power, or Britain against an expansionate Rimland power. He predicted that competition would develop between Britain and the Soviet Union for control of the Rimland, and encouraged American policy-makers to prevent the region from falling under Soviet control, anticipating the American containment policy.

Sophistication and a renewed emphasis on dynamic process were added to the Heartland–Rimland debate by Meinig.[28] A less extensive continental Heartland was seen to be surrounded by a Rimland which divided into functionally different maritime and continental portions. It was recognised that within the Rimland the orientations of states could change from the maritime to the continental, and *vice versa*, as reflected in the change of the Chinese orientation from an outward maritime to an inward continental one following the communist revolution and during the *entente* with the Soviet Union, while contemporary events suggest a return to the maritime perspective. Since Meinig's approach derives most from objective reality and allows flexibility by drawing the least upon geographical determinism, emphasising instead the volitional aspects of state behaviour, it constitutes the least unacceptable statement of a Heartland concept.

A global geopolitical approach which dispenses with any Heartland concept, and which probably was more applicable to conditions in the 1950s and early 1960s, was presented by de Seversky.[29] He replaced the geopoliticians' traditionally favoured Mercator projection with an azimuthal equidistant projection centred on the North Pole, and a startlingly different view of the world resulted. The spheres of air dominance of the respective superpowers, based on the ranges of contemporary aircraft, were plotted, and these overlapped to produce an 'area of decision', the entire territory of each superpower being shown to be within reach of the bombers of the other. De Seversky advocated a policy of American air supremacy at the expense of all other forms of defence, and considered that land forces need only be deployed to defend the Arctic fringes of the continent in the region of the Bering Straits. A number of developments, not least the introduction of mobile Polaris-type missile launching bases, and the increasing American dependence upon external sources of raw

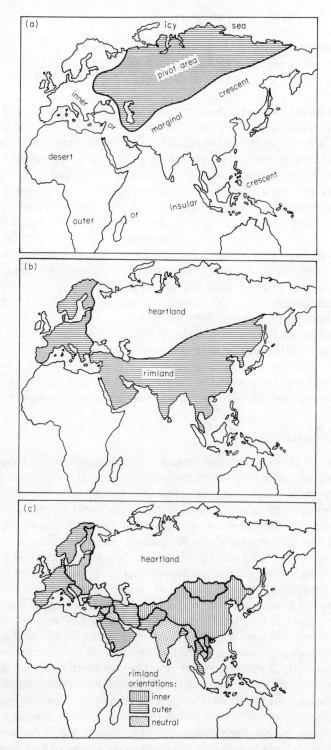

Figure 8.1.   Versions of the geopolitical world. (a) After Mackinder (ref. 2). (b) After Spykman (ref. 27). (c) After Meinig (ref. 28).

materials have rendered the air-supremacy theory largely redundant, and it only remains pertinent because of its suggestion that the geopolitical regions of the world should be studied from a number of different vantage points.

A continuity of approach can be traced from the writings of Mahan and Mackinder through to the works of more recent writers such as Meinig and Cohen. The uniqueness of the approach does not entirely derive from the fact that most geopoliticians have been motivated by the desire to influence government policy, since other political, social and economic geographers frequently offer advice, and this would seem to be a valid part of their role in society. Rather it lies in the valuable demonstration of global unity and interaction, an antidote to the tendency of some geographers to define regions and proceed to study them in isolation, and the less desirable tendency to base political conclusions on frequently dubious and subjectively selected evidence; it is this latter failing which has led many to doubt the academic acceptability of the geopolitical approach. No one mind can comprehend all the significant interactions taking place in the world, and this human inability has tempted geopoliticians to interpret past and future history in terms of a perceived master variable and to inflate its importance disproportionately at the expense of the host of other relevant variables. Excessive subjectivity, however, is not inherent in the global approach to the world, and since there is a need for the development of geocentric viewpoints, balanced world-based analyses will be valued.

8.2 International regions

It being an obvious fact that certain political communities have closer political, cultural or economic ties with some members of international society than with others, it should be possible, without resort to any geopolitical fantasising, to delimit macro-regions of the world which are united by a measure of complementarity in outlook or behaviour, or which have a potential for further integration. An attempt in this direction was made by Cohen in 1964.[30] Considering that the nation states and small political units of the world were becoming overtaken by supranational forces which encouraged the formation of much larger groupings, Cohen attempted to divide the world in a way which would reflect the direction of these pressures and tendencies. He named a number of large 'geostrategic regions': units sufficiently large to exert a worldwide influence, over which certain elements of power could be applied and with certain minimal levels of unity in outlook and trading activity. These he subdivided into 'geopolitical regions', the individual global influence of which was tactical rather than strategic but which were associated with more advanced economic and political integration than within the geostrategic regions as a whole. Two remaining areas, the middle east and south-east Asia, were designated 'shatterbelts': large strategically located regions occupied by a number of states and caught between the conflicting spheres of influence of greater powers.

Cohen argued that peaceful global progress would involve the search for geopolitical equilibrium, an isostatic balance of power. Such isostatic forces, he thought, were present, with the regions existing in a dynamic rather than a static condition, such that when one region loses control of a portion of its sphere of influence or power, compensating reactions produce a probing and extension of influence into new areas, or renewed economic growth. For example, the Russian loss of influence in communist Albania was automatically compensated by an improvement in Russian relations with Albania's great rival Yugoslavia, and the removal of American influence in Cuba stimulated the US to strengthen its control over the remainder of Latin America. With its emphasis on a dynamic macroregionalism, and its relative objectivity, Cohen's study provided a link between geopolitics and the meticulous and monumental search for international regions described below.

Perhaps the most controversial contribution to political geography in the post-war period has come not from a political geographer but from the political scientist B. M. Russett.[31] Russett notes that the problem of defining regions is one 'which has vexed social scientists, both students of international relations and observers of national social and political systems for decades'.[32] In his study published in 1967 Russett set out to examine the existence of international regions in terms of their extent and the criteria by which they could be defined, and to identify areas with potential for further integration. In a search for regions of social and cultural homogeneity, a factor analysis of fifty-four variables for eighty-two countries was carried out. Factor analysis is a complex technique, normally requiring the use of a computer, and it produces a clustering of variables into groups according to their intercorrelations. The social and cultural variables used ranged widely, including measures of GNP *per capita*, life expectancy and birth rates; the variables were firstly arranged in a correlation matrix, and each variable was correlated with every other variable using a product-moment correlation. It was then assumed that those variables which showed a high correlation among themselves and a low correlation with other variables revealed underlying 'factors'. The factor of economic development was found to summarise 31 per cent of variation in the original data matrix, that of communism 11 per cent, size 7 per cent, intensive agriculture 6 per cent, and Catholic culture 5 per cent. Thus 60 per cent of the total variation in the original variables could be summarised by reference to five underlying factors. The size factor was discarded, since for example Luxembourg is no less 'European' through being small, and the remaining factors or dimensions were used in the delimitation of homogeneous regions. Russett used Q analysis to detect clusters of similar countries; the matrix was transposed so that each country became a column and each variable a row, using only those twenty-nine variables which were fairly highly correlated with one of the four relevant factors already identified. This analysis revealed similarities between countries and a number of factors necessary for the grouping of countries; the regional groupings defined on the basis of social and cultural homogeneity were labelled Afro-Asia, Western community, Latin America, semi-developed Latins, and Eastern Europe, while a residue of five countries including China remained unclassifiable. The Afro-Asian group, for example, emerged as highly underdeveloped, moderately non-communist, not Catholic in culture, but with variations in population density and agricultural patterns, while the Western community varied on the intensive agriculture and Catholic culture dimensions but was characterised by rather low communism scores and uniformly high levels of development, these features being common to Japan, Argentina and Australia as well as the countries of Western Europe and North America.

Regions thought to be sharing similar political attitudes or external behaviour were defined on the basis of analysis of roll-call votes in sessions of the United Nations General Assembly. Factor analysis of international airline connections was used as a basis for defining regions of geographical proximity. The focus was shifted from regions of homogeneity to the question of interdependence, and a direct factor analysis was undertaken of international trading data, measuring mutual trade as a proportion of the importing or exporting state's GNP, in order to identify groups of states with similar trading patterns; further analysis revealed those with trading interdependence. Regions of political interdependence were defined by direct factor analysis of a matrix of common memberships of international organisations.

Russett discovered a degree of congruence that was greater than expected between regions of sociocultural homogeneity, and political and economic interdependence. He predicted further integration within certain regions, particularly Western Europe, but little change in the number or composition of the principal coalitions working in world politics. He did not foresee the replacement of the nation state by international groupings; 'so far the regional subsystems of the world are far less well delineated than are the boundaries of national systems'.[33] Neither did he consider that regional integration would necessarily be a force for world peace, for while further integration at the regional level might facilitate the amicable solution of intra-regional differences, or be developed to produce a balance-of-power situation, it would also produce rigidities and heighten conflicts between groupings while weakening links between nations across regions.

Regional integration without concurrent pressures and probably deliberate effort toward integrating the entire international system would be at best a short term and at worst a highly volatile 'solution'. . . . The choice about what to do for global unity will determine whether the regional blocs will build a stable political edifice for man, or merely a shaky temple he can pull down upon his head.[34]

As a work of considerable scope and originality, Russett's study produced extreme reactions, ranging from Berry's 'this superb contribution to political geography and regional analysis'[35] to Young's 'A careful reading . . . makes it difficult to avoid being impressed by the essential futility of the exercise . . .'.[36] Russett is criticised on the broad scale for a supposed obsession with complicated data-manipulation processes at the expense of the development of adequate conceptual foundations (though the opening chapter on regional concepts is geographically authoritative), and in detail for various assumptions involved in particular calculations, such as the equal weighting of the EEC and the International Institute of Refrigeration as indicators of the strength and extent of links between states. Criticisms of Russett's work should be seen in the context of social science disciplines, which still tend to include a polarisation between quantifiers and traditionalists with each camp tending to occupy entrenched positions; any work of an advanced and quantitative nature can be expected to receive blanket criticism from the traditionalist quarter, some authoritative and some less so.

The political geographer is particularly interested in political regionalisation at the macro-scale; this involves both the formation of formal international organisations, whose functions and boundaries are clearly identifiable, and underlying tendencies towards integration and regional homogeneity of an informal nature, expressed in patterns of social and cultural similarity, trading interdependence and complementary behaviour within formal organisations. With regard to the second type of regionalisation, the political geographer may rely on subjective assessment and intuition in his estimation of the extent and scope of regional groupings, or he may apply quantitative analysis to the relevant and measurable variables. In my own opinion the latter technique is more likely to produce a more objective regionalisation and to reveal underlying tendencies which would otherwise go unnoticed. It seems quite probable that developments in political geography will validate Berry's statement that 'Russett's direction is one that promises profitable progress'.[37]

The delimination of regions has always been a central concern of geographers and a field to which political geographers have contributed regularly. Discussions of regionalism at the supranational level are complemented by studies of intranational political regionalism, as expressed by the morphological approach to the state, the delimitation of irridentist regions or the definition of vernacular provinces of the type described by Fawcett (see below). Some transnational political or quasi-political regions have also been described, particularly with reference to Europe. A fairly common factor in most such studies has been the failure to employ suitable objective criteria in the assessment of regional character and boundaries. This criticism is particularly demonstrated in the case of 'central Europe'. Sinnhuber points out that the only areas common to a sample of twelve atlas maps of 'central Europe' were eastern Bohemia,

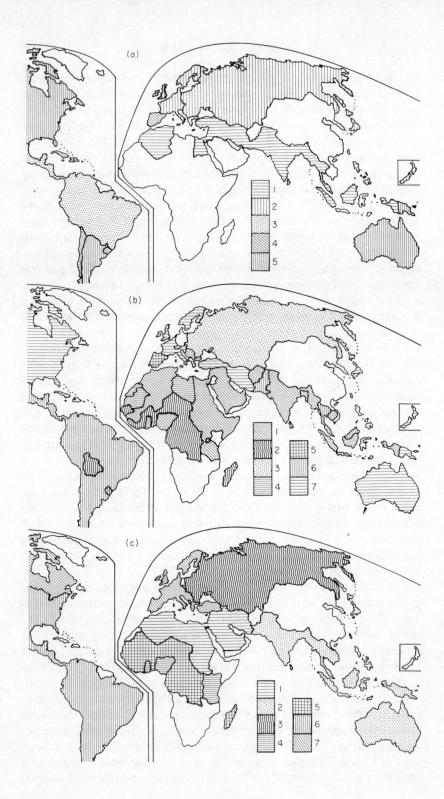

Moravia, western Slovakia, the southern margins of Poland, northern Hungary and the north-eastern fringe of Austria, while in the descriptions given by sixteen selected writers the only part of the continent not included by any was Iberia and the only part common to all was Austria, Bohemia and Moravia. Hanslik and Mackinder denied the existence of 'central Europe', while according to Steers it had ceased to exist; Kossman thought it emerged as a distinctive politico-cultural region in Roman times, though Lhéritier dated this emergence to the sixteenth century.[38]

Some descriptions of transnational political regions have distinct political overtones; descriptions of *Mitteleuropa* by German geographers have either reflected an attempt to delimit the region in terms of a unifying German culture spread over an area of geographical diversity, or used the concept of *Mitteleuropa* as support for German expansion into Slav-ruled lands. Objective and authoritative transnational studies may also be produced, as for example East's description of the character, emergence and changing status of the east-central European shatter zone.[39]

8.3 Electoral geography

During the post-war period, when general interest in political geography has tended to stagnate or to decline, the study of electoral geography has expanded greatly. The relationship of electoral geography to political geography as a whole appears to be somewhat confused; to some it is an integral part of the discipline, to others it seems to be a discipline in its own right, while others still would seem to imply that electoral geography is the very core and substance of political geography.[40] It has also been suggested, with some justification, that electoral geography 'seems to belong more to the realm of sociology than political geography',[41] and equally it could be argued that many studies in electoral geography do not have sufficient geographical content to allow their differentiation from studies in political science.

Certainly one of the important reasons underlying the eruption of interest in electoral geography concerns the ready availability of statistical electoral data. Students eager to test and apply statistical concepts and

---

Figure 8.2.   Russett's international regions.

(a) Grouping of sociocultural homogeneity. 1: Afro-Asians; 2: Eastern Europe; 3: Latin America; 4: semi-developed Latins; 5: Western community.

(b) United Nations voting groupings (1963). 1: Afro-Asians; 2: Brazzaville Africans; 3: Communists; 4: conservative Arabs; 5: Iberia; 6: Latin America; 7: Western community.

(c) International organisation membership groupings (1962). 1: Arabs; 2: Asia; 3: Eastern Europe; 4: former British Africa; 5: former French Africa; 6: Latin America; 7: Western community.

See ref. 31.

with an interest in spatial and political phenomena may have (wrongly) considered that the remainder of political geography contains few areas amenable to advanced quantitative analysis. Yet if electoral geography is a fundamental branch of political geography, its growth has been disproportionate in relation to the more general needs for the development of relevant techniques, models and theories in the subject as a whole.

Election statistics provide material for a variety of analyses, and studies relevant to political geography are those which focus on the more direct spatial causes and implications of electoral behaviour. Most commonly, electoral geographers have assumed that voters' choices are made according to their perceived best interests, and these perceptions and choices are then related to the sociological, economic or ethnic characteristics of electorates. This approach has been criticised on the grounds that in concentrating upon the generalised voting patterns of groups geographers overlook the behaviour of the individual, and that they should develop approaches which emphasise distinctly environmental factors.

For the purpose of voting, states are divided up into constituencies, wards, districts, precincts, or their equivalents, and the spatial characteristics of such divisions are of geographical interest. Though it would be impossible to devise a set of divisions each reflecting a balance between opposed party political viewpoints, in many cases deliberate attempts have been made to misrepresent expressions of political choice. Firstly, this may be achieved through the 'gerrymandering' of electoral boundaries (the term itself is derived from a Governor Gerry of Massachusetts, an early exponent of the gerrymander, who manipulated boundaries in his party's favour in the early nineteenth century). Though most common in the USA, gerrymandering occurs elsewhere; it is achieved in a variety of ways, the general effect being that the party perpetrating the gerrymander makes the most effective use of votes cast in its favour while wasting votes cast for the opposition. This may be achieved by linking together islands of party support within irregularly shaped divisions to create a majority within a generally unsympathetic environment, as was the case with the attenuated and curving original Massachusetts gerrymander. Alternatively, areas of concentrated opposition support may be made to constitute single divisions, which are won with enormous majorities, while neighbouring divisions produce slight majorities for the gerrymandering party. Thirdly, opposition strongholds may be divided and linked to adjacent areas in such a way that the opposition vote nowhere constitutes a majority. Prescott has described the gerrymandering of electoral boundaries in Armagh in Northern Ireland, where between 1920 and 1934 the urban council had an anti-partition majority which won two of the three wards until the council was disolved in 1934. In 1946 the ward boundaries were extended to include surrounding rural areas and the number of wards was increased to five, though urban and population growth during the period in question was minimal. At the ensuing election the Unionist party gained control of the council by winning in three wards.[42]

Election results may also be manipulated through the operation of a system of weighting, according to which the votes cast by certain groups count for much more than those cast by others. Under article 25 of the 1918 constitution of the RSFSR, which provided a model for the constitutions of the other Russian Union Republics, urban deputies were elected directly to the Congress of Soviets on the basis of one deputy to 25 000 inhabitants, while provincial deputies were elected indirectly by electorates of 125 000 inhabitants. The reason for the weighting was that the Bolsheviks found strongest support among Russian industrial workers while the peasant majority in the population was regarded with considerable distrust.[43] Under the abortive Central African Federation, Southern Rhodesia had 34 per cent of the population, Northern Rhodesia 30 per cent and Nyasaland 36 per cent, while the distribution of the federal electorate between them was 75 per cent, 23 per cent and 2 per cent. The extremely restricted franchise virtually debarred the African population from voting; thus settler-dominated Southern Rhodesia controlled three-quarters of the electorate, while the more populous Nyasaland controlled only one-fiftieth.[44]

Uneven growth and population movements will cause some district electorates to expand and others to contract, and to counter this natural tendency towards weighting it is necessary to undertake a periodical revision of boundaries and a redistribution of constituencies. In 1954 the Boundary Commission for England aimed at the creation of constituencies as close as possible in size to the mean electoral quota of 55 670 voters per constituency, and the actual recommendations included constituencies ranging between populations of 40 000 and 80 000; by 1969 four constituencies had electorates of between 90 000 and 100 000, and three had electorates of less than 30 000, while thirty-one had electorates of between 80 000 and 90 000.[45] Though migration had created serious imbalances, the Labour government argued that a wholesale redistribution of constituencies should wait upon the finalisation of plans for local government area reform, and the 1970 election was fought on the existing constituencies. New constituencies were introduced for the February 1974 election, though strong objections from the Labour party were raised when it was thought that the Conservative party might fight the election on an out-of-date electoral register of voters. In Australia a system of weighting is openly practised to avoid the creation of impossibly vast districts in interior areas of light rural population density.[46]

The most obvious product of the statistical or cartographic analysis of voting figures is material descriptive of spatial variation in voting behaviour, through time or in a spatial context or in both ways. Few investigators would consider their brief to be as limited as this, while such descriptive material, though interesting, would not justify the considerable input of effort to electoral geography or the diversion of effort from backward areas of political geography which are fraught with opportunity. For voting patterns to be of more particular political-geographical interest they should be capable of revealing more than just aggregate voting decisions, notably the effect of environment and culture upon voting and, possibly, the effects of voting upon environment. It may also be inferred that voting decisions are indicative of the distribution of both narrower and wider attitudes.

To relate the question of voting to sociological and environmental contexts, an investigation of the distribution of the Labour vote in Britain will, in a loose fashion, reveal the general distribution of the working class if national election results are used, or the intra-urban distribution of the class if local government voting patterns are used. Kish has pointed out that the left-wing vote in Emilia in Italy was associated with lowland areas worked by tenants, share-croppers and hired labourers, while the centre-right vote was strongest in upland areas farmed by independent peasant farmers.[47] However, information on sociological and economic distributions and densities is available, frequently in more detailed and direct forms, from sources other than voting returns, and such studies are useful in demonstrating interrelationships rather than in revealing otherwise unknown socioeconomic distributions.

In most cases the relationship between popular voting decisions and specific political decisions affecting the environment is indirect, since it is normally considered that representatives once elected, though sensitive to constituency pressures, have a mandate to vote in accordance with their own or party judgments, while parties generally come to power as a result of overall perceptions of their sympathies and policies. Thus, in 1970 a Conservative government was elected which was pledged to EEC membership despite the substantial majority of the British public's opposition to such membership. In a minority of cases the relationship between popular voting and political-geographical change is direct and profound. This category includes plebiscites of the sort held in East Prussia and Upper Silesia after the 1914–18 war to decide on the partitions of territory between new nation states, or of the kind promised to the British population by the Labour party during the February 1974 election to decide on the acceptance of renegotiated EEC membership terms. It would also include elections of the type held in Pakistan in December 1970, which produced a majority for the Bangladesh-separatist Awami League party.

One branch of electoral geography is concerned with the study of voting behaviour within national and international assemblies. The main geographical justification for such studies would seem to lie in the expectation that the voting patterns might elucidate the existence of regional interest groupings. Russett's work on United Nations voting as indicative of shared political attitudes or external behaviour has been mentioned, while in 1932 Paullin produced an atlas which included maps showing the pattern of voting in Congress on a series of issues and which partially reflected the regional outlooks current in the USA.[48] In 1967 Friedheim carried out a factor analysis of roll call votes at the United Nations Law of the Sea Conference. He clarified the issues of conflict and related them to the attitudes of the various groups of states. The basic alignment to emerge was an east–west conflict, primarily on the issues of the territorial sea and contiguous zone, with a secondary north–south conflict on the fishing rights of coastal states, and five less clearly divisive issues.[49]

The limitations affecting such studies are that votes cast by representatives in national assemblies need not necessarily reflect the majority sentiments of their constituents, but rather the personal judgments of the representatives; or the votes may be affected by party loyalty or the operation of a party whip. Votes cast in international assemblies like the UN may not always reflect the true opinions of governments represented; they may be conditioned by diplomatic or propaganda considerations, often in the knowledge that no further action is likely to follow the passing of a particular resolution.

Conventional approaches in electoral geography were criticised by Cox on the grounds that the study of aggregate voting decisions does not necessarily reflect the outlooks of the individual; for example, not all negroes vote Democrat, and not all of the British upper class is Conservative.[50] Secondly, he considered that a political-geographical approach to voting should be distinguishable from the types of study being practised within political science, and he advocated concentration on the relationship between the spatial context and the voting decision.[51] One of the conclusions of his 1968 investigation was that individuals belonging to both formal and informal social networks at the local level will be much more influenced in their partisan attitudes by the political *milieu* at that local level than will those belonging to social networks at the extra-local level. In 1969, while admitting the speculative nature of much of his work, Cox attempted to relate the voting decisions of individuals to their location in an information flow network. He wrote

. . . an approach which emphasises the space in which areal units or voters are embedded and the relationships of these units across space, not only provides electoral geography with a justification for an existence independent of comparative studies in political science; it also places the systematic field in the spatial mainstream of current geographical methodology and makes available the accumulating body of ideas relating to the geometry and the duality of spatial structure and spatial interaction.[52]

The new approaches in electoral geography are criticised by Prescott on the grounds that geographers are generally much more concerned with aggregate than with individual behaviour, while the concentration upon spatial processes and contextual influences is as yet in an early stage and may lead more in the direction of sociology than that of geography. However, the relevance of much of the earlier work in electoral geography is rather marginal, and if electoral geography is to be considered a part of political geography there is a definite need for approaches which will demonstrate the links between environment and voting behaviour; if such links do not emerge as being significant, the case for electoral studies outside the other social sciences is weak.

Political geographers are anxious to obtain information concerning the political attitudes of populations, since such attitudes are likely to be influential in the development of political processes affecting environments and indicative of spatial variations in political outlooks. However, the information which can be derived from election results frequently falls short of our requirements. The information obtainable from national elections in Britain indicates how, on a constituency basis, electorates divide between three or four leading parties at intervals generally of three or four years. From this information it is impossible to measure with any certainty popular feeling on particular issues, for voters are influenced by their overall perceptions of the relative performance of parties and their own perceived best interests. Many of the issues involved in the voting decision, such as divorce law reform, censorship or pensions, have only the most marginal geographical significance, while results in particular constituencies may be greatly affected by non-geographical factors such as the popularity in his own constituency of a particularly effective member of parliament. The results of national elections have considerable political-geographical implications, though it is seldom possible to disentangle the relative importance of specific processes and issues in producing these results. For example, it is suspected but not confirmed that the Conservatives won the British election of 1970 because the issue of inflation was raised shortly before polling, when insufficient time remained for an effective Labour government reply; inflation was also probably a determining factor in the next election, in February 1974, when Labour emerged as the largest single party. In local government elections there is a tendency, in Britain at least, for results to be influenced more by national party performance than by particular issues relating to the locality. The political geographer is generally more likely to obtain more useful information on popular opinion and its relationship to contextual factors through the use of well-constructed questionnaires than through the study of voting patterns.

Elections have an added political-geographical interest in campaigns involving a minority nationalist party, where voting patterns may reflect the strength and distribution of pressures for political change on the issue of nationalism. This is not always the case; many regimes will not tolerate the existence of national minority parties which might threaten the constitutional status quo or territorial integrity of their states, while voting for the nationalist party, where it exists, may not reflect the detail of nationalist sentiments. In the Scottish local government elections of May 1968 the Scottish Nationalist Party, campaigning on the issue of Scottish independence, won 36 per cent of votes cast in the four leading cities, which contain almost one-third of the Scottish electorate. In the same year a poll conducted by the *Glasgow Herald* revealed that only 21 per cent of Scots polled wanted complete independence from England; 38 per cent wanted home rule within the UK; 27 per cent wanted greater local and regional freedom; and 14 per cent wanted no change.[53] Taylor has demonstrated a high correlation between voting for *Plaid Cymru* and the use of the Welsh language, and has investigated the electoral histories of PC and the SNP, concluding that 'The Scottish Nationalist Party appears mainly as a vehicle for protest, whereas Plaid Cymru is more an expression of a threatened culture'.[54]

It is extremely difficult in electoral geography to develop studies which have a degree of universality, while for a large number of states electoral statistics are of little if any practical value. The latter point applies to states such as the communist states which have a one-party system of government; military or civil dictatorships; cases such as Rhodesia where the franchise is offered to a restricted segment of the population; or states where restrictions and the uneven provision of polling facilities discriminate against opposition parties and their supporters. Prescott suggests that there are seventy-one states where electoral results are theoretically suitable for geographical examination, while in fifty-seven countries the nature of the voting system renders the investigation of results worthless.[55] Further difficulties result from the fact that each state has tended to develop fairly distinctive parties, institutions and electoral arrangements. The UK, for example, has tended in recent years to have an alternation of political power between right-centre and left-centre parties, and, with the exception of the February 1974 election, to have one party in an overall majority. Most other West European states have functioned through coalition government, Italian politics being characterised by the formation of unstable coalitions between larger and smaller parties, of which there are several. Also in contrast, the Irish Republic has generated two powerful right-centre parties and a weaker Labour party.

There are estimated to be at least fourteen different ways of electing representatives, and various further permutations of these. In the UK, only the individual in each constituency who polls the largest number of votes is elected to Parliament; this system is likely to produce stable government by one party, since minority parties are unrepresented in Parliament unless they can win one or more seats with more votes than any other party. In some ways the system is unfair in discriminating against minority choices; for example, in the February 1974 election, the Liberal party received around six million votes and would have gained 123 of the 635 parliamentary seats under proportional representation rather than the fourteen seats actually gained. Election outcomes will vary considerably according to the system of election employed, as table 8.1 (overleaf) shows.[56]

The Irish Republic operates a single transferable vote system, according to which each constituency, depending on its size, returns between three

Table 8.1

	1970			February 1974		
	actual result	proportional representation	single transferable vote	actual result	proportional representation	single transferable vote
Con.	330	292	326	296	241	279
Lab.	287	271	280	301	236	299
Lib.	6	47	14	14	123	33
others	7	20	10	24	35	24
results	Con. win	Con. largest party	Con. win	Lab. largest party	Con. largest party	Lab. largest party

and five deputies, the major parties nominating two to four candidates; the electorate ranks the candidates in order of preference. The surplus votes of deputies elected and the transfer votes from the candidates with the lowest votes are allocated to the remaining contestants, making for a system which is more favourable to smaller parties, with the last seat in each constituency being closely contested.[57] The West German system is a combination of simple relative majority voting and proportional representation, with each voter casting two votes, one for the constituency representative to the Federal Parliament, elected by direct vote, and one for a candidate from the party lists, these candidates being elected by proportional representation. Each party receives a number of seats proportional to the votes cast in its favour; half the 496 seats in the Federal Parliament are filled by directly elected representatives, and half are divided between parties on the basis of proportional representation.

Rowley warns against rash generalisation between different political systems, pointing out that in the USA, as opposed to the UK, the main parties are not explicitly linked to social classes or appeals to support on the basis of class, and the salience of class divisions is further reduced by political regionalism, expressed for example in the Republicanism of the midwest and the characteristically southern form of Democratic support found in the deep south.[58]

I am attempting here not to devalue the usefulness of electoral studies but to question whether much of the research conducted is part of the mainstream of political geography. Unless voting decisions can be clearly related to spatial contexts, their geographical relevance is unproven. Some recent work is of distinctly geographical interest, such as McCarty's investigation of the degree to which voting for Senator McCarthy in Wisconsin in 1952 was a function of distance from McCarthy's home town,[59] or Cox's demonstration that in the English Midlands the Conservative vote varies as a direct function of the proportion of the labour force employed in agriculture, while in Wales it varies as an inverse function. The English rural populations tend to look towards Tory landowners and Anglican churchmen for leadership, while in nonconformist Wales such establishment figures are often despised.[60] Geographical voting studies can be developed for the micro and macro-scales of individuals in neighbourhoods and members of national and international assemblies, and it will be interesting to study the development of relevantly geographical studies at the meso-scale.

8.4 Internal administrative divisions

All but the smallest states are internally subdivided for reasons of administrative convenience, and the divisions, as forms of political regions, are amenable to geographical analysis. Such analysis may involve generic studies seeking comparisons between different sets of divisions, may concern the shape and morphology of selected divisions, or may be of a more dynamic nature—historically based and concerning the evolution of administrative divisions through time, or functionally based and studying the divisions in respect of the functions which are operated within their boundaries. Students concerned with the practical applications of political geography will find questions of administrative area reform to be responsive to their talents, and the section which follows is devoted to this topic. Many of the techniques developed by political geographers working at the state or meso-scale can be adapted to apply at the intra-state or micro-scale, though others, particularly those relating to the international behaviour of states, are rendered inappropriate by the non-sovereign nature of administrative subdivisions. The opportunities for methodological and theoretical advance in political geography must be almost as great at the micro as at the meso-scale, while students involved with postgraduate or undergraduate dissertations will find that the study of administrative divisions is relevant, rich in sources of data and practicable in most localities.

The comparative study of administrative areas reveals a surprisingly high degree of diversity from state to state; this renders the global classification of such areas difficult, and states which may appear similar in geographical, cultural and political respects may be found to have adopted completely different systems of internal administration. Any system and pattern of administrative units represents the outcome of human decisions, though once established, a pattern may become entrenched and survive long after its *raison d'être* has been forgotten, as did the English counties. Reference to a wide range of variables, effective in different combinations, is necessary in the explanation of such patterns, and these include geographical factors, cultural factors, and political considerations of both an evolutionary and a revolutionary nature. Consequently administrative areas can be understood only within their *milieu* and with regard to the purposes for which they were adopted, the functions operated within them, and the influences affecting their survival. Administrative areas favoured by governments which place a high premium on tradition, continuity and market forces are unlikely to resemble, either in form or function, those adopted to serve in state-planned economies.

Therefore it is not surprising that the limited similarities between different local government systems tend to be outweighed by contrasts, though all originate in the need to devolve power regionally from central agencies. Imitation and imposition have been important in determining the favoured forms of administrative system in recently sovereign states, while the *département* of Revolutionary France was copied by a number of states and the Soviet *oblast* reappears in a variety of adaptations in Eastern Europe, such as the *Bezirke* of East Germany. Humes and Martin have detected a number of basic models.[61] The 'Anglo-Saxon' model, embracing the UK and USA and exported to most former British colonies, is characterised by the 'council committee' form of government, with the popularly elected council as the formal centre of local government but with effective power delegated to various subcommittees of the council. The 'south European' form, also adopted in France and diffused to the former French territories, is associated with highly centralised national government and considerable restrictions on the powers vested in elected committees, with a large proportion of decision-making responsibility being vested in a single official, the mayor, who may be appointed by the local council or the national government. The 'East European' model involves a greater emphasis on public participation and initiative in a system of local government which tends to embrace many functions that are the prerogative of private enterprise in the capitalist world. At the same time, central government interference and coercion are also more evident than in most other forms. In the formulation of more advanced forms of classification the use of factor analysis would seem to be recommended, and this might provide the basis for a useful doctoral research project.

The most obvious uniformity between different systems of internal administration is that they are hierarchical, involving a division of responsibilities between larger and smaller areas and between higher and lower administrative tiers. The basic divide is between unitary states, within which all other levels of government lie in a direct chain of command downwards from the central government, and the federal state, within which there is normally an agreed division of responsibility between the federal and state governments. The number of administrative tiers employed varies considerably and need not be related solely to the size of the state concerned. Usually at least three tiers are involved, though some micro-states have no administrative subdivisions, while parts of India, Burma and Ethiopia have six tiers of administrative areas in their hierarchies.

In the course of their comparative study Humes and Martin searched for a common denominator or basic administrative unit, which they termed the 'municipality'. Included in this category were the old urban and rural districts of England, old districts of Scotland, the *communes* of France and *Powiats* of Poland. Units smaller and less influential than the municipalities were termed 'sub-municipal units', and included the English parish and Turkish *mahalles*. Between the federal or state governments and the municipalities are administrative areas of 'intermediate' status, which include the old English counties and the new counties, the French *département, arrondissement* and *canton*, and the Spanish *provincia*. Equivalent status is sometimes given to urban units, such as the old English county borough, Scottish county of city or German *Kreisfreie Städt*, and these were termed 'quasi-intermediate units'. (See table 8.2, overleaf.)

Though the Humes and Martin classification is as effective a classification as can be defined without recourse to quantification of a complex variety, few administrative systems fit comfortably into the framework; for example, three different French and three Turkish administrative areas all occupy the intermediate category, while many countries lack quasi-intermediate or sub-municipal levels of local administration. The populations of 'municipal' units vary from zero for some unpopulated French *communes* to almost 100 000 for some USA townships, and one must question whether like is being grouped with like. Further, some units in the intermediate category, such as the old counties, have elected administrations charged with a wide range of responsibilities, while others, such as the provinces of Iran or of Portugal, exist solely for the implementation of provincial legislation by a permanent bureaucracy.

Many states include examples of special-purpose authorities which exist outside the tiered structure of administrative divisions and handle specific duties for which the basic administrative structure is unsuitable. Examples include the English regional crime squad or USA school board areas, or special regional development authorities such as the Tennessee Valley Authority, the Highlands and Islands Development Board and the Regional Development Commissions (CODER) of France. Such bodies may have elected or governmentally appointed authorities, though the latter is the norm.

The techniques discussed in section 3.7 for the measurement of shape are as applicable at the micro as at the meso-scale of political region, and other shape indices or methods of defining centres of gravity can be substituted.[63] The spatial forms of administrative units are not arbitrary, but related to particular functions, even if these functions have since been forgotten. In the chalklands of eastern Cambridgeshire, elongated rectangular parishes, dating from the Saxon period, have a short river frontage and extend backwards at right angles to the rivers to incorporate zones of water meadow, arable land and upland grazing.[64] The parish boundaries thus define areas of small community self-sufficiency in addition to their provision of an ecclesiastical subdivision. The theme of self-

Table 8.2

Country	Intermediate unit	Quasi-intermediate unit	Municipality	Sub-municipal unit
England	County (former) new County new District	County Borough (former) new Metropolitan County new Metropolitan District	Urban District (former) Rural District (former)	Parish
Scotland	County (former) new District	County of City (former)	Large Burgh (former) Small Burgh (former) District (former)	
France	Département Arrondissement Canton		Commune	
Italy	Provincie (Regioni)		Comuni	
USA (federation of states)	County		Township	
West Germany (federation of states)	Landkreis Regierungsbezirk	Kreisfreie Städt	Gemeinde (combine to to form Aemter)	
Spain	Provincia		Municipio	Entidades locales menores
Turkey	Vilâyets Kazas Nahiyes		Belediye Köy	Mahalles

sufficiency is repeated more recently on a much larger scale by the Soviet *oblast*.

Alternatively the shape of administrative units may reflect the sphere of influence of a focal administrative centre, such as the county-town residence of the King's sheriff, situated at the heart of the old English county. A half-digested city regionalism has influenced the form of new English counties, while the French *département* was adopted as the outcome of a debate in post-revolutionary France in 1790 and rooted in a suggestion by Mirabeau that France should be divided into eighty-three units of roughly equal area. His suggestion that the administrative focus of each *département* should be rotated to avoid inter-city rivalry was not adopted;

instead each *département* focused on a central town which was within one day's travel time of all other locations within it.[65]

In other cases still the shape of administrative units may represent a fossilisation of a pattern of territorial division, the origins of which are obscure. The old counties of north-east Scotland evolved from sheriff-doms, themselves derived from pre-feudal 'mormaerships' which were based on a Pictish or pre-Pictish division of the landscapes, the origins of which are lost but probably falsified in the Pictish myth that the seven children of the legendary Cruithne divided Alba into seven districts.[66]

Studies of the shapes of administrative units are not common. Rasheed examined the shapes of administrative districts in Bangladesh to test three hypotheses: that the administrative districts had a tendency for elongation towards the relatively central capital of Dacca; that the district headquarters would tend to be located nearer to the boundary closest to Dacca than that furthest from the capital; and that the greater the elongation of the district, the greater the departure of its headquarters from a central position.[67] The first premise was tested by joining the mid-point of the longest axis of each district to the capital and measuring the angle between the resultant line and the longest axis; an angle of less than 45° indicated elongation in the direction of the capital. The second premise was tested by simple linear measurement, and the third by using Haggett's shape index $S = (1.27A)/L^2$ (see p. 53). Then the degree of departure of the district headquarters from the geographic centre was estimated by measuring the shortest and longest distance between the headquarters and the boundary—the two measures were compared and the ratio between them used as an index of departure (I^d) from the geographic centre. Product moment correlation coefficients of S and I^d were calculated to establish the relationship between shape and the location of the headquarters.

The mean of the angles of 34.75° gave a positive result in respect of the first of the premises, and positive results were also obtained for the second premise, though only weak positive results were established in testing the third premise. Though an imaginative and potentially productive use was made of shape measurements, the exercise foundered as a study of causal relationships because the district boundaries and the establishment of district headquarters preceded Dacca's elevation to capital status, and the districts and headquarters did not evolve in response to Dacca.

Administrative divisions may be studied in terms of their contacts with neighbouring units; Haggett took a sample of Brazilian *municipios* and counted the number of neighbours touching each unit. Thirty of the sample of one hundred had six neighbours, and the mean was 5.71 contacts.[68] Pedersen, in an examination of communes in Denmark, produced a closely similar mean of 5.83,[69] though it was subsequently suggested that the tendency towards mean values of 6.0 need not imply a tendency towards a hexagonal net structure among administrative areas, since a blurring of a triangular or quadratic net structure could produce

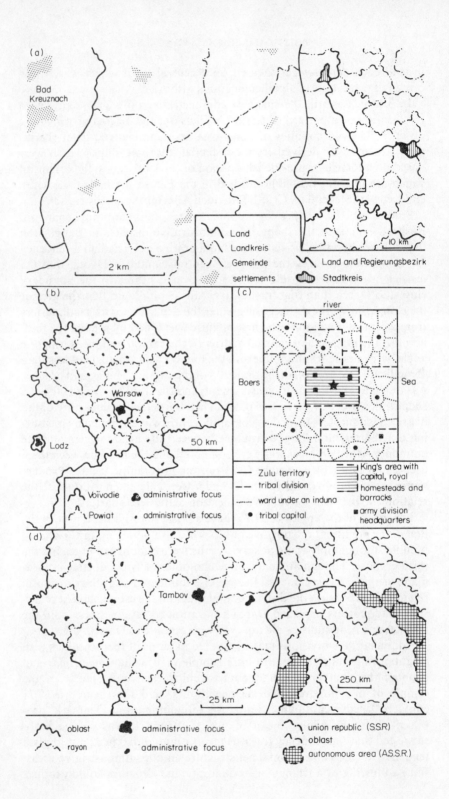

(a)

Bad
Kreuznach

2 km

10 km

		Land	
		Landkreis	
		Gemeinde	Land and Regierungsbezirk
		settlements	Stadtkreis

(b)

Warsaw

Lodz

50 km

(c)

river

Boers

Sea

	Zulu territory		King's area with capital, royal
	tribal division		homesteads and barracks
	ward under an induna		army division headquarters
	tribal capital		

(d)

Tambov

25 km

250 km

	oblast		administrative focus		union republic (S.S.R.)
	rayon		administrative focus		oblast
					autonomous area (A.S.S.R.)

Voïvodie	administrative focus
Powiat	administrative focus

similar means.[70]

Studies of the evolution of systems of administrative areas are likewise in short supply, particularly with regard to attempts to trace back successive evolutionary stages. At the federal level Robinson has described the development of federal divisions in Australia, and has suggested that the states are in some respects more geographically distinct than at the time of federation.[71] Haggett studied the progressive territorial subdivision of Santa Caterina state in Brazil between 1872 and 1960, and demonstrated a tendency for administrative divisions to become smaller as population density increased, with the number of contacts which each unit had with different neighbours also tending to increase. The increase in the number of *municipios* between 1950 and 1960 was from 1761 to about 3000.[72]

I have analysed the development of administrative areas in north-east Scotland from the dark ages to the present day.[73] From about the sixth century Pictland was divided into a well-authenticated sevenfold subdivision, and a longer-established twofold division of Pictland into northern and southern sections, probably along the lines of the Mounth, can be traced back to the Roman invasion. The seven Pictish provinces were said to be ruled by underkings, and comprised Angus and Mearns; Atholl and Gowrie; Strath Earn and Menteith; Fife and Kinross; Mar and Buchan; Moray and Ross; and Caithness. Though Pictland fell to the Scots in the ninth century, its provinces retained their identity, and their names are still in common usage.

Each of the seven Pictish provinces, except Caithness, was composed of two districts, and one or both of these districts emerged in the Scottish period as the territory governed by a mormaer, an important tribal leader whose exact function is obscure but which may have been related to a regionally organised system of coastal defence. About the late eleventh century, with the penetration of feudal influences into Scotland, the mormaers became converted into earls, and linked to the Scottish kings by feudal obligations. The next stage in the political-geographical evolution of north-east Scotland involved the introduction of sheriffdoms, the Scottish equivalent of the English county. Each sheriffdom represented the claimed sphere of influence of a king's sheriff, and their diffusion was crucial to the processes by which an insecure Scotto-Norman monarchy based in and around the Central Lowlands expanded its effective state area, using feudalism as a vehicle for the subjugation and absorption of unruly Celtic provinces to the north and west.

Figure 8.3. Examples of administrative areas. (a) West Germany. (b) Poland. (c) Zulu territory in the mid-nineteenth century (ref. 62). (d) USSR. Note that West Germany and the USSR are federal states, and the federal division is represented by the Land and SSR levels respectively. The division of Zulu territory is a very stylised plan, not a map.

Effective centralised control penetrated northern Scotland along the east-coast lowlands, the zone of least resistance, and sheriffdoms were established, each of which focused on a caput, a town housing a largely intrusive feudal population and containing the stronghold of the royal sheriff. It is tentatively suggested that in the twelfth century the sheriffdoms of Angus, Mearns (Kincardine), Aberdeen and Banff were established, and that the correspondence of the two former with the Pictish regions of the same name is clear: that of Aberdeen incorporated the linked regions of Buchan and Mar, while Banff guarded the eastern margins of the troublesome Celtic province of Moray. In the thirteenth century the power of Moray was broken, and the province was split up between the sheriffdoms of Elgin, Forres and Nairn. In the centuries which followed the basic pattern of the north-east sheriffdoms was little changed, though exclaves appeared as sheriffs brought lands which they owned in neighbouring sheriffdoms under their own jurisdictions. No wholesale modification of the basic feudal system of administrative areas came until the reform of Scottish local government of the early 1970s, and administrative areas such as Aberdeenshire (Buchan and Mar), Kincardineshire (Mearns) and Angus have been in continuous usage, but with vastly changed functions, for over a thousand years. The tenacity of the old division was evident in the successful Kincardineshire campaign to resist the division of the old county between two new administrative districts in the course of the recent reform.

Manuscripts of the dark ages and medieval land charters provided the main sources of data; the relative dating of the appearance of sheriffdoms relied upon the search for the earliest historical mention of a particular sheriffdom, and the northward, north-westward and southern diffusion of sheriffdoms clearly emerged. At a future date it is hoped to apply trend surface analysis to the dates obtained to produce an objective contouring of the diffusion of feudal influences from a central Scottish power focus. The shapes of the medieval counties were deduced from a laborious study of land grant charters, each of the early charters normally containing the phrase 'terra de "x" infra vicecomitatus [sheriffdom] de "y"'. As each charter also normally bears a date, it was possible to determine within which sheriffdom a particular parcel of lands lay at a particular point in time; when sufficient such information is mapped, it becomes clear that the counties of north-east Scotland changed little in outline after the early medieval period, apart from the abolition of the county of Forres which was absorbed by Moray and the later resumption of exclaves to their surrounding counties in the nineteenth century.

A conceptual framework which relates stages in the development of administrative areas to stages of demographical and economic development has been devised by Massam.[74] Though the framework is valuable in its identification of a number of basic trends and relationships, it does not make provision for the revolutionary changes in administrative area policy which may result from a radical change in government, such as occurred with the Russian revolution, or from the ultimate realisation that a system of administrative areas has become hopelessly outmoded and must be swept away despite the objections which will be raised by influential vested interests, as occurred in the UK at the beginning of the 1970s (see table 8.3).

Massam indicates two main standpoints from which changes in the administrative system can be viewed: firstly with reference to changes in the spatial pattern of areas, and secondly with reference to changes in the control and organisation of the system.[75] The study of administrative divisions becomes largely meaningless unless reference is made to the functions which the administrative areas actually operate. Though there were few

Figure 8.4.   The expansion of the sheriffdoms. The earliest traceable recorded mentions of sheriffdoms are shown, along with estimates of their shapes, and their caputs are shown by dots. The combination of some sheriffdoms at certain times is shown by braces and dates. Some sheriffdoms are probably considerably older than their earliest surviving mention, for example the Mearns of Kincardineshire will be older than 1165–73. (See ref. 66.)

changes in the spatial forms of many English counties from the Norman
period, until 1 April 1974, changes in the functions of the counties were so
profound that spatial form probably remains the only basis for meaningful
comparison over the centuries. Norman counties basically represented the
spheres of influence of kings' sheriffs, whose duties included the collection

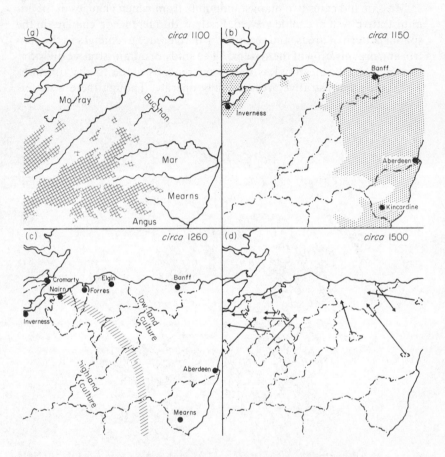

Figure 8.5.   Evolution of administrative areas in north-east Scotland.
    (a) Early feudal earldoms. These were directly derived from areas ruled by mor-
maers developed from an earlier Pictish division. The main rivers are shown, and
land over 500 metres shaded.
    (b) The appearance of sheriffdoms. The estimated extent of their effective state
area is shaded.
    (c) The division of Moray. The troublesome Celtic province is divided between
sheriffdoms. The shaded zone is the approximate divide between highland and lowland cultures.
    (d) Complication. The pattern of administrative areas becomes complicated by
the appearance of exclaves, frequently formed by sheriffs obtaining the annexation
to their own jurisdiction of lands they owned outside their own sheriffdoms.
    See ref. 66.

of taxes, arbitration at the county courts and the raising of the county levy. In subsequent centuries, while the duties of the sheriff became increasingly ceremonial, the counties became the basic units for the operation of steadily more complex and onerous legislation, operated firstly by the landed gentry of the county and later by democratically-elected officials supporting a growing bureaucracy and labour force and charged with social, sanitary and environmental services. It would be quite pointless to equate the sheriff, his castle and retinue with a modern county council establishment and service infrastructure. Most studies concerned with the functions of administrative areas are cast in terms of plans and techniques for the designation of improved systems of administrative areas, and for this reason, function is included in a separate section devoted to administrative area reform.

Case study

The system of internal administration in the Soviet Union is particularly interesting, for it has been developed in the context of an excep-

Table 8.3. A conceptual framework for the spatial evolution of administrative systems

Time	State of the area	Stage of administrative system
t_1	Unknown and unsettled	No spatial units
t_2	Explored, but unsettled	Some boundaries may be shown on maps to claim sovereignty of area
t_3	Settled in part	The settled part may be subdivided into distinct units
t_4	(a) Expansion of settlement	New areas defined
	(b) Density of settlement increases	Subdivision of existing areas to maintain small units
t_5	(a) Density of settlement increases	Amalgamation of small units to take advantage of economies of scale
	(b) Communication systems improve with transportation innovations	Centralisation and standardisation in the quality of the administrative service
t_6	Modification of demand and supply as values change, population density changes and distribution mechanisms change	Areas may be modified to amalgamate different functions. Areas may be kept at a level which *explicitly* does not take advantage of economies of scale, but provides local standards of service. Affluence of communities may encourage quality to dominate quantity–cost considerations of pure economic reasoning

tionally large and ethnically diverse state by a government which took a revolutionary view of the problem of internal administration and totally disregarded earlier systems of administration. Inconsistency has resulted from the attempts to reconcile a federal and subfederal ethnically based division of territory with administrative–economic regions appropriate to the operation of a planned economy.

Before the Russian revolution the Bolshevik party was opposed to the federation of the Soviet Union along national lines, but in the course of the post-revolutionary disturbances several national minorities virtually established their *de facto* independence. The federation of the former Tsarist empire along national republican lines was then seen as an expedient to the reunification of Russia as a proletarian state; it was expected that, with the offer of linguistic and administrative autonomies, the various national minorities would come to recognise that their true loyalties related to social class rather than nationality. However, the federal division of the country became entrenched in the provisions of the 1936 constitution, which confirmed the Union Republics with the formal but unreal rights of secession, independent diplomacy and independent military formations.[76]

Since the Union Republics or Soviet Socialist Republics (ssRs) had the formal right to secession, the award of ssR status was made conditional upon the possession of a common boundary with a foreign power; otherwise secession might theoretically have led to the formation of hostile enclaves within the ussR. Smaller national minorities and those which lacked a common boundary with a foreign power were awarded non-sovereign national territories: Autonomous Soviet Socialist Republics (assRs), which have constitutions, Autonomous Oblasts, which retain the right to use the national language in official business, and National Okrugs, in descending order of importance. No national minority is subjected to another, and national territories are subordinate only to the ssR of which they form a part.

Coexisting uncomfortably with the federal and subfederal national divisions is a set of economic and administrative areas. As might be expected, the national territories (largely defined on linguistic bases) rarely correspond with geographical or economic regions; for example, the Azerbaydzhan ssR is split in two by the Armenian ssR, the Caucasus region is divided between three ssRs, and natural units such as the Fergana valley are often divided between several republics. The boundaries of national republics are regarded as inviolable, and consequently economic and administrative boundaries may not cut across them.

The main economic–administrative divisions of the Soviet Union are oblasts, krays and rayons; all but the smallest ssRs are internally subdivided into *oblasts*, while a larger counterpart of the oblast, the kray, exists in some of the more backward parts of the RSFSR. Oblasts are defined as units of complex economic character containing both manufacturing and agricultural components (the relative importance of each naturally varies from region to region), and most focus on a central industrial town which is supposed to serve as a focus for the dissemination of current political dogma and planning policy. The oblasts are in turn divided into rayons which also have both urban and rural components. Towns are slotted into the hierarchy at various levels. Republican capitals and towns of over 300 000 population in the RSFSR are subordinate only to the SSR administration and are subdivided into urban rayons; the smaller towns are subordinate to rayons, and the remaining larger towns to the oblasts.

Schemes for large economic planning regions have been introduced at various times; a scheme devised by the Kalinin Commission in the early 1920s for macro-regions to be used for planning in conjunction with the national plan for electrification was never fully implemented because some of the proposed regions involved the unacceptable incorporation of SSRs into larger units—for example, the inclusion of Byelorussia with the RSFSR—though later economic regions have linked, subdivided, but not partially amalgamated SSRs. Regionalisation made little headway under the extreme centralisation of power which characterised the Stalin period, though in 1940 a series of thirteen macro-regions were introduced in an attempt to create regional self-sufficiency and reduce interregional strains on the inadequate transport system. The plan was not successful, and the unwieldy regions were increased in number to seventeen in 1947. A decade later, attempts were made to decentralise the top-heavy administrative system through the introduction of 105 sovnarkhozy regions which provided a framework for intra-regional planning and cooperation. Disagreement followed between planners, who favoured regional approaches to regional problems, and the aparatchiks of the bureaucracy, who were distrustful of any delegation of power and favoured large-scale regional

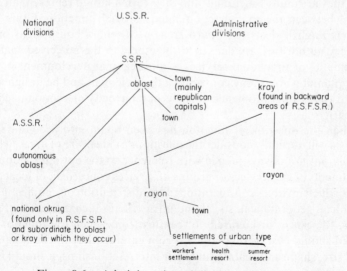

Figure 8.6.   Administrative subdivisions of the USSR

self-sufficiency. In 1963 the sovnarkhozy were consolidated into forty-seven Industrial Management Regions, with nineteen major economic regions to handle the broader aspects of regional development, and since the demise of Khrushchev there has been a retreat from the regional devolution of power.[77]

8.5 Administrative area reform

Much of the content of political geography is of a descriptive or theoretical nature and is unlikely to find practical application. In the case of suggestions for administrative area reform, even more so than that of international boundary studies, the political geographer has much to offer to the politician and the planner, though his talents have too often gone unsung and uninvited. Many administrations are realising the need to attune administrative areas of various types to changing social and economic circumstances, and political geographers can draw upon a potent armoury of geographical techniques suited to this task. No other single political-geographical field offers more opportunities to the student of planning and applied geography.

Administrative areas are to be understood only by reference to the functions which are discharged within them, and in the investigation of such areas, political geographers will be obliged to ask: 'what functions are operated within these areas? what are the spatial requirements of these functions? how can we achieve a harmony between the areas and the functions?' Different sets of administrative areas exist for the discharge of a great variety of functions. Most local government areas are used for the operation of a considerable range, from education and planning to sanitation; they are multi-functional, and their forms should represent an equilibrium between the spatial requirements of each function. Other areas, such as English electricity board areas, USA school board areas or Thai sanitary authorities, are defined with respect to the perceived spatial requirements of individual services, while regional development or economic planning areas may constitute a third element and be designed with regard to regional problems, areas of homogeneity or economic complementarity.

When the question of function has been taken into account, further analysis will normally consider the questions of ideal size of areas, which is usually but not always judged with reference to the optimum population catchments of the services or groups of services concerned; of ideal spatial form, which involves consideration of the distribution of significant demographical, geographical, social and infrastructural characteristics; and of focus, the centre or hierarchy of centres from which the functions concerned should best be discharged. From careful study of these aspects of ideal size, shape and centres, and their interrelationships, it should be possible to approximate a best-fit set of administrative areas.

The bulk of functions operated within the administrative subdivisions of the state involve services to the public, such as education, welfare, hygiene and protection, and consequently ideal size is generally best expressed, primarily but not necessarily solely, in respect of an optimum number of consumers for the services in question. Certain functions, however, must be operated in areas whose size and form are not related to population catchments; for example, river boards operate in areas which represent river catchment basins, and economic development boards may correspond to particular economic regions, such as the Highlands and Islands Development Board which operates over an area characterised by particular development problems and within which tourism, crofting, fishing, estate management, forestry and cottage industries are the main economic activities. Each public service or function probably has its ideal population catchment, though this statistic is likely to be affected by patterns of population distribution, and in areas of light or uneven population density, the requirements of consumer access may necessitate the adoption of suboptimal population catchments.

Massam has approached the problem of optimum size through the use of concepts of economies of scale and long-run average cost curves (see figure 8.7a).[78] The basic premise involved is that, as the quantity of output of an organisation increases, economies of scale begin to operate up to a point beyond which diseconomies are increasingly encountered. In the case of an administrative system the economies of scale relate to the number of consumers for a particular service which will dictate in turn the output of that service. The long-run average cost curve is the envelope curve of a series of short-run curves. If the above premise is correct, the curve will have a U shape, and it will be possible to discern the optimum size for a service in terms of consumers served. The form of such a curve is described by the formula

$$y = a - b_1 x + b_2 x^2$$

where y is the cost per unit output and x is the quantity of output produced. Data relating to specific administrative services can be collected and plotted in the form of a scatter graph of quantity against cost per unit output for each case, and a best-fit line added. This will either reveal the optimum size requirements of a particular service through a U-shaped long-run average cost curve, show that economies of scale do not exist (the l.a.c. is horizontal), or show that they operate at low or high levels of output (an inverted U curve). Using cross-sectional data from the Ontario Hydro Electrical Commission, Massam found that there appeared to be little relationship between efficiency and the size of Municipal Electrical Utilities areas, but that a U-shaped l.a.c. applied in the case of rural operating areas.[79]

The assessment of optimum size has other dimensions than the calculation of the size of population catchment which will produce the best economies of scale in respect of a particular service. Firstly, local government areas are usually shared by a range of functions, and secondly, the provision of services must also be judged in relation to the quality of the service offered and the sociogeographical characteristics of the area within which it is being provided. The 'Seebohm Report' recommended that the personal social services, for example education, housing, welfare and health services, in the UK could be organised together in decentralised units of 50 000 to 100 000 population, while the 'Maud Report' considered that for all the main services, minimum population catchments of 250 000 were desirable, and that while authorities serving populations of less than this number would lack the resources for effective planning, those serving populations of more than one million would face difficulties in centralising work and maintaining effective managerial control.[80] Senior, who dissented from the majority opinion on many issues, believed that realistic optimum figures could not be obtained, and preferred to look for realistic sociogeographical units.

Where the patterns of settlement, communications and activity have created a coherent town district embracing anything over 100 000 people, the sacrifice of that unit's convenience and democratic viability by its amalgamation with a neighbouring unit, merely to attain a predetermined population size, is unlikely to be compensated by any greater efficiency in the running of its social services.[81]

The optimum size figures as visualised for particular services by their respective ministries in the UK were tabulated by Mackintosh, and table 8.4 is an extract.[82]

Table 8.4

Function	Most appropriate unit (population)
principal roads	approx. 1 000 000
fire	1 000 000
education	300 000–500 000
local health and welfare service	200 000+
clean air legislation	60 000+
public parks	40 000+
refuse collection	40 000+

There is a general lack of consensus available, and though long-run average cost curves might be employed to test for economies of scale in particular services where, as is usually the case, a number of services are grouped together in a single set of areas, subjective systems of weighting would have to be employed in a search for rough equilibrium between the size optima for each of the services. Evidence available from official British sources would seem to imply that the personal services are best grouped in units of at least 100 000 population, and that economies of scale will be encountered if this figure is doubled, while the environmental services, including planning, transport and water, require larger units, and for effective long-term planning, units of 250 000 to 4 million population have been recommended. Local recreation and amenity services, on the other hand, can operate effectively in units of around 40 000 population.

The most effective and generally acceptable local administration will result if the cost advantages accruing from economies of scale are tempered where necessary with the consideration of the quality of service provided. Deterioration in the quality of the services offered will result if consumers are obliged to sacrifice time and effort in order to avail themselves of a service, or feel remote and dissociated from local democracy through the operation of over-large units. The quality of personal services can be improved if the size and distribution of centres dispensing services is geared to patterns of consumer utilisation. An index of traffic intensity can be derived from the formula

$$\text{traffic intensity} = \frac{\text{average service time}}{\text{average inter-arrival time}}$$

where service time is the time taken to provide a customer with service, and average inter-arrival time is the average time between the arrival of each customer. From these the average waiting time spent by each customer can be calculated.[83]

Knowing the functions which are to be operated, and the size requirements of each function, administrative area reform can proceed to the allocation of administrative centres and area boundaries. Depending upon the functions involved and the particular geographical characteristics of the environment concerned, one set, or a hierarchy of areas and centres, may be required. Where the problem is simply one of providing a set of areas and dispensing centres for the operation of a single service, such that the mean distance between centres and customers is minimised and each centre serves a similar number of customers, then 'The tool is linear programming and the particular problem we are dealing with is the transportation problem'.[84] A matrix is used in which the alternate centres are listed on one axis, and a set of points representing customers' locations on a second axis (figure 8.8).

In column R_1 we list the number of customers at each location; the total is 45. In row R_2 we list the number of customers that will be served by each center. If we wish each center to service the same number we assign 15 to each. The box at the bottom right-hand corner tells us that all customers have been assigned to a center. By examining all possible allocations from I, II, III and IV to A, B and C so that in each case $R_1 = R_2$, and knowing the cost of moving people to the centers we can draw the administrative boundaries.[85]

Increasing sophistication can be added by introducing constraints such as the focusing of units on points of mean aggregate travel.[86] Though linear programming may be used effectively to delimit catchment areas for single *ad hoc* or special purpose authorities, the construction of local government areas presents problems more subtle and complex than the allocation of

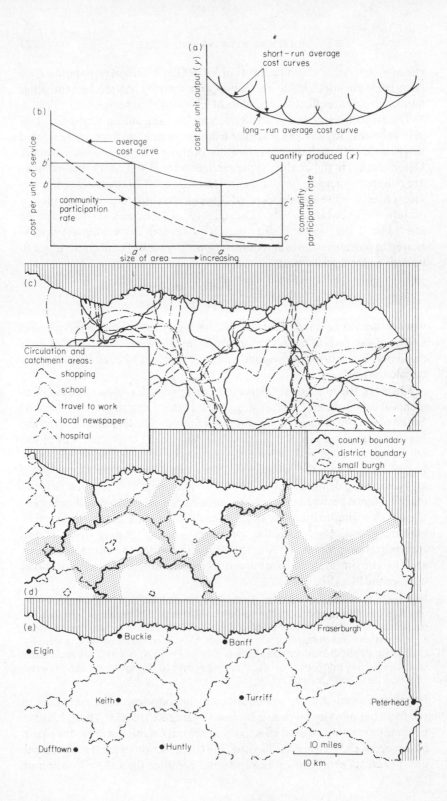

(a)

cost per unit output (y)

short-run average
cost curves

long-run average
cost curve

quantity produced (x)

(b)

cost per unit of service

average
cost curve

b'

b

community
participation
rate

community participation rate

c'

c

a' a

size of area ⟶ increasing

(c)

Circulation and
catchment areas:

⌒ shopping

⌒ school

⌒ travel to work

⌒ local newspaper

⌒ hospital

━━ county boundary

┈┈ district boundary

◌ small burgh

(d)

(e)

• Elgin

• Buckie

• Banff

Fraserburgh •

Keith •

• Turriff

Peterhead •

Dufftown •

• Huntly

10 miles

10 km

people in bundles of the right size to appropriate centres. Areas suitable for the organisation of local democracy should respect and enhance existing associations between people and places, and should express and adapt to the circulation fields generated by real-life patterns of circulation and identification. Through the recognition of these facts, it should be possible to devise sets of areas which reconcile the economies of effective planning with sociogeographical realities.

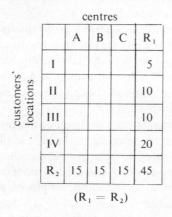

centres

	A	B	C	R_1
I				5
II				10
III				10
IV				20
R_2	15	15	15	45

customers' locations

$(R_1 = R_2)$

Figure 8.8

Several recent studies of city regions have shown that in most populated and developed parts of the earth, patterns of urban–rural and inter-urban association and interaction exist, the identification and mapping of which can form an excellent basis for local government area reform. Two leading exponents of city regionalism are Dickinson and Senior; the former, writ-

---

Figure 8.7.   Techniques for administrative area reform.

(a) Average cost curves.

(b) Cost *versus* quality of service. Note that the greatest economies are achieved at *a*, but with a low community participation rate at *c*. Less economy is obtained at *a'*, where the cost per unit of service rises to *b'* but the community participation rate rises to *c'*.

(c), (d) and (e) Stages in the reform of administrative areas in the north of northeast Scotland. In (c) various circulation fields and catchment area boundaries are superimposed. In (d) the zones of indifference, where loyalties to particular centres are blurred, have been detected through a study of (c), and are here superimposed on a map of the pre-1974 administrative divisions. In (e) the recommended boundaries for the low-order administrative divisions have been delimited through a process of introducing boundaries within the zones of indifference to take account of local relief and water barriers to interaction and the retention intact of village service areas. District service centres are shown.

For (a) and (b), see ref. 63. For (c), (d) and (e), see ref. 66.

ing in 1967, stated that 'The unity of the areas focussed on the cities has not yet been recognised as a basis for defining new units of metropolitan government',[87] and the latter that '[the city region] represents a new form of civilised life, one which constitutes a highly significant entity for the purposes of physical planning, and one whose structure and functioning we consider capable of being deliberately shaped by public opinion'.[88] This view was supported by James, who wrote that '[new local government areas in England and Wales must] embrace all people who look to the central city as their regional capital'.[89]

City regionalism has its critics among geographers as well as its supporters; Hall referred to the city region as 'a mythical beast' (though he found much to approve of in Senior's city region based scheme for administrative area reform),[90] while Minshull has doubted that social intercourse can be measured or mapped, though the advocates of the city region consider it to be a natural social unit.[91]

The problem of detection is not so difficult as Minshull might have imagined; most social contacts are made in the course of day-to-day movements which can be measured and mapped, as can the spatial interactions produced by retailing, travel to work and other movements, and as can the infrastructures which exist for retailing, employment, recreation, education and so on. From the vantage point of city regionalism, the landscape appears as a cellular pattern of territories linked by economic and social bonds to nuclear towns. Each regional centre has about it a maze of functional areas, each of which represents the operational area of a different city-based service, and all of which have dependence on the city as their common denominator; 'we may refer to this area of functional association with the city as the city region'.[92]

The city region has much to recommend itself to the local government area reformer. It provides a viable basis for local democracy, since it expresses the patterns and associations of everyday life as represented in circulation fields which centre upon the regional city; it unites town and country and reflects the symbiosis which exists between the city and its urban field, and consequently allows the integration of urban and rural planning. Thirdly, the concept can provide a unified basis for the definition of a hierarchy of administrative areas, with tiers of areas often being conveniently based upon city regions and town districts of various orders.

> . . . the idea of the regional metropolis is that of leadership over neighbouring tributary towns. Hence functions of leadership are graded in towns which fall into a series, based on their importance as regional centres.[93]

In terms of size, it was suggested above that in the UK population catchments of at least 100 000, and preferably double this figure, are desirable for the operation of the personal group of services, and catchments of at least 250 000 for the environmental services, a figure which can be greatly exceeded. Senior has demonstrated the feasibility of a division of England

and Wales on the basis of city regions into personal service authorities of (projected 1981) populations ranging from 97 000 to 908 000, with the median lying at exactly 250 000, and environmental service areas of (projected) populations ranging from 312 000 to 3 993 000, with the median at 990 000.[94]

Since city regions exist as the total of circulation fields generated by a focal town, the best way to map the extent of city regions is to begin by mapping each circulation field. Particularly relevant are those generated by journeys to work, shopping and recreation after work, while local newspaper circulation areas, hospital and school catchment areas should also be plotted. Each of the fields mapped is likely to be slightly different in form, but when the different sets of boundaries are superimposed, city regional core areas should become apparent, while between the areas which clearly gravitate to one or another regional centre are zones of indifference within which loyalties are transitional and blurred. Within these zones, city regional boundaries should be drawn to take account of convenient physiographical divides such as rivers and watersheds, while respecting the integrity of lower-order service areas. The researcher may consider that certain indicator boundaries, such as those delimiting retail or travel-to-work catchment areas, should receive special weighting. The selection of a particular city-regional boundary within the zone of boundary overlap may be achieved by quantitative or non-quantitative methods, though in my experience it is preferable to adjust the final boundary to geographical characteristics occurring within the zone of indifference rather than to adopt a median or arithmetic boundary which may cut across patterns of terrain or local socioeconomic association.

Case studies

An application in depth of the city region concept to the problem of administrative area reform in north-east Scotland was made between 1968 and 1970.[95] An Aberdeen city region was defined through the investigation of the gravitational watersheds existing between Aberdeen and Dundee, in respect of a range of city-based services, though to the west the absence of a Highland city of comparable status to Aberdeen created a void in the cellular pattern of city regions, and recourse was made to more conventional geographical and economic considerations in establishing the western boundary. The resultant region was considered suitable for the operation of the environmental group of services, but too large for the operation of the personal group of services for which consumer access to dispensing centres is of basic importance, and consequently separate personal service areas were defined, based on the spheres of influence of Elgin and of Aberdeen as a lower-order service centre. A lower tier of authorities, based on town districts, the miniatures of city regions and centred on smaller central places, was considered suitable to form units for the operation of grass-

roots local democracy, being sufficiently large to operate a range of administrative services, largely those connected with local amenities, and
sufficiently small to provide intimate government. It was considered that
such units, too small to produce remoteness of government and yet large
enough to operate locally important functions, would favour a resurgence
of popular participation in local government. The population sizes of the
proposed administrative areas were: first tier, 440 000; second tier, 90 000
to 350 000; third tier, 5000 to 20 000.

The methods of academic and of officially appointed administrative
area reformers are likely to differ. The Royal Commission on Local
Government Reform in Scotland presented its report to Parliament in
1949, after three years of deliberation; the commission had a membership
of nine people, distinguished in public life and some branches of administration, but not in the theoretical techniques appropriate to administrative
area reform. Their evidence was drawn from four main sources: visits to
local authorities in Scotland, London, Rotterdam and Scandinavia; written evidence submitted by interest groups and individuals; oral evidence in
public hearings; and research material produced by a commissioned intel-
ligence unit. The written evidence derived from more than 330 bodies,
vested interests and individuals, most of which were preoccupied with the
protection of their own corporate, personal or idiosyncratic interests
rather than with the improvement of local government. The commissioned
research was of variable usefulness, and it is doubtful that most geographers acquainted with the field would agree with the chairman of the
commission that this material was adequate to the task of defining new administrative areas upon the city-regional basis which the commission evi-
dently favoured.

The official and the academic approaches to administrative area reform
each have their strengths and their weaknesses (though I may be biased
regarding their relative merits). The government commission enjoys better
circumstances of financial support and of access to official material; no
single dogmatic viewpoint is likely to dominate their enquiries, and the collective approach has the advantage that a number of different experiences
are brought to bear on the problem. Consensus is not an end in itself (many
would regard the Senior report as superior to that produced by the majority of commissioners working on local government in England and
Wales), and the commission in question produced one note of dissent and
four notes of reservation. The academic, unlike the public personages
chosen to sit upon a commission, begins his task equipped and competent
in the tools of the trade, and can be expected to pursue a logical sequence of
enquiry. The role of the commission is more passive, the members being
the recipients of a barrage of largely uninvited information of which only a
fraction is of real value. Perhaps it is significant that the only member of
the English commission with prior academic experience in depth of the
problems and possibilities of administrative area reform felt obliged to

produce a separate dissenting report embodying a separate set of proposed areas and functions.

The continuing failure of the English system of local government to adapt to changed social and economic conditions throughout the first seven decades of this century prompted writers of considerable ability to present their views on how the system should be recast, to the extent that it is possible to recognise a developing English school of regionalism. The failings of the local government areas (which preceded the introduction of reformed areas in April 1974) were both numerous and serious. The top tier of authorities consisted of counties and county boroughs. Most of the former had evolved directly from the administrative areas of Norman or late-Saxon England, and since their foundation most had retained their original forms despite minor changes in their detail such as the removal of enclaves; though these counties may have reflected the political realities of early medieval England, they were unrelated to the socioeconomic realities of the twentieth century. Most were too small to offer the necessary economies of scale essential to efficient adminis-tration, and frequently their boundaries cut across economic regions, such as the south-east Lancashire–north-east Cheshire industrial area and the Newcastle and Bristol city regions. The county boroughs dated from legislation of 1888, which detached the major towns from their sur-rounding counties, and endowed them with comparable status; this status was a considerable prize, and as corporations competed for the honour, it became a norm that a population of at least 100 000 was a prerequisite for elevation. The creation of county boroughs disregarded the symbiotic re-lationship between the city and its region and substituted competition and clashes of interest for cooperation in the planning of urban and rural amenities, destroyed natural planning units, and gave rural-dwelling com-muters immunity from the payment of higher rates required for the upkeep of the urban amenities which they regularly used.

Lower levels in the administrative hierarchy were occupied by metropo-litan boroughs, whose status frequently derived from feudal manipu-lations or medieval rather than modern grandeur; urban and rural districts, which were frequently too small for the effective operation of many services; and parishes, which were virtually devoid of powers and had frequently fallen into administrative disuse. The inadequacy of the system was further evidenced by the low polls associated with local govern-ment elections; by the erosion of local democracy, as functions that the local government areas were too small to handle were removed to *ad hoc* boards; and by the burdening of Parliament with matters that should have been handled locally. *The Times*, quoting the previous day's parliamentary business, noted that 'Between 8.55 and 9.20 p.m. on Dec. 19th, 1957, the Mother of Parliaments became seized of an argument about the Byram-cum-Sutton bus shelter'.

The long involvement between Fabian socialists and administrative area reform originated in their campaign for municipal socialism; early in the twentieth century several vital municipal services such as electricity, water and gas were divided between numerous small private and civic enterprises, and it was considered that the municipalisation of these services would be hampered by irrational administrative boundaries. Sanders in 1905 produced the first in a sequence of tracts on local government reform, and urged the introduction (in a future socialist Britain) of seven provincial authorities in England through two stages of reform, the first involving the amalgamation of adjacent municipal authorities to facilitate the planned growth of entire urban units, followed by the sevenfold provincial division. Though no map was provided, it was suggested that each province should focus on a great provincial city, so here we have a primitive version of city regionalism.[96]

The first major work on English regionalism was C. B. Fawcett's *The Provinces of England*, produced in 1919 and developed from a lecture of 1917. In 1917 the suggested provinces numbered eleven; they were increased to twelve in 1919, and reduced to eleven in Fawcett's final statement of 1942 (see figure 8.10a).[97] Fawcett was sensitive to the ethos and sentiment of the regions of England, and fearful of the erosion of regional identity through the standardisation and centralisation of English life on London. He believed that these tendencies could be reversed through the devolution of power from the capital to the provinces. The strength with which these views were held is evident in his statement that

... the man or woman who has no love for and pride in his or her home region is not thereby qualified for wider views of life. Provincialism is in itself a good thing, and a necessary factor in the well being of humanity.[98]

Since little space or serious analysis was given to the spatial requirements of local government systems or the provision of a suitable hierarchy of administrative areas and associated functions, despite Fawcett's being remembered as a supremely rational man, his provinces are probably best understood as his representation of areas associated with particular regional sentiments rather than as areas suited to administrative efficiency.

While Fawcett had concentrated on devising large provinces which would have proved too unwieldy for the efficient operation of most local government functions, two leading Fabians, Sydney and Beatrice Webb, were working on a now-forgotten scheme which took the opposite approach, recommending the fragmentation of local government into fundamental units, each including about 2000 to 5000 families and coming together in various different combinations to provide each particular function with a near-ideal area of operation.

Wherever there is a question of determining the unit of area or population to be adopted for any particular service, the wards themselves should be grouped . . . in such a way as to form, for each function, the area in which the administration can be made most efficient and most truly economical.[99]

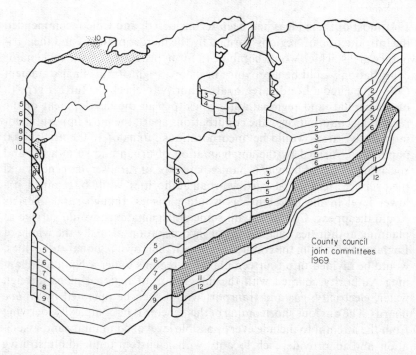

Figure 8.9.   County council joint committees. The map emphasises the problem caused by administrative areas which are too small to function efficiently and result in the combination of authorities to share work on a piecemeal basis. In addition to the county council joint committees shown, regional boards handled planning, gas, water, hospitals, electricity and river purification, all of which were directly or indirectly removed from democratic local government control. This is an oblique view of the five counties of north-east Scotland, looking southwards. Each tier represents a separate county council joint committee.

1: joint county council; 2: library committee; 3: weights and measures committee; 4: health committee; 5: police board; 6: fire board; 7: valuation committee; 8: North East Civil Defence Group Control Committee; 9: development committee; 10: library committee; 11: Moray Firth Civil Defence Joint Committee; 12: bridges committee.

Another prominent Fabian, economist G. D. H. Cole, presented a different plan in 1921, another in 1941, and a more thorough restatement in 1947.[100] His 1921 proposals were for larger and smaller local government units, with a top tier of nine large regions and a bottom layer of parishes and urban wards, which would become political units with elected councils. The middle tier comprised 'county districts' formed by the elimination of counties and most urban districts, and their replacement by areas formed from the amalgamation of rural districts and comparable in size to parliamentary constituencies; all but the smallest county boroughs would be retained, but their boundaries would be extended to include entire built-up areas. Within the revised administrative areas, the health, trading and educational services would each be operated by elected *ad hoc* boards. By

1941 most of these ideas had been reconsidered, and Cole recommended the introduction of 'regions' formed by the merger of towns and their tributary areas, which would combine to form 'provinces', while each major conurbation would be a province in its own right. In his final statement Cole advocated a London regional authority to check the further growth of the capital, and regional authorities to plan the development of the remaining conurbations. The conurbations apart, the most important administrative areas would be 'incorporations', units of 10 000 to 250 000 population, formed by the amalgamation of urban and rural areas and consisting either of heavily urbanised areas or of rural service centres and their service areas. Most existing urban authorities would be retained at a lower level in the hierarchy, as would parishes, though rural districts would disappear. Counties, with some amalgamations, would survive as planning authorities over groups of incorporations. Finally the whole of England, apart from the conurbations with their own regional authorities, would be divided into fourteen planning regions under a National Planning Authority charged with the integration of regional plans, though water, electricity, gas and transport would each be operated by *ad hoc* boards. The obvious shortcoming of this scheme is its complexity, deriving from the attempt to include every possible level of community and association and to provide each locality with a custom-built administrative system.

Various other blueprints for administrative area reform appeared between the ends of the first and second world wars, by Ashby, Robson, and yet another Fabian, 'Regionaliter', though these lacked the impact of Fawcett's and Cole's.[101] Gilbert and Taylor presented maps of proposed planning regions in 1942,[102] though these tended to emphasise the fact that

---

Figure 8.10.   English local government areas.

(a) Provinces suggested by C. B. Fawcett in 1919 (ref. 97).

(b₁) The old counties of England.

(b₂) An example of the complicated system of administrative areas in operation before April 1974. The heavy broken line is the county boundary between Northumberland and Durham. Stipple: county boroughs; diagonal shading: municipal boroughs; cross-hatching: urban districts; unshaded: rural districts. Parishes are not included.

(c) D. Senior's city regions (ref. 88). Heavy lines delimit proposed planning regions, lighter lines proposed counties. Broken lines show alternative areas in each case. Squares: major service centres; circles: proposed 'little Whitehalls'.

(d) Redcliffe-Maud commission areas, 1969. Broken lines delimit provincial divisions, continuous lines the proposed unitary authorities. Metropolitan areas are shaded.

(e₁) New counties of England and Wales, 1974.

(e₂) Inset for part of north-east England. Heavy lines show county boundaries, lighter lines district boundaries. Note that the pattern is hardly more complex than in (b₂), though the scale is five times larger.

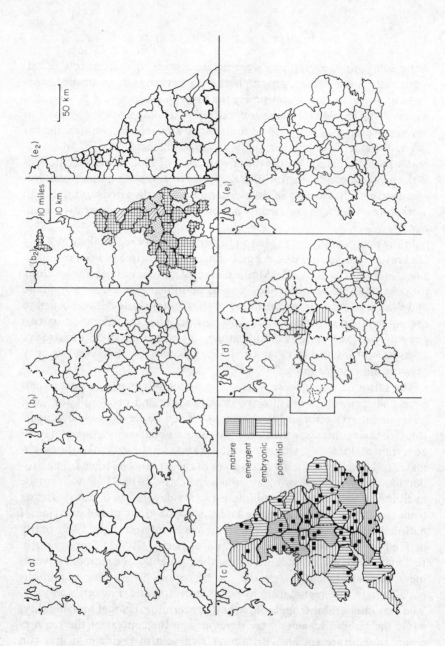

(a)

(b₁)

(b₂)

(c)

(d)

(e₁)

(e₂)

50 km

10 miles
10 km

mature
emergent
embryonic
potential

while some non-geographers were neglecting the spatial aspects of administrative area reform, geographers were devising administrative areas without adequate consideration for the functions that would be operated within them. In 1949 Lipman produced the first comprehensive analysis of criteria essentially involved in administrative area reform, emphasising the size requirements of the various local government services.[103] More recently Douglas demonstrated the effectiveness of geographical techniques in the problem of administrative area reform by revealing the lack of correspondence of the existing middle-order administrative divisions in South Yorkshire with the areas used by a number of local administrative agencies.[104]

In the post-war period the baton passed to the city regionalists, notably Dickinson and Senior, whose basic concepts have already been outlined. Then in 1969 the Redcliffe-Maud Commission announced far-reaching proposals for the wholesale revision of administrative areas in England and Wales, and Senior, as a member of the Commission, felt compelled to present his own scheme in a minority report. After consideration by two governments and various modifications, a new system of administrative areas was introduced in 1974, which more closely resembled the majority than the minority proposal.

The introduction of these revised areas probably marks at least a temporary suspension of the flow of private ideas and proposals for local government area reform. The schemes outlined above can only be understood in their contexts, which were the contexts of an ailing system of local government operating within inadequate areas, of the general political climate, and of the personality and values of the writers concerned. The production of several works on regionalism in the 1919–21 period can be attributed partly to the general interest in the devolution of power arising from the Irish Home Rule issue and the applications of the doctrine of national self-determination, while the renewed interest in the 1940s partly derived from the wartime introduction of twelve Civil Defence regions; regionalists were both encouraged by their potential for regional government, and apprehensive lest the use of regions in wartime conditions should stigmatise regionalism as being undemocratic. Fawcett's regionalism was inseparable from his love and concern for regional individuality, while the Fabian schemes were developed in the context of the requirements of a future socialist Britain. A rich vein of regionalism has run through British academic writing during this century, though it is only recently that analytical techniques have been developed which could be applied to forge a link between efficiency and sentiment.[105]

Before the introduction of reformed administrative areas in England and Wales, local government was operated through more than 1300 elected councils. The reforms abolished the county boroughs, metropolitan boroughs, and urban and rural districts. The new spatial administrative structure consists of forty-seven counties, subdivided into 333 districts, and six metropolitan counties covering the main conurbations, divided into thirty-six metropolitan districts; parishes have been extended to include urban as well as rural areas. The difference between the metropolitan and non-metropolitan districts is that, in the latter, education and the personal social services are administered by county councils, while in the former these functions devolve upon the districts. Permanent boundary commissions have been appointed to keep the question of administrative area reform under constant review.

Unfortunately, 'By adhering to existing county structure as far as was possible, meaningful city regions were effectively ruled out . . . there was no attempt at matching boundaries with . . . logical tributary areas'.[106] Also ignored were the recommendations of the majority report from the 'Kilbrandon Commission' on the constitution, which favoured the creation of legislative assemblies for Scotland and Wales and advisory councils in eight English planning regions. In fact the plans for administrative area reform were finalised before the release of the controversial report, though the commission concerned with the original plans for administrative area reform stressed the importance of considering the constitutional recommendations before introducing new administrative areas.

Appendix

The systems approaches

At various places in the text, reference has been made to systems approaches, and the following brief guide to some of these approaches may be found useful. A *system* comprises parts or elements, the relationship between them, and the process of interaction on which that relationship rests. In the case of *open systems*, the system is set in an *environment*, which is regarded as external to the system and includes those elements that interact occasionally rather than regularly with any part of the system. In international relations it is customary to think in terms of a closed international system composed of *subsystems*, which are parts of the larger system but also constitute systems in their own right and contain their own subsystems. The subsystems of the international system may be termed *actors*, and none is wholly subordinate to other actors. States form the most distinctive and important group of actors in the international system, though other actors include formal international organisations, cartels, international religious groupings and so on, and there is disagreement on the importance of non-state elements.

The contemporary international system is worldwide, since various technological innovations have permitted the establishment of international patterns of economic, political and social interaction, leading to the transformation of an earlier situation in which various forms of political region constituted regional systems, each set in its own environment. It is nevertheless still possible to recognise a number of regional subsystems within the international system, such as the EEC or the middle east.

Included with the actors as *independent variables* in every system are *structures*, characteristic relationships among actors across time, which in the international system tend to be informal rather than formal; *processes*, forms and modes of interaction, including individual interactions which cannot be classed as characteristic relationships; and *context*, which may be economic, social, cultural or geographical. The *dependent variables* of the international system are generally classed as power; management of power, relating to its distribution in the system; stability; change; and system transformation, which involves a qualitative change in one or more essential variables.

One development of the systems approach is the linkage approach: a *linkage* involves a recurring sequence of behaviour that has its initial or *input* stage in one system, and its *output* or terminal stage in another. In the case of a *penetrative* linkage, one participant is able to share directly in determining developments within another, for example Russian guidance of economic development in east-central Europe. In the case of a *reactive* linkage, those responsible for output react to an input within an unpenetrated unit, for example British preparation for an anticipated German invasion; while in that of an *emulative* linkage, the actions of one unit are emulated or imitated in another, as in the case of the US attempt to emulate the Russian success with Sputnik I. If the patterns of behaviour are designed deliberately, the inputs and outputs are said to be *direct*; if these patterns are unanticipated, the inputs and outputs are termed *indirect*.

The systems approach and its many variants are useful as analytical frameworks which facilitate the detection of order in a reality that apparently is hopelessly complicated. They encourage the analysis of units within their own settings, and emphasise their interactions with other units within the system. International relations is normally concerned with interaction between the state subsystems, but systems approaches can also be applied to the study of the relationship between the state and its own subsystems.

In studies at the state and intra-state level, the systems approach devised by Easton is one which may be conveniently adopted; a brief outline of it follows. Among the *attributes* of the political system are its *units*, which are political actions; its *boundaries*, which include within the system all those actions that are more or less related to the making of binding decisions for a society; *inputs* and *outputs*, the inputs being converted by the processes of the system into outputs, authoritative decisions which have important consequences for society; *differentiation* within the system, a division of labour by members of the system providing a structure within which action can take place; and *integration*, a minimal degree of cooperation necessary to offset the disintegrative effects of differentiation and to allow members of the system to make authoritative decisions.

The inputs of a political system are of two basic kinds, *demands* and *support*, and these provide the system with its dynamic nature, furnishing it with energy and with information to process. *External* demands arise in the systems of the environment, and *internal* demands within the system itself; the latter are 'withinputs' rather than inputs in the stricter sense. Some demands become *issues*, demands that members of a political system are prepared to deal with as serious items for discussion through

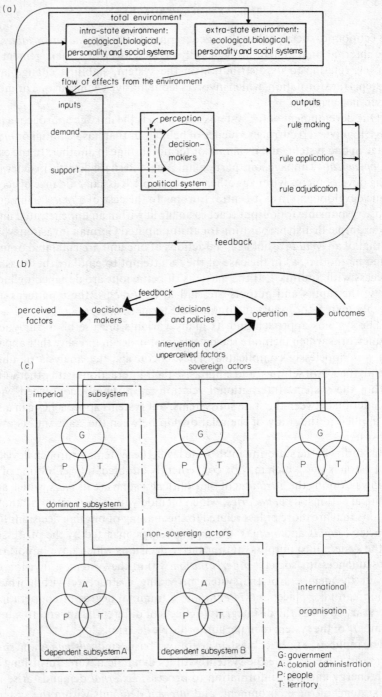

Figure A.1. Systems, process and decision-making. (a) Model of a political system (developed from ref. 1). (b) Relationship between public policy and geography (after ref. 2). (c) Model of a portion of the international system. Some writers would include among the non-sovereign actors organisations such as international cartels, churches and trade union associations.

established channels in the system. Change in the type of demand inputs is one of the sources of change in the political system.

Without support, demands could not be satisfied or conflicts created. Supportive behaviour may involve overt action for the promotion of certain goals, interests or actions, or it may not involve external observable acts but a state of mind embracing deep-seated attitudes or predispositions. Support directed into a political system involves support for the political *community*, a group which must attract the identification of its members (a nation is an example); for the *regime*, which consists of those arrangements that regulate the way in which demands put into the system are settled and decisions put into effect (equating in the west to constitutional principles); or for the *government*.

Without a steady flow of support, a system will not absorb sufficient energy for its members to be able to convert demands to decisions. Without a minimal satisfaction of demands, a society may not generate support for the system; thus the outputs or political decisions constitute inducements to the members of a system to support the system. Inducements may be negative, involving coercion, or positive, involving the satisfaction of demands; so long as a system has stored up a reserve of support it need not meet all or even any demands, but a persistent inability by a government to produce satisfactory outputs may lead not only to the removal of the government but also to demands for a change in the regime and the dissolution of the political community. The process of *politicisation* includes the ways in which political patterns are learned by members of a society, and is part of the process of socialisation which establishes certain norms of social behaviour. Attachment to a political system is built into a maturing member of society and constitutes legitimacy for that system, an important reserve of support for the system at times when it is not meeting with success in the satisfaction of demands.

Further reading

J. W. Burton, *Systems, Diplomacy and Rules* (1968).
D. Easton, An approach to the analysis of political systems, *World Politics* (April 1957), 383–400.
J. Frankel, *Contemporary International Theory and the Behaviour of States*, University Press, Oxford (1973), 32–47.
M. A. Kaplan, *System and Process in International Politics*, Wiley, New York (1957).
J. N. Rosenau, *Linkage Politics* (1969).
R. N. Rosencrance, *Action and Reaction in World Politics*, Little, Brown, Boston (1963).

References

Part 1   Introductory

1. R. Hartshorne, Political geography, in *American Geography: Inventory and Prospects* (ed. P. E. James and C. F. Jones), Syracuse, NY (1954), p. 178.
2. L. M. Alexander, *World Political Patterns*, Chicago (1957), p. 32.
3. W. A. D. Jackson, Whither political geography?, *Annals Assoc. Am. Geogr.*, **48** (1958), 178–83.
4. S. B. Cohen and L. D. Rosenthal, A geographical model for political systems analysis, *Geogr. Rev.*, **61** (1971), 6.
5. H. H. Sprout, Political geography, in *International Encyclopaedia of the Social Sciences*, New York (1968), 116.
6. J. P. Cole and C. A. M. King, An operational framework for political geography, in *Quantitative Geography*, London (1968).
7. R. Hartshorne, The functional approach in political geography, *Annals Assoc. Am. Geogr.*, **49** (1950), 99.
8. R. Hartshorne, Recent developments in political geography, *Am. Pol. Sci. Rev.*, **29** (1935), 785–804, 209–50.
9. See ref. 7, 99.
10. S. B. Jones, A unified field theory of political geography, *Annals Assoc. Am. Geogr.*, **24** (1954), 111–23.
11. R. W. McColl, Political geography as political ecology, *Professional Geographer*, **18** (1966), 143–5.
12. See ref. 4.
13. S. B. Cohen: Personal communication (17 July 1973).
14. F. Ratzel, *Politische Geographie* (1897).
15. I. Bowman, *The New World*, New York (1921); D. S. Whittlesey, *The Earth and the State*, New York (1939).
16. R. Kjellen, *Der Staat als Lebensform*, Leipzig (1917); *Die Grossmächte vor und nach dem Weltkriege*, Berlin (1921).
17. This point is emphasised in C. Troll, Geographic science in Germany during the period 1933–45: a critique and justification, *Annals Assoc. Am. Geogr.*, **39** (1949), 99–137.
18. Commander Roncagli, Physical and strategic geography of the Adriatic, *Geogr. J.*, **53** (1919), 211.

19. A. Demangeon, Géographie politique, *Annales de Géographie*, **41** (1932), 23.
20. I. Bowman, Geography *vs* geopolitics, *Geogr. Rev.*, **32** (1942), 658.
21. Quoted in H. H. Sprout, Geopolitical hypotheses in technologiçal perspective, *World Politics*, **15** (1963), 190.
22. O. Maull, *Das Wesen der Geopolitik*, Leipzig (1936), p. 31.
23. See ref. 21, 190–1.
24. See ref. 1.
25. See ref. 3, 183.
26. See ref. 11, 143.
27. B. J. L. Berry, Geographical reviews, *Geogr. Rev.*, **59** (1969), 450.
28. P. Schat, Political geography: a review, *Tijdschr. Econ. Soc. Geogr.*, **60** (1969), 255.
29. See ref. 21, 191.
30. J. R. V. Prescott, *Political Geography*, London (1972), p. 14.
31. See ref. 27, 451.
32. See ref. 4.
33. See ref. 30, p. 2.
34. F. Burghardt, *Borderland: A Historical and Geographical Study of Burgenland, Austria*, Madison (1962).
35. See ref. 30, p. 40.
36. E. W. Soja, Communication and territorial integration in East Africa: an introduction to transaction flow analysis, *East Lakes Geogr.*, **4** (1968), 39–57; B. O. Witthuhn, The spatial integration of Uganda as shown by the diffusion of postal agencies, 1900–55, *East Lakes Geogr.*, **4** (1968), 5–20; R. L. Merritt, Systems and the disintegration of empires, *General Systems*, **3** (1963).
37. See ref. 30, pp. 42–4.
38. W. G. East, The geography of land-locked states, *Trans. Inst. Br. Geogr.*, **28** (1960), 1–20.
39. See J. Frankel, *Contemporary International Theory and the Behaviour of States*, Oxford (1973), 33–45, for an evaluation of the systems approach in political science.
40. Main sources used were: C. Harman, The Eastern bloc, in *World Crisis* (ed. N. Harris and J. Palmer), Hutchinson, London (1971); F. E. I. Hamilton, Location policy in the Socialist world, in *Models in Geography* (ed. R. J. Chorley and P. Haggett), London (1967); W. B. Walsh, *Russia and the Soviet Union*, Ann Arbor (1968); E. H. Carr, *The Bolshevik Revolution*, London (1950).

Part 2   Political regions and time

1. S. B. Jones, Boundary concepts in the setting of place and time, *Annals Assoc. Am. Geogr.*, **49** (1959), 119.
2. D. Morris, *The Human Zoo,* London (1969).
3. R. Ardrey, *The Territorial Imperative*, New York (1966).
4. J. Bleibtrau, *The Parable of the Beast*, London (1968).
5. W. Kirk, The primary agricultural colonisation of Scotland, *Scot. Geogr. Mag.*, **73** (1957), 65–90.
6. R. Muir, *The political geography of north-east Scotland*, PhD thesis, University of Aberdeen (1970).
7. H. de Blij, *Systematic Political Geography*, New York (1967), p. 4.
8. S. B. Jones, A unified field theory of political geography, *Annals Assoc. Am. Geogr.*, **44** (1954), 111–23.
9. See ref. 7.
10. J. R. V. Prescott, *The Geography of Frontiers and Boundaries*, London (1965), pp. 49–53.

11. See ref. 10.
12. See A. Cobban, The nation state, *History*, **29** (March 1944), for further discussion on this point.
13. See ref. 7, p. 5.
14. L. Oppenheim, *International Law*, 7th edition, vol. 1, London (1952).
15. C. H. Alexandrowicz, New and original states, *Internat. Affairs*, **45** (1969), 465–80.
16. V. I. Lenin, *The State*, a lecture at Sverdlovsk University (1919), Peking (1965).
17. See ref. 2.
18. J. E. Hertz, Rise and demise of the territorial state, *World Politics*, **9** (1957), no. 4, 473–93.
19. L. D. Kristof, The nature of frontiers and boundaries, *Annals Assoc. Am. Geogr.*, **49** (1959), no. 31, 269–82.
20. See ref. 19.
21. D. W. Meinig, Heartland and rimland in Eurasian history, *Western Pol. Q.*, **9** (1956), 553–69.
22. C. F. G. Whebell, Flashpoints for future world conflict, *Geogr. Mag.* (June 1970).
23. M. Freeberne, Minority unrest and Sino-Soviet rivalry in Sinkiang, in *Essays in Political Geography* (ed. C. A. Fisher), London (1968).
24. F. W. Carter, An analysis of the medieval Serbian oecumene: a theoretical approach, *Geografiska Annale*, **51B** (1969), 39–56.
25. See ref. 6.
26. F. Ratzel, The laws of the spatial growth of states (1896), English translation in *The Structure of Political Geography* (ed. R. E. Kaspersen and J. V. Minghi), Chicago (1969).
27. D. S. Whittlesey, *The Earth and the State*, New York (1939), p. 597.
28. See ref. 27, p. 2.
29. N. J. G. Pounds and S. S. Ball, Core areas and the development of the European states systems, *Annals Assoc. Am. Geogr.*, **54** (1964), 24–40.
30. See ref. 8, 111–23.
31. The main circumstances and events are outlined in: M. S. Rajan, Bangladesh and after, *Pacific Affairs*, **45** (1972), no. 2, 191–205; G. W. Choudhury, Bangladesh: why it happened, *Internat. Affairs*, **48** (1972), 242–50.

Part 3   Political regions and structure

1. J. G. Starke, *Introduction to International Law*, 7th edition, London (1972), pp. 192ff.
2. A. F. Burghardt, The bases of territorial claims, *Geogr. Rev.*, **63** (1973), 225–45.
3. See ref. 2.
4. M. Jefferson, The law of the primate city, *Geogr. Rev.*, **29** (1939), 226.
5. O. H. K. Spate, Factors in the development of capital cities, *Geogr. Rev.*, **22** (1942), 622–31.
6. H. de Blij, *Systematic Political Geography*, New York (1967), pp. 410–11.
7. See ref. 5, pp. 622–31.
8. V. Cornish, *The Great Capitals: An Historical Geography*, London (1923).
9. See ref. 5, pp. 622–31.
10. K. C. Kearns, Belpoman: perspective on a new capital, *Geogr. Rev.*, **63** (1973), 151.
11. See ref. 10, 169.
12. A. C. G. Best, Gaberone: problems and prospects of a new capital, *Geogr. Rev.*, **60** (1970), 1.
13. See ref. 12.

14. D. Turnock, Bucharest: the selection and development of the Romanian capital, *Scot. Geogr. Mag.*, (1970).
15. See ref. 6, p. 371.
16. R. Hartshorne, The functional approach in political geography, *Annals Assoc. Am. Geogr.*, **40** (1950), 116..
17. N. J. G. Pounds and S. S. Ball, Core areas and the development of European state systems, *Annals Assoc. Am. Geogr.*, **54** (1964), 24–40.
18. A. K. Philbrick, Principles of areal functional organisation in regional human geography, *Econ. Geogr.*, **53** (1957), 299–336.
19. I. H. Zaidi, Towards a measure of the functional effectiveness of a state: the case of West Pakistan, *Annals Assoc. Am. Geogr.*, **56** (1966), 24–40.
20. F. Ratzel, Gesetze des raumlichen Wachstums der Staaten, *Petermanns Geogr. Mitteilunge*; for details of a recent English translation, see part 2, ref. 26.
21. D. S. Whittlesey, *The Earth and the State*, New York (1939).
22. See ref. 19.
23. N. J. G. Pounds, *Political Geography*, New York (1963), pp. 181–2.
24. (a) from J. S. Gregory, *Russian Land, Soviet People*, London (1968). (b) from R. Hartshorne, The Polish corridor, *Journal of Geography*, **36** (1937), 161–76. (c): population centre of gravity from R. Estall, *A Modern Geography of the United States*, Penguin, Harmondsworth (1972).
25. A. Burghardt, The core concept in political geography: a definition of terms, *Canadian Geogr.*, **63** (1969), 349–53.
26. L. D. Kristof, The nature of frontiers and boundaries, *Annals Assoc. Am Geogr.*, **49** (1959), no. 3, 269–82.
27. C. F. J. Whebell, Core areas in intrastate political organisation, *Canadian Geogr.*, **52** (1968), 99–112.
28. D. S. Whittlesey, The impress of effective central authority upon the landscape, *Annals Assoc. Am. Geogr.*, **25** (1935), 453–4.
29. The English Pale in medieval Ireland was the coastal portion effectively controlled by the English; in 1515 it ran from Dublin to Naas, Navan and Ardee.
30. See ref. 21, p. 10.
31. P. E. James, *Latin America*, 3rd edition, New York (1959), p. 11.
32. See ref. 19.
33. E. J. Hobsbawm, *Bandits*, Penguin, Harmondsworth (1972), p. 19.
34. See ref. 19.
35. G. W. S. Robinson, Exclaves, *Annals Assoc. Am. Geogr.*, **49** (1959), 288.
36. See ref. 35.
37. See ref. 35, 294.
38. See ref. 35, 288.
39. H. M. Catudal, Jr., The Berlin agreement: an exchange of exclaves and enclaves, *Geoforum*, **2**(1972), 78–80.
40. G. W. S. Robinson, West Berlin: the geography of an enclave, *Geogr. Rev.*, **43** (1953), no. 4, 540–57.
41. R. L. Merritt, Infrastructural changes in Berlin, *Annals Assoc. Am. Geogr.*, **63** (1973), no. 1, 58–70.
42. C. F. J. Whebell, Models of political territory, *Proc. Assoc. Am. Geogr.*, **2** (1970), 152–6.
43. J. V. Minghi, Point Roberts, Washington: the problem of an American exclave, *Yearbook Assoc. Pacific Coast Geogr.*, **24** (1962), 39–44.
44. J. Ross Mackay, The interactance hypothesis and boundaries in Canada: a preliminary study, *Canadian Geogr.*, **2** (1958), 1–3.
45. F. E. I. Hamilton, guest lecture, Trinity College, Dublin (1 March 1971).
46. R. R. Boyce and W. A. V. Clark, The concept of shape in geography, *Geogr. Rev.*, **54** (1964), no. 4, 561–72.

47. See ref. 46, 568.
48. P. Haggett and R. J. Chorley, *Network Analysis in Geography*, London (1969).
49. J. P. Cole, The study of major and minor civil divisions in political geography, paper presented to the Twentieth International Geography Congress (1964).
50. See ref. 23. p.46.
51. For further discussion on centres of gravity, see: J. P. Cole and C. A. M. King, *Quantitative Geography*, London (1968), chapter 4; B. H. Massam, The Spatial Structure of Administrative Systems, Research Paper no. 12, Assoc. Am. Geogr. (1972).
52. R. E. Kasperson, The Dodecanese: diversity and unity in island politics, Research Paper no. 108, Dept. of Geography, University of Chicago (1966).
53. C. G. Clarke, Political fragmentation in the Caribbean: the case of Anguilla, *Canadian Geogr.*, **55** (1971), 13.
54. P. G. Bradshaw, *Geography and international politics: an attempt at synthesis*, PhD thesis, University of Southampton (1971), 32.
55. R. T. Holt and J. E. Turner, Insular politics, in *Linkage Politics* (ed. J. N. Roseman), New York (1969).
56. B. M. Russett, *International Regions and the International System*, Chicago (1967), p. 160.
57. W. G. East, The geography of land-locked states, *Trans. Inst. Br. Geogr.*, **28** (1960), no. 1, 1–22.
58. E. H. Dale, Some geographical aspects of African land-locked states, *Annals Assoc. Am. Geogr.*, **58** (1968), no. 3, 485–505.
59. United Nations, Report of the Committee on the Preparation of a Draft Convention to Transit Trade of Land-locked States (1965).
60. See ref. 24 (Hartshorne).
61. N. J. G. Pounds, A free and secure access to the sea, *Annals Assoc. Am. Geogr.*, **49** (1959), 256–68.
62. D. Hilling, The problem of West Africa's land-locked states, in *Essays in Political Geography* (ed. C. A. Fisher), London (1968).
63. J. W. B. Perry (publication pending).
64. J. W. B. Perry, Malawi's new outlet to the sea, *Geography*, **56** (1971), no. 2.
65. *Time Magazine* (12 February 1973).
66. See ref. 42.

Part 4   Political process, perception and decision-making

1. S. B. Cohen and D. Rosenthal, A geographical model for political systems analysis, *Geogr. Rev.*, **61** (1971), 31.
2. See ref. 1.
3. D. S. Whittlesey, The impress of central authority upon the landscape, *Annals Assoc. Am. Geogr.*, **25** (1935).
4. D. S. Whittlesey, *The Earth and the State*, New York (1944), p. 556.
5. H. H. Sprout and M. Sprout, Environmental factors in the study of international politics, *J. Conflict Resolution*, **4** (1957), 309–28.
6. K. E. Boulding, National images and international systems, *J. Conflict Resolution*, **6** (1959), no. 3.
7. H. E. Koch, R. C. North and D. A. Zinnes, Some theoretical notes on geography and international conflict, *J. Conflict Resolution*, **4** (1957), 4–14.
8. See ref. 6.
9. B. P. FitzGerald, *Developments in Geographical Method*, Oxford (1974), p. 65.
10. G. Wirsing, ed., *Der Krieg 1939–41 in Karten*, Munich (1941).
11. H. Speier, Magic geography, *Social Research*, **8** (1941), 310–30. For a discussion on the importance of subjectivity in mapmaking, see: J. Kirtland Wright,

Human Nature in Geography, Cambridge, Mass. (1966), 33–52; R. Prestwich, Maps and the perception of space, in *An Invitation to Geography* (ed. D. Lanegran and R. Palm), New York (1973).

12. R. C. Snyder, H. V. Bruck and B. Sapin, *Foreign Policy Decision-Making*, New York (1954).
13. F. E. I. Hamilton, guest lecture, Trinity College, Dublin (1 March 1971).
14. See ref. 7.
15. P. G. Bradshaw (1971), *Geography and international relations: an attempt at synthesis*, PhD thesis, University of Southampton, 88–122.
16. A. Wilson, *War Gaming*, Penguin, Harmondsworth (1970); originating from A. Rapoport, *Strategy and Conscience*, Schocken, New York (1964).
17. G. T. Allison, Conceptual models and the Cuban missile crisis, *Am. Pol. Sci. Rev.*, **63** (1969).
18. R. Muir, As we see others, *Geogr. Mag.*, **46** (1974), no. 7, 364–5.

Part 5 Political process and the state

1. A. M. Scott, *The Functioning of the International Political System*, New York (1967), 18–19.
2. J. D. Singer, The global system and its sub-systems: a developmental view, in *Linkage Politics* (ed. J. N. Rosenau), New York (1969), pp. 26–7.
3. K. E. Boulding, *Conflict and Defense*, New York (1962), p. 79.
4. See ref. 2. p. 29.
5. U. Kitzinger, *Britain and the Common Market*, London (1967), p. 69.
6. M. Weber, Politics as a vocation, in *From Max Weber* (ed. H. H. Gerth and C. Wright Mills), New York (1946), p. 78.
7. G. A. Almond, A functional approach to comparative politics, in *The Politics of the Developing Areas* (ed. G. A. Almond and J. S. Coleman), Princeton, N. J. (1960), pp. 6–7.
8. D. S. Whittlesey, *The Earth and the State* (1939); cited in 1949 edition, New York, p. 556.
9. R. Hartshorne, The functional approach to political geography, *Annals Assoc. Am. Geogr.*, **40** (1950), 95–130.
10. F. Ratzel, *Politische Geographie*, 1923 edition, Munich, p. 6.
11. J. Gottman, The political partitioning of our world: an attempt at analysis, *World Politics*, **4** (1952), 512–19.
12. G. A. Lanyi and W. C. McWilliams, *Crisis and Continuity in World Politics*, New York (1966), p. 40.
13. J. S. Mill, *Representative Government*, London (1861).
14. N. J. G. Pounds, *Political Geography*, New York (1963), p. 11.
15. K. W. Deutsch, *Nationalism and Social Communication*, Cambridge, Mass. (1953).
16. K. W. Deutsch, The growth of nations, *World Politics*, **5** (1953), 169.
17. K. R. Minogue, *Nationalism*, London (1967), p. 25.
18. J. M. Keynes, cited in ref. 17, p. 24.
19. See ref. 17, pp. 13–17.
20. J. Frankel, *International Relations*, London (1964), p. 16.
21. See ref. 14, p. 12.
22. S. H. Beaver, Railways in the Balkan peninsula, *Geogr. J.*, **97** (1941), 287.
23. H. E. Syed Abdus Sultan, Bangladesh: reconstruction and development plans, *Commonwealth* (August 1972), 106
24. H. G. Johnson, Economic nationalism in new and developing states, *Pol. Sci. Q.*, **80** (1965), 169.
25. See ref. 24.

26. I. Wallerstein, *Africa: The Politics of Independence*, New York (1961); condensed as Independence and after, in *The Structure of Political Geography* (ed. R. E. Kosperson and J. V. Minghi), Chicago (1969), p. 275.
27. See ref. 26, p. 277.
28. E. Shils, On the comparative study of the new states, in *Old Societies and New States* (ed. C. Geertz), New York (1963), 3.
29. See ref. 26, p. 275.
30. C. A. McClelland, *Theory and the International System*, New York (1966), p. 120.
31. See ref. 20, p. 117.
32. N. Bethell, *Gomulka, his Poland and his Communism*, London (1969), p. 223.
33. K. Mehnert, The Chinese and the Russians, *Annals Am. Assoc. Pol. Sci.*, (1963), 349.
34. A. Lösch, Differences in natural character, in *Political and Geographic Relationships* (ed. W. A. D. Jackson), Prentice-Hall, Englewood Cliffs, N.J. (1964).
35. E. Piasecki, Peoples of the world and an attempt to define ethnic differentiation of territories, *Czasopismo Geograficzne*, **35** (1964), 73–85.
36. L. A. Kosinski, Changes in the ethnic structure in East Central Europe, 1930–1960, *Geogr. Rev.*, **59** (1969), 388–492.
37. W. G. Runciman, *Relative Deprivation and Social Justice*, Berkeley, Calif. (1966).
38. G. K. Bertsch, The revival of nationalism, *Problems of Communism*, **22** (1973), 1–15.
39. A. H. Taylor, The electoral geography of Welsh and Scottish nationalism, *Scot. Geogr. Mag.*, **89** (1973), 145.
40. A. Cobban, *The Nation State and National Self Determinism*, revised edition, London (1969), p. 115.
41. F. C. Innes and J. Lundgren, Montreal: the national and international city, *Geogr. Mag.* (October 1970), 47.
42. G. Young, Enigma in the sun, *Observer* (4 April 1971).
43. M. Lipton, Independent Bantustans?, *Int. Affairs*, **47** (1972), 6.
44. A. C. G. Best, South Africa's border industries: the Tswana example, *Annals Assoc. Am. Geogr.*, **61** (1971), 329–43.
45. R. Conquest, *The Nation Killers*, London (1970).
46. M. A. Busteed, Northern Ireland: geographical aspects of a crisis, Research Papers, no. 3, School of Geography, University of Oxford (1972), 20.
47. E. Jones, The distribution and segregation of Roman Catholics in Belfast, *Sociol. Rev.*, **9** (1956), 167–89.
48. See ref. 47, 168.
49. See ref. 47, 186.
50. Adapted from D. Timms, Quantitative techniques in urban social geography, in *Frontiers in Geographical Teaching* (ed. R. J. Chorley and P. Haggett), London (1965).
51. K. W. Robinson, Sixty years of federation in Australia, *Geogr. Rev.*, **51** (1961), 1–20.
52. See W. S. Livingston, A note on the nature of federalism, *Pol. Sci. Q.*, **67** (1952), 81–95, for further discussion on this theme.
53. R. D. Dikshit, Geography and federalism, *Annals Assoc. Am. Geogr.*, **61** (1971), 104.
54. See ref. 52, 94.
55. C. D. Tarlton, Symmetry and asymmetry as elements of federalism, *J. of Pol.*, **27** (1965), no. 4.
56. R. D. Dikshit, The failure of federalism in Central Africa: a politico-

geographical postmortem, *Professional Geogr.*, **23** (1971), 224–8.
57. See K. F. Cviic, The missing historical dimension in Yugoslavia, *Int. Affairs*, **48** (1972), 414–23, for further discussion; also ref. 38.
58. R. Marshall, The Commonwealth Caribbean: prospects of a new political grouping, *Commonwealth* (August 1972), 95–8.
59. J. C. Davies, Toward a theory of revolution, *Am. Sociological Rev.*, **27** (1962), 5–19.
60. R. W. McColl, The insurgent state: territorial bases of revolution, *Annals Assoc. Am. Geogr.*, **59** (1969), 613–31.
61. E. W. Soja, Communications and territorial integration in East Africa: an introduction to transaction flow analysis, *East Lakes Geogr.*, **4** (1968), 39–57.
62. J. Ross Mackay, The interactance hypothesis and boundaries in Canada: a preliminary study, *Canadian Geogr.*, **2** (1958), 1–8.
63. See ref. 15.
64. See ref. 38, 6–9.

Part 6   Frontiers and boundaries

1. J. R. V. Prescott, *The Geography of Frontiers and Boundaries*, London (1965), pp. 34–9.
2. P. E. James, *Latin America*, 3rd edition, New York (1959).
3. M. W. Mikesell, Comparative studies of frontier history, *Annals Assoc. Am. Geogr.*, **50** (1960), 62–74.
4. R. Hartshorne, Suggestions as to the terminology of political boundaries, *Annals Assoc. Am. Geogr.*, **26** (1936), 56–7.
5. See ref. 3.
6. L. D. Kristof, The nature of frontiers and boundaries, *Annals Assoc. Am. Geogr.*, **49** (1959), 269–82.
7. See ref. 6, 269.
8. F. J. Turner, The frontier in American history, New York (1893).
9. B. O. Witthuhn, The spatial integration of Uganda as shown by the diffusion of postal agencies, 1900–65, *East Lakes Geogr.*, **4** (1968), 5–17.
10. D. Wishart, The changing position of the frontier of settlement on the Eastern margins of the Central and Northern Great Plains, 1851–1896, *Prof. Geogr.*, **21** (1969), 155.
11. D. R. Reynolds and M. L. McNulty, On the analysis of political boundaries as barriers, *East Lakes Geogr.*, **4** (1968), 31.
12. P. D. Wood, Frontier relics in the Welsh border towns, *Geography*, **47** (1962), 54–62.
13. See R. P. Beckinsale, Rivers as political boundaries, in *Water, Earth and Man* (ed. R. J. Chorley), London (1969), for further discussion.
14. See ref. 4.
15. See Col. Sir T. Holdich, *Political Frontiers and Boundary Making*, London (1916); L. W. Lyde, *Some Frontiers of Tomorrow: An Aspiration for Europe*, London (1915).
16. S. C. Gilfillan, Duration of land boundaries in Europe, *Pol. Sci. Q.*, **39** (September 1924), 458–84.
17. A. T. A. Learmonth and C. Hamnett, *Approaches to Political Geography*, Bletchley (1971), pp. 28–32.
18. See ref. 1.
19. See ref. 4, and W. G. East, The nature of political geography, *Politica*, **2** (1937), 259–86.
20. J. W. House, A local perspective on boundaries and the frontier zone, in *Essays in Political Geography* (ed. C. A. Fisher), London (1968), p. 329.

21. S. B. Jones, *Boundary Making: A Handbook for Statesmen*, Washington DC (1945).
22. See ref. 6, 136.
23. A. Cobban, *The Nation State and National Self-Determination* (1945), revised edition, London (1969), pp. 57–75.
24. H. R. Wilkinson, Jugoslav Kosmet, *Trans. Inst. Br. Geogr.*, **21** (1955), 171–93.
25. D. S. Whittlesey, *The Earth and the State* (1939), 1944 edition, New York, 331.
26. S. W. Boggs, *International Boundaries: A Study of Boundary Functions and Problems*, New York (1940), 66.
27. P. Odell, Europe sits on its own energy, *Geogr. Mag.*, **46** (1974), no. 6, 244.
28. R. S. Yuill, A simulation study of barrier effects in spatial diffusion processes, Discussion Paper no. 9, Michigan Inter-University Community of Mathematical Geographers (1964).
29. A. P. Brigham, Principles in the delimitation of boundaries, *Geogr. Rev.*, **7** (1919), no. 4, 201–19.
30. See ref. 26.
31. See ref. 11, 24.
32. J. Ross Mackay, Interactance hypothesis and boundaries in Canada: a preliminary study, *Canadian Geogr.*, **2** (1958), 1–8.
33. A. Lösch, *The Economics of Location*, New Haven, Conn. (1954).
34. E. J. Soja, Communication and territorial integration in East Africa: an introduction to transaction flow analysis, *East Lakes Geogr.*, **4** (1968), 39–57.
35. See ref. 11, 33–4.
36. See ref. 33, p. 192.
37. F. E. Oxtoby, The role of political factors in the Virgin Islands watch industry, *Geogr. Rev.*, **60** (1970), no. 4, 463–74.
38. W. Franke, *Forschungen zur deutschen Landeskunde*, Bad Godesberg (1968).
39. See ref. 33.
40. J. E. Martin, Industrial employment and investment in a frontier region: the Franco-German example, *Geography*, **58** (1973), 55–8.
41. For (a), N. J. G. Pounds, *An Historical and Political Geography of Europe*, London (1947); for (c), A. E. Moodie, *Geography behind Politics*, London (1957); for (d), A. Shearer, *Guardian* (11 March 1972); for (e), R. Muir, *The political geography of north-east Scotland*, PhD thesis, University of Aberdeen (1970).
42. K. E. Boulding, *Conflict and Defense: a General Theory*, New York (1962).
43. P. G. Bradshaw, *Geography and international relations: an attempt at synthesis*, PhD thesis, University of Southampton, 84–5.
44. S. Hoggart, Bordering on the impossible, *Guardian* (9 October 1971).
45. I. Claude, Jr., *Swords and Ploughshares*, New York (1964), 348.

Part 7   Political geography and the international system

1. J. Gottman, Geography and international relations, *World Politics*, **3** (1951), 153–73.
2. See C. A. McClelland, *Theory and the International System*, New York (1966), 16–20, for a definition of the aims of international relations.
3. M. A. Kaplan, Traditionalism *vs* science in international relations, in *New Approaches to International Relations* (ed. M. A. Kaplan), New York (1968), p. 16.
4. H. J. Morgenthau, *Politics among Nations*, 3rd edition, New York (1960), p. 27.
5. J. Frankel, *International Politics*, Penguin, Harmondsworth (1973), p. 178.
6. F. C. German, A tentative evaluation of world power, *J. Conflict Resolution*, **4**

(1960), 138–44.

7. W. Fucks, *Formeln zur Macht*, Stuttgart (1965).
8. Computer investigation by political geography students at the Cambridgeshire College of Arts and Technology.
9. M. A. Kaplan, *System and Process in International Politics*, New York (1957).
10. See ref. 9.
11. R. M. Dikshit, Geography and federalism, *Annals Assoc. Am. Geogr.*, **61** (1971), 101.
12. B. M. Russett, Delineating international regions, in *Quantitative International Politics* (ed. J. D. Singer), New York 1968), p. 321.
13. See ref. 5, pp. 245–6.
14. D. Jay, *After the Common Market*, Penguin, Harmondsworth (1968), p. 67.
15. E. Deakins, EEC problems for British agriculture, *Fabian Tracts*, no. 408, London (1971).
16. See R. Mathews, H. D. Black and D. Austen, in *From Commonwealth to Common Market* (ed. P. Uri), Penguin, Harmondsworth (1972), for further discussion of this point.
17. J. M. Montias, *Economic Development in Communist Romania*, Cambridge, Mass. (1967), pp. 187–229.
18. H. Alker, Jr., and D. Puchala, Trends in economic partnership: the North Atlantic Area, 1928–63, in ref. 12 (Singer), p. 290.
19. R. N. Taafe and R. C. Kingsbury, *An Atlas of Soviet Affairs*, London (1965), p. 22.
20. T. Cliff, *Russia: a Marxist Analysis*, London (1964), p. 277.
21. J. H. Weaver, How to stay the richest country in the world, *Commonwealth* (4 April 1969), 67.
22. *Sunday Times* (13 December 1970).
23. See ref. 21.
24. R. I. Savage and K. W. Deutsch, A statistical model of the gross analysis of transaction flows, *Econometrica*, **28** (1960), no. 3.
25. See ref. 18.
26. See ref. 18, pp. 298, 305.
27. R. Prestwich, *America's dependency on foreign sources of metallurgical minerals: patterns and policies*, PhD thesis, University of Minnesota (1971).
28. See T. Kemp, *Theories of Imperialism*, London (1967), for further discussion, and for a recent geographical appraisal of explanations for imperialism, see S. Folke, First thoughts on the geography of imperialism, *Antipode*, **5** (1973), no. 3, 21–32.
29. V. I. Lenin, *Imperialism: the Highest Stage of Capitalism* (1916).
30. S. H. Frankel, *The Concept of Colonisation*, Oxford (1949).
31. S. B. Cohen, *Geography and Politics in a World Divided*, New York (1963), 204.
32. L. D. Kristof, The nature of frontiers and boundaries, *Annals Assoc. Am. Geogr.*, **49** (1959). 269–82.
33. R. L. Merritt, Noncontiguity and political integration, in *Linkage Politics* (ed. J. N. Rosenau), New York (1969), 266.
34. R. C. Tiuvari, Distance in decisions: some aspects of colonial administration in tropical Africa, *Scot. Geogr. Mag.*, **88** (1972), 208–10.
35. H. de Blij, *Systematic Political Geography*, New York (1967), pp. 495–508.
36. See ref. 35, p. 498.
37. I. Wallerstein, *Africa: The Politics of Independence*, New York (1961); condensed as Independence and after, in *The Structure of Political Geography* (ed. R. K. Kasperson and J. V. Minghi), Chicago (1969), p. 275.
38. R. L. Merritt, Systems and the disintegration of empires, *General Systems*, **8** (1963).

39. *The Observer Atlas of World Affairs*, London (1971), p. 6.
40. M. Westlake, Commodity boom redresses balance, *The Times* (14 November 1973).
41. See ref. 21, 68.
42. See ref. 21.
43. See ref. 39, p. 8.
44. W. T. W. Morgan, Aid with trade for needy nations, *Geogr. Mag.* (1974); for Russian aid, M. Korner, in *The Soviet Union under Brezhnev and Kosygin* (ed. J. W. Stamp), New York (1971), p. 69.
45. M. Walker, Where death knows no bounds, *Guardian* (11 April 1974).
46. H. M. Pachter, Imperialism and neocolonialism: a reexamination, in *Crisis and Continuity in World Politics* (ed. G. A. Lanyi and W. C. McWilliams), New York (1973), p. 119.
47. See R. C. North, The behavior of nation states: problems of conflict and integration, in *New Approaches to International Relations* (ed. M. A. Kaplan), New York (1968), pp. 303–56, for an example of a theoretical appraisal of conflict.
48. See ref. 39, p. 21.
49. United Nations, *Economic and Social Consequences of Disarmament*, New York (1962), p. 3.
50. M. Kidron, *Western Capitalism since the War*, Penguin, Harmondsworth (1970), p. 152.
51. T. Geraghty, Supersalesmen of death, *Sunday Times* (13 January 1974).
52. See ref. 32.
53. L. C. D. Joos, Are national frontiers natural frontiers?, *European Community* (March 1973), 20–2.
54. D. Wood, *Conflict in the Twentieth Century*, Institute for Strategic Studies, London (1968).
55. W. A. Douglas Jackson, *The Russian–Chinese Borderland*, Princeton (1968); Liu P'ei-hua, ed., *A Short History of China*, Peking (1954); L. Freedman, *Guardian* (22 May 1974).
56. J. R. V. Prescott, *The Geography of Frontiers and Boundaries*, London (1965), p. 109.
57. See ref. 56, p. 114.
58. J. D. Eyre, Japanese–Soviet territorial issues in the Southern Kurile Islands, *Prof. Geogr.*, **20** (1968), 11–15.
59. B. W. Hodder, The ewe problem, in *Essays in Political Geography* (ed. C. A. Fisher), London (1968).
60. R. P. Beckinsale, Rivers as political boundaries, in *Water, Earth and Man* (ed. R. J. Chorley), London (1969); W. D. Rushton, Defining a frontier in the Andes, *Geogr. Mag.*, **40** (1968), 972–81.
61. J. W. House, The Franco-Italian boundary in the Alpes Maritimes, *Trans. Inst. Br. Geogr.*, **26** (1959).
62. See ref. 56, pp. 110–13.
63. M. Freeberne, Minority unrest and Sino-Soviet rivalry in Sinkiang, in ref. 59 (Fisher).
64. Tass dispatch (March 1969) concerning an incident on the Ussuri river.
65. N. Maxwell, *Sunday Times* (30 September 1973).
66. See ref. 39.
67. The main sources used were: A. Lamb, *Asian Frontiers*, London (1968); ref. 63; H. Salisbury, *The Coming War between Russia and China*, London (1969); F. Watson, *The Frontiers of China*, London (1966); Peking Foreign Languages Press, *On Khrushchev's Phoney Communism and its Historical Lessons* (1964).
68. The main sources used were: R. D. Hayton, Polar problems and international

law, *Am. J. Internat, Law*, **52** (1958), no. 4; O. J. Lissitzyn, The American position on outer space and Antarctica, *Am. J. Internat. Law*, **53** (1959), no. 1; O. Svarlein, The sector principle in law and practice, *Polar Record*, **10** (1960); P. C. Daniels, The Antarctic treaty, *Bull. Atomic Sc.*, **26** (1970), 11–16.

69. See ref. 60 (Beckinsale), p. 350.
70. S. W. Boggs, *International Boundaries*, New York (1940), p. 272.
71. J. Simsarian, The division of waters affecting the United States and Canada, *Am. J. Internat. Law*, **32** (1938), 488–518.
72. C. G. Smith, The disputed shores of the Jordan, *Trans. Inst. Br. Geogr.*, **40** (1966), 111–28.
73. W. M. Ross, The management of international common property resources, *Geogr. Rev.*, **61** (1971), 332.
74. J. E. S. Fawcett, International conservation: question of method, *Internat. Affairs*, **48** (1972), 217–25.
75. L. M. Alexander, Geography and the law of the sea, *Annals Assoc. Am. Geogr.*, **58** (1968), 177.
76. S. W. Boggs, National claims in adjacent seas, *Geogr. Rev.*, **41** (1951), 18.
77. N. J. G. Pounds, *Political Geography*, New York (1963), p. 107.
78. Main sources used were: I. Ashwell, Saga of the cod war, *Geogr. Mag.* (May 1973), 550–6; L. Marks, *Observer* (27 May 1973); D. Blundy, *Sunday Times* (30 September 1973).
79. B. Gray and C. Booker, The North Sea sell-out, *Observer* (10 February 1974).
80. See ref. 35, p. 294.

Part 8   Political regions and scale

1. G. Modelski, The promise of geocentric politics, *World Politics*, **20** (1970), 617–35.
2. H. J. Mackinder, The geographical pivot of history, *Geogr. J.*, **23** (1904), 421–4.
3. N. J. G. Pounds, *Political Geography*, New York (1963), p. 410.
4. L. D. Kristof, The origin and evolution of geopolitics, *J. Conflict Resolution*, **4** (1960), 632–45.
5. R. Hartshorne, What is political geography? (1954); also in *Politics and Geographic Relations* (ed. W. A. D. Jackson), Englewood Cliffs, N. J. (1964), p. 56.
6. G. J. Martin, Political geography and geopolitics, *J. Geogr.*, **58** (1959), 441–4.
7. Discussion of the Heartland concept is one of the main elements in the geographical component of the basic social science course of the Open University.
8. H. J. Mackinder, *Democratic Ideals and Reality*, New York (1919).
9. See ref. 2, 431.
10. See ref. 2, 437.
11. See ref. 2, 432. Mackinder was influenced by earlier geopolitical writing on sea power by A. T. Mahan, *The Influence of Sea Power upon History*, Boston, Mass. (1900); but he did not consider that sea power remained as potent as Mahan suggested.
12. See ref. 2, 433.
13. See ref. 2, 433.
14. See ref. 2, 433.
15. See ref. 2, 436.
16. See ref. 2, 437.
17. See ref. 8.
18. See ref. 8, p. 113.

19. H. J. Mackinder, The round world and the winning of the peace, *Foreign Affairs*, **21** (1943), 595–605.
20. S. B. Jones, Global strategic views, *Geogr. Rev.*, **45** (1955), 493.
21. W. G. East, How strong is the Heartland?, *Foreign Affairs*, **29** (1950), 78–93.
22. D. J. M. Hooson, A new Soviet Heartland, *Geogr. J.*, **128** (1962), 19–29.
23. See ref. 19.
24. J. C. Malin, The contriving brain as the pivot of history, in *Issues and Conflicts*, Lawrence, Kansas (1959), p. 339.
25. See ref. 22, 19.
26. See ref. 2, 422.
27. N. J. Spykman, *The Geography of the Peace*, New York (1944).
28. D. W. Meinig, Heartland and Rimland in Eurasian history, *Western Pol. Q.*, **9** (1956), 553–69.
29. A. P. de Seversky, *Air Power: Key to Survival*, New York (1950).
30. S. B. Cohen, *Geography and Politics in a Divided World*, London (1964), 56–87.
31. B. M. Russett, *International Regions and the International System: a Study in Political Ecology*, Chicago (1967).
32. B. M. Russett, Delineating international regions, in *Quantitative International Politics* (ed. J. D. Singer), New York (1968), p. 317.
33. See ref. 31, p. 228.
34. See ref. 31, p. 232.
35. B. J. L. Berry, Geographical reviews, *Geogr. Rev.*, **59** (1969), 450.
36. O. R. Young, Professor Russett: industrious tailor to a naked emperor, *World Politics*, **21** (1969), 486.
37. See ref. 35, 450.
38. K. A. Sinnhuber, Central Europe, Mitteleuropa, Europe Centrale, *Trans. Inst. Br. Geogr.*, **20** (1954), no. 1, 5–37.
39. W. G. East, The concept and political status of the shatter zone, in *Geographical Essays on Eastern Europe* (ed. N. J. G. Pounds), Birmingham, Al. (1967), pp. 1–27.
40. K. R. Cox, A spatial interactional model for political geography, *East Lakes Geogr.*, **4** (1968), 58ff.
41. G. R. Crone, *Background to Political Geography*, London (1967).
42. J. R. V. Prescott, Functions and methods of electoral geography, *Annals Assoc. Am. Geogr.*, **49** (1959), 301.
43. R. Conquest, ed., *The Soviet Political System*, London (1968), p. 13.
44. R. D. Dikshit, The failure of federalism in Central Africa, *Prof. Geogr.*, **23** (1971), 227.
45. *The Times* (20 May 1969).
46. J. R. V. Prescott, *Political Geography*, London (1972), p. 78.
47. G. Kish, Some aspects of the regional political geography of Italy, *Annals Assoc. Am. Geogr.*, **43** (1953), 178.
48. C. O. Paullin, *Atlas of the Historical Geography of the United States*, Washington DC (1932), plates 112–31.
49. R. L. Friedheim, Factor analysis as a tool in studying the law of the sea, in *The Law of the Sea* (ed. L. M. Alexander), Columbus, Ohio, (1967), pp. 47–70.
50. See ref. 40.
51. K. R. Cox, The voting decision in a spatial context, in *Progress in Geography* (ed. R. J. Chorley, P. Haggett and D. R. Stoddart), London (1969), vol. 1, pp. 96–117.
52. See ref. 51, p. 112.
53. Quoted in J. P. Mackintosh, *The Devolution of Power*, Penguin, Harmondsworth (1968), p. 155.

54. A. H. Taylor, The electoral geography of Welsh and Scottish nationalism, *Scot. Geogr. Mag.*, **89** (1973), 44.
55. J. R. V. Prescott, Electoral studies in political geography, in *The Structure of Political Geography* (ed. R. K. Kasperson and J. V. Minghi), Chicago (1969).
56. P. Kellner, If the system were different, *Sunday Times* (3 March 1974) (with adaptations).
57. A. J. Parker, Irish way of voting, *Geogr. Mag.* (May 1973), 600.
58. G. Rowley, Electoral behaviour and electoral behaviour: a note on some recent developments in electoral geography, *Prof. Geogr.*, **21** (1969), 398–9.
59. H. H. McCarty, quoted in E. N. Thomas, Maps of residuals from regression: their characteristics and uses in geographical research, Report no. 2, Dept. of Geography, State University of Iowa (1960).
60. K. R. Cox, *Regional anomalies in the voting behavior of the population of England and Wales, 1921–1951*, PhD thesis, University of Illinois (1967).
61. S. Humes and E. M. Martin, *The Structure of Local Government throughout the World*, The Hague (1961).
62. M. Gluckman, The kingdom of the Zulu of South Africa, in *African Studies* (ed. M. Forbes and E. E. Evans-Pritchard), Oxford (1970).
63. See B. H. Massam, *The Spatial Structure of Administrative Systems*, Assoc. Am. Geogr. Resource Papers, no. 12 (1972), for a further range of techniques.
64. J. Mitchell, *Historical Geography*, London (1954).
65. F. Doré, G. Dupuis and V. Chagny, *Le Département*, Paris (1963), p. 30.
66. R. Muir, *The political geography of north-east Scotland*, PhD thesis, University of Aberdeen (1970), 1–17.
67. K. B. Sajjadur Rasheed, An examination of the shapes of the administrative districts of Bangladesh, *Geografiska Annaler*, **44B** (1972), 104–8.
68. P. Haggett, *Locational Analysis in Human Geography*, London (1965), p. 51.
69. P. O. Pedersen, On the geometry of administrative areas, MS report, Copenhagen (1967).
70. P. Haggett and R. J. Chorley, *Network Analysis in Geography*, London (1969).
71. K. W. Robinson, Sixty years of federation in Australia, *Geogr. Rev.*, **51** (1961), 1–20.
72. See ref. 68, pp. 51–3.
73. See ref. 66.
74. See ref. 63, 27.
75. See ref. 63, 27.
76. 1936 Constitution, chapter 2, articles 17, 18a and 18b respectively.
77. Main sources used were: ref. 43; R. E. H. Mellor, *Geography of the USSR*, London (1964); J. C. Dewdney, Patterns and problems of regionalisation in the USSR, Durham University Research Paper Series, no. 8 (1967).
78. See ref. 63, 19–26; B. H. Massam, A test model of administrative areas, *Geogr. Analysis*, **3** (1971), 402–6.
79. See ref. 78.
80. Royal Commission on Local Government in England and Wales, 1966–1969, Report, HMSO, London (1969).
81. D. Senior, Memorandum of Dissent, ref. 80, vol. 2, p. 66.
82. See ref. 53, pp. 49–50.
83. See ref. 63, 23.
84. See ref. 63, 10.
85. See ref. 63, 10.
86. See P. R. Gould and T. R. Leinbach, An approach to the geographic assignment of hospital services, *Tidschrift voor Econ. en Soc. Geogr.*, **57** (1966), 203–6, for further developments of linear programming.

87. R. E. Dickinson, *The City Region in Western Europe*, London (1967), p. 389.
88. D. Senior, *The Regional City*, London (1968), p. 16.
89. J. R. James, Regions and regional planning, *Geography*, **54** (1969), 130.
90. P. Hall, Geography illogical?, *New Society* (19 June 1969), 954.
91. R. Minshull, *Regional Geography*, London (1969), p. 61.
92. See ref. 87, p. 11.
93. See ref. 88.
94. See ref. 88.
95. See ref. 66.
96. W. S. Sanders, Municipalisation by provinces, Fabian Tracts, no. 126, New Heptarchy Series, no. 1 (1905).
97. C. B. Fawcett, *The Provinces of England*, London (1919); Natural divisions of England, *Geogr. J.*, **49** (1917), 124–41; Regional boundaries in England and Wales, Assoc. of Planning and Reconstruction Broadsheet, no. 9 (1942).
98. See ref. 97 (1919), p. 151.
99. S. Webb and B. Webb, *A Constitution for the Socialist Commonwealth of Great Britain*, London (1920).
100. G. D. H. Cole, *The Future of Local Government*, London (1921); The Future of Local Government, *Pol. Q.*, **12** (1941), no. 4; *Local and Regional Government*, London (1947).
101. E. Ashby, Regional government, or the next step in public administration, *Public Admin.* (1929), 365ff; W. A. Robson, *The Development of Regional Government*, London (1931); 'Regionaliter', Regional government, Fabian Research Series, no. 63 (1942).
102. E. W. Gilbert and E. G. R. Taylor, Discussion on the geographical aspects of regional planning, *Geogr. J.*, **99** (1942), no. 2.
103. V. D. Lipman, *Local Government Areas, 1834–1945*, Oxford (1949).
104. J. N. H. Douglas, Political geography and administrative areas: a method of assessing the effectiveness of local government areas, in *Essays in Political Geography* (ed. C. A. Fisher), London (1968).
105. Condensed from R. Muir, The evolution of theories for regional local government in England, Occasional Papers, no. 1, Dept. of Geography, Cambridgeshire College of Arts and Technology (1975).
106. M. Blacksell, Reformed England and Wales, *Geogr. Mag.* (March 1974), 239.

Appendix The systems approaches

1. D. Easton, An approach to the analysis of political systems, *World Politics* (April 1957), 291–9; J. Frankel, *Contemporary International Theory and the Behaviour of States*, Oxford (1973), p. 65.
2. J. R. V. Prescott, *Political Geography*, London (1972), p. 97.

Index